DEATH
IN THE
SAHARA

Also by the same author

Get Rommel
Shoot to Kill
The Real Bravo Two Zero
Lawrence: The Uncrowned King of Arabia

DEATH
IN THE
SAHARA

THE LORDS OF THE DESERT
AND THE TIMBUKTU RAILWAY EXPEDITION MASSACRE

Michael Asher

Foreword by Dean King

Skyhorse Publishing

To Mariantonietta Peru,
The First Woman to Cross the Sahara Desert
From West to East by Camel

Originally published as *Sands of Death*
in Great Britain in 2007
by Weidenfeld & Nicolson

Skyhorse Publishing books may be purchased in bulk at special discounts for sales promotion, corporate gifts, fund-raising, or educational purposes. Special editions can also be created to specifications. For details, contact the Special Sales Department, Skyhorse Publishing, 307 West 36th Street, 11th Floor, New York, NY 10018 or info@ skyhorsepublishing.com.

Skyhorse® and Skyhorse Publishing® are registered trademarks of Skyhorse Publishing, Inc.®, a Delaware corporation.

Visit our website at www.skyhorsepublishing.com

10 9 8 7 6 5 4 3 2

Paperback ISBN: 978-1-61608-594-0

Library of Congress Cataloging-in-Publication Data
Asher, Michael 1953–
Death in the Sahara: the story of the massacre of the colonial railway expedition at the hands of the vicious lords of the desert / Michael Asher.
p.   cm.
Includes bibliographical references and index.
ISBN-13: 978-1-60239-630-2 (alk. paper)
ISBN-10: 1-60239-630-2 (alk. paper)
I. Railroads—Algeria—History.
2. Railroads—Sahara—History. I. Title.

HE3412.A674   2008
385.0966'09034—dc22
2007050717

Printed in the United States of America

Contents

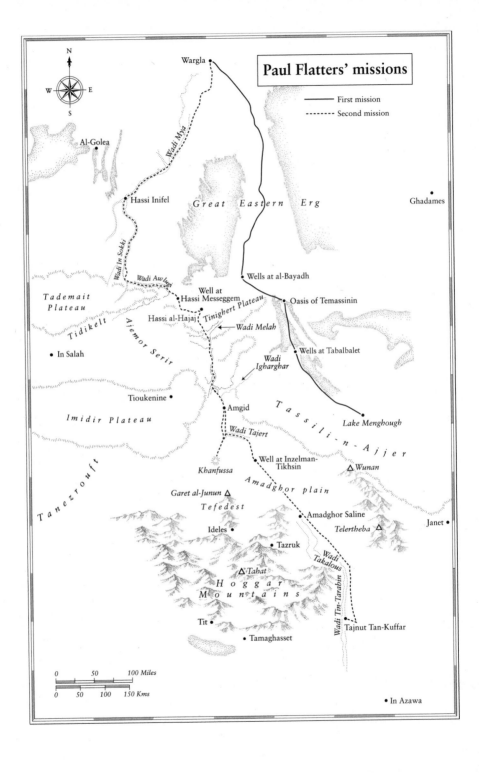

N
W · E
S

Wargla

Al-Golea

Paul Flatters' missions

———— First mission
- - - - - Second mission

Hassi Inifel

Great Eastern Erg

Ghadames

Wadi Mya

Wadi In Sokki

Wadi Awlan

Wells at al-Bayadh

Tademait Plateau

Well at Hassi Messeggem

Oasis of Temassinin

Tidikelt

Hassi al-Hajaj

Tinighert Plateau

Wadi Melah

Ajemor Serir

In Salah

Wadi Igharghar

Wells at Tabalbalet

Tioukenine

Imidir Plateau

Amgid

Tassili-n-Ajjer

Lake Menghough

Wadi Tajert

Tanezrouft

Well at Inzelman-Tikhsin

Khanfussa

△ Wunan

Amadghor plain

Garet al-Junun △

Tefedest

Amadghor Saline

Janet

Ideles

Telertheba △

Tazruk

Wadi Takalous

△ Tahat

Hoggar Mountains

Tit

Wadi Tin-Tarabin

Tajnut Tan-Kuffar

Tamaghasset

0   50   100 Miles
0   50   100   150 Kms

In Azawa

Acknowledgments

I would like to thank my editor at Weidenfeld & Nicolson, Ian Drury, for accepting this book, which I have wanted to write for more than twenty years. I must also thank him for his patience in waiting for it. Once again, I could not have succeeded without the support of my agent, Anthony Goff, of David Higham Associates, and his assistant, Georgia Glover.

I am particularly grateful for the friendship of H. E. Mohammad Hassan, Algerian Ambassador in Kenya, for facilitating my journey to Algeria, and for providing me with a full list of French sources on the Tuareg and the Flatters Mission. I would like to thank my guides and camel-men in the Hoggar Mountains, Assaya of the Ait Lowayen, and Ahmadu of the Issekermaren, for finding Tajnut Tan-Kuffar and proving that local knowledge is still better than GPS. I am grateful to Messek Sidi Mohammad of Tazruk for his hospitality and assistance.

Thanks also go to Nigel Morris for pointing me in the right direction in my research, and to Esmond and Chryssee Bradley Martin for the loan of books from their private library.

I would like to thank my French teachers at Stamford School, particularly the late Bill Packer, whose gift became unexpectedly apparent after thirty years, when I set to work on the research for this book. As always, I could not have written it without the patience of my wife, Mariantonietta, and my children, Burton and Jade.

Michael Asher
Langata, Nairobi
November 2006

Foreword

In 1875 a Scottish merchant named Donald Mackenzie proposed cutting a canal from the Atlantic Ocean into the interior of the Sahara and flooding it to create a shipping lane to Timbuctoo. For a brief while his fanciful notion was the rage of London newspapers. Steamers would soon be carrying British goods and civilization into the heart of Africa, they crowed, and returning with ivory, gold, and gum. Fortunately for the British, sanity prevailed and this chimerical dream evaporated like rain on the *hammada* before any lives were lost trying to accomplish it.

At around the same time, fresh from their success constructing the Suez Canal, which opened in 1869 (the same year that the U.S. trans-continental railroad began operation), the French envisioned building a trans-Saharan railroad from Algeria to Timbuctoo to access that same ivory, gold, and gum. Already substantially invested in North Africa, the French created a national commission to study the possibilities, setting in motion a fine example of debacle by committee.

A taut and remarkably detailed account of the disastrous expedition that followed, Michael Asher's *Death in the Sahara* shows how Western hubris, political complexities, and naiveté concerning desert geography and culture doomed the expedition led by Major Paul Flatters. *Death in the Sahara* carries the reader deep into the Sahara and into the vortex of follies committed by Flatters as the ambitious Frenchman and his French and Arab soldiers and native cameleers descended into the jaws of death. Asher not only captures the horrific beauty and brutality of the central Sahara and the fierce and cunning Tuareg who inhabit it, he explores man's reckless pursuit of adventure and glory, the nature of betrayal, and the limits of human endurance. Underpinning it all is man's obsession with the unknowable desert.

Having walked the entire breadth of the Sahara himself (chronicled in *Two Against the Sahara,* 1989) and examined the lives of Wilfred Thesiger (*Thesiger,* 1995) and T. E. Lawrence (*Lawrence,* 1999), two of the great desert explorers of the past century, Asher understands this passion, this place, and these people as well as any Westerner alive. *Death in the Sahara* is a masterful analysis of the East-West clash and should be standard reading for any Westerner dealing with cultures tempered in the desert heat.

—Dean King
author of *Skeletons on the Zahara* and *Unbound*

A note on transliteration

I have preferred to use English rather than French phonetics in transliterating Arabic and Tamahaq, as a more effective guide to their actual pronunciation. The Arab tribe *Shamb*a (singular: *Shambi*), for instance, spelt *Chaanba* in French, is often mispronounced by English-speakers as if it began with *ch* (cheese), when, in fact, this phoneme does not even exist in Arabic (except in some Middle East dialects). This is, of course, because French *ch* = English *sh*.

My consonant system is as follows:

French *ch* = English *sh*: *Chaanb*a = *Shamba*

French *gu* = English *gi/ge*: *guerba* = *girba*; *guelta* = *gelta*; *Amguid* = *Amgid*; *Aguendis* = *Agendis*

French *dj* = English *j*: *Djanet* = *Janet*; *djunun* = *junun*; *djinn* = *jinn*

French *c/k* = q (pronounced *k* or *g* depending on context): *Abdelkacem* = 'Abd al-Qassim; *caid* = *qa'id*; *Abdelcader* = 'Abd al-Qadir

French *r* = *gh*: *Aitarel* = *Aitaghel*; *Tamanrasset* = *Tamanghasset*

French *c* = English *ss*: *Belkacem* = *Bul-Qassim*; *Attici* = *Atissi*

'('ayn) usually missed out in French transliteration, is a very common Arabic consonant produced by a slight retching in the throat.

For vowels:

French *ou* = English *w/aw*: *Ouargla* = *Wargla*; *Ouillimidden* = *Awlimmidden*

Technically there is no short 'e' (bed) in Arabic. The definite article, often represented as *el*, is *al* in my text.

We came to the country of Haggar, who are a tribe of Berbers. They wear face-veils and there is little good to say about them. They are a rascally lot.

Ibn Battuta, 1353

Prologue

They glided out of the heat-haze on their camels like spectres. There were twenty of them, and they were Tuareg. Their faces were hidden by black veils that left only slits for the eyes, and they wore purple robes that fluttered in the desert wind. They carried swords, muskets and seven-foot iron spears, and wore stilettos in sheaths on their left forearms. They were an impressive, sinister sight.

Alexander Gordon Laing watched them as they drifted nearer. He and his fellow caravaneers had been expecting an attack by bandits ever since they had set off two weeks earlier. There had been persistent rumours that a party of robbers was tracking them. Now, it seemed, the moment of truth had arrived.

It was January 1826, and the caravan was more than three hundred kilometres south of the oasis of In Salah in the central Sahara. Laing, a thirty-one-year-old Scotsman, a major in the British West Indies Regiment, had set out from Tripoli the previous August. He was determined to become the first European to reach Timbuctoo – the legendary 'golden city', whose name had been a byword for centuries for remoteness and mystery.

Laing had set himself no mean task. To Europeans the Sahara was still beyond the pale of the known world – as fearful as the dark side of the moon. It was a three-million-square-mile blank on the map, an uncharted ocean of sand-dunes, gloomy mountain chains and endless thirsty black plains whose emptiness befuddled the senses. Water was scarce. Oases could be hundreds of kilometres apart. Whole caravans of camels, thousands strong, could vanish into the maw of terrifying sandstorms capable of blinding a man.

Laing had picked the wrong time to make the first European crossing of the central Sahara. The country south of In Salah was more troubled than it had been in years. The Ottoman Dey of Algiers, the nominal ruler of the area, had suspended trade with the south for a year because of a war between the Tuareg and the Awlad Dulaim, a Moorish tribe. As a Christian, Laing's life had been in constant danger at the oasis, yet he had been obliged to wait there five weeks to collect a group of traders courageous enough to defy the ban and make the crossing south. Even after the caravan had got under way, Laing's companions had been in a constant state of nervous tension, always on the verge of turning back. On two occasions, Laing had prevented them from doing so by threatening to continue alone. He suddenly began to wish that he had not been so headstrong.

To Laing's astonishment, the Tuareg did not attack. Instead, they couched their camels and walked over to shake hands. They seemed friendly. They offered their protection to the caravan for a price based on the value of the goods it carried. The price was agreed on, and the forty-six caravaneers, including Laing, heaved a collective sigh of relief. The caravan-leader, an Arab called Babani, told him that the danger had passed, and he need no longer keep his weapon loaded. Laing foresaw no further obstacles now these guardians were with them. 'My prospects are bright and expectations sanguine,' he wrote. 'I do not calculate on the most trifling difficulty between me and my return to England.'[1] He never dreamed that he had already fallen foul of a classic Tuareg trick.

The Tuareg considered themselves the lords of the desert and superior to all other peoples, whose possessions were theirs by right. Their modus operandi was trickery and deceit. Frequently Tuareg bands would simply attach themselves to caravans, displaying the greatest friendliness, eating and drinking with the caravaneers, until they had gained a degree of trust. Then, having pinpointed the richest pickings, they would strike suddenly, by night, murdering the men with whom they had so recently eaten bread and salt. Loading their booty on to their camels, they would beat a hasty retreat into the Hoggar Mountains, a labyrinth of crags and ravines whose geography was known only to themselves.

The attack came on the sixth night, at about five o'clock in the morning. The first Laing knew of it was a musket-ball crashing into his hip. He jerked to his feet, screaming, as blood pulsed from the wound. His assailants were masked shadows, moving inexorably in on him. A sword-blade slashed his thigh. He staggered, trying desperately to defend his head with his right arm. More sword-cuts came thick and fast, almost severing his right hand, smashing his jaw, slicing open his earlobe, snapping his left arm like a dry twig. Laing fell, and did not get up again. Blows rained down on his head and hands and across his neck. Mercifully, he lost consciousness.

When he finally came round, white as a ghost and slick with his own blood, the robbers had vanished. Almost all of his money was gone. He crawled numbly from under what was left of a tent to find a scene of utter carnage. His baggage had been broken open, rifled and scattered across the desert. His camel-man was lying senseless with a wound in the head. His assistant, a West African sailor, had been hacked and stabbed to death. His Jewish interpreter was dead from three sword-cuts. A second West African sailor had managed to crawl away, despite a musket-ball in his leg, and a third had vanished into the desert.

Laing stared around in stupefaction as he realized that the other members of the caravan, whose camps were spread around him, had not been touched. He alone had been attacked and robbed, and none of his travelling companions had lifted a finger to help. It was only then that he remembered Babani's counsel not to keep his gun loaded. The caravan-leader must have been in on the plot.

Laing had suffered no fewer than twenty-four wounds, eighteen of them severe. The musket-ball in his hip had worked its way round to his back, narrowly missing the spine. His jaw, left arm and three fingers on his right hand were fractured, and the bones of his right wrist had been cut right through, leaving his right hand hanging off. He had five deep lacerations in his head and three more on his left temple. That he had survived at all was a miracle.

What followed is one of the most remarkable tales of survival in the history of exploration. Tied on to to his camel, never far from death, Laing struggled behind the caravan for another 650 kilometres, until he reached a village north-east of Timbuctoo. He was recuperating there when plague struck, carrying off, among others, the headman of the village and Laing's two surviving West African assistants. Laing himself lay in bed, delirious, for nine days, but by sheer willpower he pulled through. It was the second miracle within as many months.

Alexander Gordon Laing rode into Timbuctoo on 13 August 1826, the first European to enter the legendary town as a free man for three hundred years. It was the most dazzling feat of exploration of its time, but Laing did not live to tell the tale. On 22 September, three days into his homeward trek, he and the Arab youth with him were set upon by their travelling companions while they slept. Laing was decapitated and his headless body was left under a tree, where it was later found and buried by a passing Arab.

Two years later, the Frenchman René Caillié succeeded in reaching Timbuctoo disguised as a Muslim, and returned home unscathed. In 1830, two years after Caillié's journey, thirty-seven thousand French troops were landed in Algeria, forcing the Dey into exile and ending for ever the rule of the Ottoman Turks.

For the next half-century the French consolidated their position in northern Algeria, spreading their influence steadily south across the Saharan Atlas Mountains to the shores of the great desert. By the time they had begun to turn their eyes towards the Sahara, and the riches that lay beyond it in the African interior, there were few left who recalled the fate of Alexander Gordon Laing.

PART
ONE
TERRA
INCOGNITA

1

Paris to Timbuctoo
in Six Days!

In early 1877, M. Adolphe Duponchel, engineer, arrived at the oasis of Laghouat in a public diligence, having spent three days being jolted over the execrable mountain roads from Algiers. In his valise he carried a letter of introduction to the local commandant, Major Paul Francis Xavier Flatters.

The oasis lay spread across the pastel landscape before him like a green stain. The town, standing at over seven hundred metres, was sited on a deep wadi where the heads of fifty thousand palm trees waved gently like feather dusters in the breeze. To the north, in a haze of dust, lay the broken outer ramparts of the Saharan Atlas Mountains; to the south, the endless shimmering plain of the desert. Laghouat was the most southerly French garrison in Algeria. Beyond this point, the Sahara stretched on for more than fifteen hundred miles.

Duponchel was fifty-six years old, a hulking, genial, vigorous man with a thick grey beard trimmed square. A Chief Engineer of the Corps of Bridges and Tunnels by profession, he was an early graduate of the École Polytechnique, the school system inaugurated after the French Revolution to embody the new ideas of scientific enlightenment. His views on everything, from engineering to politics and morality, were original, and decided. If he was lacking in anything, it was in subtlety – he was a man convinced that his way was right.

This was Duponchel's first visit to Algeria. He had spent some time in the French colonial towns on or near the Mediterranean – Algiers, Oran, Constantine – but this journey away from the coast had been his first glimpse of the authentic 'Orient'. In Boukhrari, he had seen exotic Awlad Na'il girls in clinking gold bracelets and brilliant scarlet dresses, dancing in the streets with sensuous abandon. He had been astonished to learn that for these Arab nomads of the hills it was perfectly acceptable for the women to earn their dowry in the towns by prostitution. At Boghari, he had rested for the night in the shadow of a Turkish fortress. He had wandered in the moonlight under glittering stars, among Moorish cafés from whose doorways drifted the babble of Arabic, the scents of coffee, tobacco, absinthe and barbecued meat. He had been captivated by the sights, sounds and smells of the steppe. Now he was stunned by his first view of the Sahara.

As the carriage bumped over the last open ground before the oasis, Duponchel stared, overawed by the hugeness of the landscape, the brilliance of the light, the fractal patterns on the surface, the quicksilver shimmer of the heat-haze. The desert was the first true wilderness he had ever seen. It was more compelling than the ocean or the mountains, both magnificent and frightening at the same time.

Laghouat was a last redoubt on the desert's edge, dwarfed by the epic dimensions of the Sahara. Beyond the teetering perimeter walls, the living quarters were built on a series of hillocks along two sides of the wadi. On one side, block-shaped minarets rose above a maze of windowless mud houses that seemed to have grown out of each other organically. On the other was a neat grid of streets built by the French after they'd captured the town in 1852.

After being deposited with his valise in the square, Duponchel shouldered his way through seething crowds, donkeys, goats and camels, to the Headquarters of the Cercle of Laghouat. It was here, in a spotless white colonial building under the fluttering *tricolore*, that the engineer introduced himself to Major Paul Flatters.

Flatters was a head shorter than Duponchel and ten years younger. An upright, broad-shouldered, blocky man, he wore the loose-fitting blue tunic and baggy trousers of the French Armée d'Afrique. His face was rose-pink and wrinkled from years in the sun, and there was something Germanic about the high cheekbones, the brilliant blue eyes, the pepper-and-salt hair, and the sharp military moustache and goatee. He appeared genuinely pleased to see his visitor, and assigned Duponchel quarters among the officers. He invited him for dinner in the mess that evening.

After sunset, Duponchel joined the officers at the long table for mutton and red wine. After introductions, he explained his visit. He had been authorized by the Ministry of Public Works in Paris, he said, to make a feasibility study for a railway that would cut directly across the untamed desert between Algiers and Timbuctoo, the first railway ever to be built across the Sahara. Flatters and his fellow officers stared at him, astounded. One or two may have chuckled and some might privately have consigned Duponchel to the crackpot category – but not Paul Flatters. He leaned forward and listened with interest.

Duponchel spoke with expansive eloquence. At home, he had a reputation for shooting off ideas like sparks off a Catherine wheel. In years past he had come up with a suggestion for the use of high-pressure water jets to cut a canal through Panama, and he had proposed washing the topsoil off the Pyrenees into the marshes of southern France to create a fertile breadbasket for his country. He had even conceived a pipeline project to carry wine directly from French vineyards to Paris. The Trans-Saharan Railway was his magnum opus.

Duponchel's plan had not met with instant popularity – at the 2nd International Congress of Commercial Geography in Paris he had been laughed off stage – but he had stuck to his guns. A few months before his visit to Algeria, he had placed his proposal before members of the Geographical Society of Lyon, to a tumultuous reception. The wind, it seemed, was changing. There were rumours of Italian and German plans to lay a railroad across the Sahara from Tripoli to Chad – the territory that would one day be named Libya, but which was, in Duponchel's day, a vilayet of the Ottoman Turks. No Frenchman wanted to be outdone by foreigners, and especially not the Germans; still smarting from their defeat in the Franco-Prussian War six years earlier, the French needed a high-profile venture to restore their sense of national pride.

Duponchel's scheme had reached the ears of the Minister of Public Works, who had sent him to Algeria for an initial survey. Duponchel had studied the existing railway line, running east–west from Algiers to Oran, and had deduced from his maps that a branch line could be diverted south, breaching the hills not far from Laghouat. He was happy to tell Flatters that everything he had seen so far had indicated that his assumption was correct.

To Duponchel the Trans-Saharan Railway was a serious business. This was the high summer of steam-and-steel technology, and the world was the engineer's oyster. There was no ocean that could not be crossed, no river that could not be spanned, no mountain that could not be tunnelled. Three hundred years of unrelenting scientific progress had produced a boundless confidence. The wilderness existed only as a challenge to man's ingenuity: it was there to be tamed, mastered and controlled. In 1869 another French engineer, Ferdinand Marie de Lesseps, had revolutionized world travel by cutting a canal through the isthmus of Suez, unlocking a new door to the Far East. The opening of the Suez Canal had been the beginning of a railway bonanza in Europe as companies vied to connect the great cities of the west to the Mediterranean ports. Not to be deterred by the barrier of the mountains, railway engineers had bored vast new tunnels through the belly of the Alps at Mont Cenis, Simplon and Saint-Gothard. The year the Suez Canal opened was also the year the Americans completed a railroad from San Francisco to New York, connecting the world's two greatest oceans. Boldly negotiating obstacles of every conceivable variety, the American Pacific ran for nearly three thousand kilometres – more than twice the length of the proposed Trans-Saharan.

The railway, Duponchel believed, would be an umbilical cord that would open up to France a market of at least fifty million consumers in the African interior. The export to the sub-Saharan lands of dates and salt alone would be enough to justify its construction, and the moral benefits that would accrue from its civilizing presence would include the suppression of the slave trade. The line from Algiers to Timbuctoo would require 2570 kilometres of rail, and would cost four hundred million francs. When it was completed, travellers would be able to hop from Paris to Timbuctoo in an astonishing six days.

The lamps burned low in the mess at Laghouat that night as Flatters and Duponchel tossed ideas back and forth. The engineer was delighted to find in Major Flatters not only a fascinated listener, but also a man who lived and breathed the Sahara.

2

A Man Spellbound By the Sahara

Paul Flatters had spent almost a quarter of a century in Algeria. For much of that time he had dreamed of leading an expedition to Timbuctoo. Fourteen years earlier, he had submitted a memo to the Geographical Society of Paris, proposing such an expedition. The memo had evoked no response.

Born in Paris in 1832, Flatters was the son of a sculptor, Jean-Jacques Flatters, a Prussian granted French citizenship after serving in the French Army. Jean-Jacques died when Paul was thirteen, and his education was paid for by one of his father's clients, Baron Taylor, patron of the Artists' Association. The death of his mother five years later left Flatters a penniless orphan and nudged him towards a military career. He graduated from the military academy at St Cyr in 1853 and was posted to an Algerian infantry regiment, the 3rd Zouaves, mostly recruited from *Kulughlis* – the descendants of Turkish janissaries and Arab wives. He soon found his niche in the Arab Bureau.

The Bureau suited Flatters' temperament. Brave, physically tough, a tireless hunter and an expert horseman, he was also a gifted linguist. He knew Greek and Latin, spoke fluent English, some German and Italian, and mastered colloquial and literary Arabic with astonishing speed as well as a smattering of two dialects of Berber. He liked and admired the local tribesmen, he had an absorbing interest in his surroundings, and he was an instinctive collector of information. He had published one book, *A History, Geography and Geology of Constantine Province*, and was working on another, *An Ancient History of North Africa Before the Arab Conquest*.

The Arab Bureau was a service created by Marshal Thomas-Robert Bugeaud in 1830, to replace the authority of the Ottoman Turks in the tribal areas beyond the fertile *tell*. Flatters was the military equivalent of a District Commissioner in a British colony, responsible for administration, justice and security in the Cercle, an immense area stretching as far as the seven oasis towns of the Mzab Valley and the outpost of Wargla, in the south. To him fell the task of maintaining peace between the nomads of the area, the proud and prickly Shamba and Laarba Arabs, some of whom had submitted to French authority but who were riddled with blood-feuds and tribal disputes. Once a week he presided over a local court where the natives brought their problems. Few went away disappointed – even if they had been reprimanded or fined, they were satisfied that they had received justice.

The role of benevolent autocrat suited Flatters. He was a man who needed, above all, to be liked and accepted. He got on well with both his superiors and those under his command, and all who knew him, Frenchmen and native Algerians alike, were impressed by his intelligence and confidence, his openness, honesty, enthusiasm and *joie de vivre*. He had a service record that bordered on the eulogistic – the only veiled hint of criticism to be found on any of his assessment reports was a tendency to be too 'humanitarian' in his attitude to discipline. This was par for the course with Arab Bureau officers. Though there were a few cases of tyranny and injustice, most were liberal-minded men who regarded the tribes they administered as their protégés.

Flatters spent much of his time in the saddle, moving between the outposts of the Cercle. He was never happier than when he was able to join local chiefs on gazelle or ostrich hunts. He preferred to collect live animals, though, and had started his own small zoo at Laghouat, containing not only leopards, foxes, antelope and ostrich, but also lizards, snakes, insects and scorpions.

On market days, when the nomads swept into the oasis on their donkeys and camels, bringing with them the odours of sour milk and uncured leather, Flatters was always to be found in their midst, an imposing figure in a native *shesh* (scarf), and burnoose (white hooded cape). He listened to complaints, sorted out disputes and asked endless questions. He was captivated by the smallest detail of nomadic existence, but what appealed to him most was the simplicity of desert life. Quite often all these men owned, apart from their camels, goats and sheep, was a few cups and bowls, a rug, a burnoose to sleep in, a camel-saddle and saddle-bags, home-made ropes and hobbles, a dagger, a rifle and a camel-stick. Their black tents, woven out of goats' hair, were the property of the women.

In the evenings he would sit by a campfire with Arab sheikhs, drinking tea, eating *mashwi* – whole roasted sheep – and talking for hours about events in the Cercle. Often he asked about conditions in the Sahara far to the south – alliances, conflicts, personalities, disputes between the tribes. The more perceptive would notice the subtle change in his voice as the conversation turned to the great desert: they knew they were talking to a man spellbound by the Sahara.

In 1864, Flatters had married Sarah Legros, the sister of a childhood friend, and his son Etienne was born four years later. His wife was too delicate to join him in Algeria, so he rarely saw his family. The years had passed, and Flatters climbed the ladder of promotion. His passion for exploration retreated into the background. In July 1870, he was posted back to the 3rd Zouaves to fight in the Franco-Prussian War, but he was captured on 6 August at Sedan. Liberated the following year, he was promoted to commanding officer of his battalion and awarded the *Légion d'honneur* for his part in the battle against the Paris Commune.

Back in Algeria, Flatters was posted to Laghouat as Arab Bureau senior commandant. That posting coincided with a new colonial initiative in the Sahara. Caravans from the Sudan had stopped coming to Algiers since the French conquest: the ban on the slave trade had ensured that all commerce was diverted through the eastern Sahara, along Ottoman routes. Now the French wanted to attract the Saharan trade back into their sphere.

At the request of the governor, General Chanzy, Flatters began to compile detailed reports on the possibility of reviving the caravan trade from Timbuctoo to Algiers. He suggested an expedition to reopen the abandoned caravan-route to the Sudan through the Hoggar Mountains, outlined methods of organization and costs. He questioned every nomad and traveller he encountered who had come from the south. Flatters knew that few men were better qualified than he himself to lead an expedition across the unexplored Sahara, but his proposals had been turned down time after time. In Duponchel's plan he saw the workings of fate. He had spent a lifetime in Algeria and had acquired skills and experience that had been devoured by the French government, to no specific end. He craved distinction, a name beyond the run-of-the-mill soldier's lot. In the Victorian age, African explorers were superstars: Flatters longed to be counted among their number. The years had passed and no opportunity for greatness had presented itself; now, as his career reached its apex, the chance seemed to have fallen like a ripe plum into his hand.

It was obvious to Flatters that the proposed Trans-Saharan Railway would require a survey expedition to map the route to Timbuctoo, possibly through the unexplored Hoggar Mountains. Only four Europeans had ever reached the 'golden city' as free men – Laing, Caillié, Heinrich Barth and Oskar Lenz – and only one of them had been French. None of them had passed through the mysterious Hoggar range. The Trans-Saharan survey expedition would mark the end of an era: it would be the last great expedition of its kind. The railway would change the whole character of the Sahara, bringing civilization to one of the earth's last areas of wilderness. The man who led the Trans-Saharan survey mission would go down in history as the last of the great Saharan explorers. Though Flatters did not say as much to Duponchel, he wanted desperately to be that man.

However, there was one aspect of the engineer's plan that disturbed him. Lying smack across the railway's route, in the very middle of the Sahara, was the country of the northern Tuareg. They were divided into two confederations, the Kel Ajjer and the Kel Ahaggar, living side by side in two vast mountain labyrinths, the Hoggar and the Tassili-n-Ajjer. The Tuareg were truculent, chauvinistic and jealous of their prerogatives. Any expedition to the south would have to take that hostility into account.

When he explained this to Duponchel, the big man raised a thick eyebrow. He respected Flatters, but in general the views of the Arab Bureau were mistrusted in France. First of all, he told the major, the railway would not traverse the mountainous regions but would be laid through the Tuat Oasis and across the Tanezrouft, featureless gravel plains that lay to the west. The Tanezrouft, acutely arid and almost without vegetation, was uninhabited. Second, a bunch of camel-herders, he maintained, could no more halt the Trans-Saharan Railway than the Redskins had halted the American Pacific. In any case, the Tuareg were known to be good people: honest, peaceful and kind.

3

A Deliberate Campaign against Foreign Intrusion

Paul Flatters thought otherwise. Only six months earlier some Arabs hunting ostrich had come across four headless bodies in the desert near al-Golea. The bodies had lain there for months and were mummified by the heat. Three of them were Europeans, Catholic priests, Fathers Alfred Paulmier, Philippe Menoret and Pierre Bouchand, who had set off the previous year to reach Timbuctoo. The dead Arab with them was their companion. They had been travelling with Tuareg guides, who had attacked them without warning.

The priests belonged to the Society of Missionaries of Africa, or White Fathers, an order of spiritual storm-troopers created in 1868 by Charles-Martial-Allemand Lavigerie, Archbishop of Algiers, who believed that the Berbers had once been Christians and that it was his sacred duty to bring them back into the fold. In practice, the White Fathers were a *missionaria prottetiva*, paving the way for colonial expansion. They were all fluent in both spoken and literary Arabic, and they knew the Quran well enough to dispute with learned Muslims. They dressed and conducted themselves as Arabs and were trained to endure any hardship in the pursuit of their goal.

Flatters was later told that, just before they were murdered, Father Paulmier had been invited by one of the guides, a Targui named al-Wunya, to examine his sword. The priest had been bending over to look at the blade when al-Wunya had brought it down on his skull. Father Bouchand had been shot in the chest at point-blank range, and Father Menoret had been stabbed in the back by a warrior called 'Ida, then slashed to pieces. The fathers' Arab companion had been butchered for good measure. The Tuareg had burned the missionaries' meagre possessions – their Bibles and holy ornaments – and even their severed heads, in an apparent attempt to obliterate them from the face of the earth.

The most embarrassing aspect of the story was that the French government had released the fathers' treacherous guides from jail – 'Ida and al-Wunya had been arrested the year before on suspicion of having murdered two French explorers, Norbert Dournaux-Dupere and Eugène Joubert, in Ottoman territory, in 1874. They had apparently lain in wait for the French travellers and set upon them; one had been shot in the head, the other had bled to death after being viciously slashed with swords. The Tuareg had been locked up in Algiers but had been let out after a plea by the fathers, who had sought to impress upon them the nature of Christian forgiveness. Evidently, the Tuareg had not been impressed.

Four years previously, a Dutch heiress and explorer, Alexine Tinne, had been murdered further to the east, between Ghat and Murzuk. Alexine had met the chief of the local Tuareg, an old man named Ikhenoukhen, who had guaranteed her protection. On the way from Murzuk to Ghat, the chief's nephew, Abu Bakr, had ridden into her camp with a band of fifteen Tuareg. The marauders had skewered one of her Dutch assistants with a spear and shot the other. As Alexine raced out of her tent, a Targui had slashed off her hand with a sword, and another put a bullet through her head.

These killings, and others like them, had left Flatters in no doubt as to the character of the Tuareg, but he did not believe that this was a simple matter of robbery. These attacks were part of a coordinated and deliberate campaign against foreign intrusion in the Sahara. He believed the hidden hand of the Sanusiyya, a fundamentalist Islamic Sufi brotherhood based in Cyrenaica, was behind them. The sect had been founded by an Algerian Islamic scholar, Mohammad ʿAli as-Sanusi, in the 1830s, and its tentacles now stretched hundreds of kilometres along the caravan routes into Egypt, the central Sahara and the Sudan. With lodges in Ghadames and Ghat, on the currently most frequented of all the trans-Saharan routes, the brotherhood had a major investment in cross-desert trade. It was astute enough to understand that French interest in the Sahara was mainly commercial: explorers and missionaries were the pathfinders of the bigger battalions that would soon follow.

The Sanusiyya did not intend to let the French take over the lucrative Sudan trade, and neither did the Ottoman Turks. The Ottoman Bey of Murzuk had reported the murder of Alexine Tinne to the French authorities, ostensibly as a diplomatic duty but actually as a warning. He had described in his letter precisely how Miss Tinne's hand had been severed at the wrist, details that could only have come from her killer. Flatters firmly believed that France needed to attempt to restore the Sudan trade – and if it were by building a railway, so much the better. Despite the truculence of the Tuareg and the Sanusiyya, he had no doubt that it could be done – but not by a few private individuals; this would require a fighting expedition of at least three hundred trained colonial soldiers, mounted on camels and armed with quick-firing rifles. This is what Flatters had told Governor-General Chanzy in his report earlier that year.

Flatters saw Duponchel off in his diligence a few days later with some regret, and suppressed elation. It was just possible that the engineer's magnum opus might provide Flatters himself with the means to achieve his own life-long ambition.

4

'Our national genius must one day be called to rule supreme'

Duponchel arrived back in France positively effervescent with new ideas. He had seen the desert for himself, and had thought up more original uses for the railway than shifting dates and salt. Whole oases, he said, could be turned into wintering-places for tourists – cosmopolitan luxury towns that would attract the wealthy. The railway could also assume a humanitarian function, supplying the Sudan in times of famine. The Trans-Saharan, he announced, would open 'a vast colonial empire . . . rivalling the wealth and prosperity of British India, opening unlimited opportunities for our commerce and industry, giving ample space for our civilizing mission on this great continent . . . where our language and our national genius must one day be called to rule supreme'.[2]

As for the technical details, they were of secondary importance. Water could be supplied by bore-wells or reservoirs spaced at fifty-kilometre intervals and connected by a pipeline worked by pumps. Dunes could be stabilized by planting crops, avoided by tunnelling beneath them, or traversed by viaducts, though since the Sahara was mostly rocky, sand-dunes should not be a major problem. As for the labour force, it could be supplied from the ranks of

France's idle youth. Any technical problems arising could be solved by the solid application of reason: the know-how existed. After all, if the Americans could do it, so could the French.

Duponchel's proposals were essentially sound, and would probably have worked in practice had his plan been followed to cross the Tanezrouft. Ninety per cent of the railroad could have been laid through these flat plains, and the sand dunes could certainly have been stabilized by forestation. Where water was absent, locomotives could have hauled their own supplies and kept the regularly spaced reservoirs continuously full. Security could have been provided by squads of troops in block-house forts, protecting stations and water-towers. Duponchel was undoubtedly right: given sufficient funding, the Trans-Saharan was a practical proposal.

In his conviction that the Tuareg presented no threat to the railway he was to prove devastatingly wrong.

5

'Hospitable, generous, kind and peaceful'

In November 1861, a young man called Henri Duveyrier had staggered into Algiers having spent three years crisscrossing the central Sahara with the Tuareg. Unfortunately for posterity, he soon became so ill from typhoid and cerebral malaria that he suffered permanent amnesia and was unable to recall anything that had happened to him. He had to reconstruct his experiences entirely from his journals.

Henri Duveyrier was half-French, half-English; he was charming, intelligent and handsome. His father, Charles, was a businessman, poet, playwright and publicist, and a prominent member of the anti-militarist Saint-Simonist movement, which believed that science and industry would save the world. Henri had been sent to school in Leipzig, where he had shone in English, Italian and German, and had shown early promise in botany and zoology. At sixteen he had begun studying Arabic with a famous professor, and a year later his father had allowed him to visit Algeria, where his first sight of a Tuareg chief in Metlili had given him a thrill he would never forget. 'With his great height,' he wrote, 'his noble and commanding gestures, he most nearly resembled the ideal I had formed of a mediaeval knight.'[3]

Duveyrier, mesmerized by the desert and by his vision of its

romantic veiled men, had returned to Algeria in 1859. His attempt
to become the first European to reach the oasis of In Salah since
Gordon Laing was foiled when he was robbed and turned back at
al-Golea in the Mzab. He had refused to be intimidated, returning
the following year with a commission from the French government
to collect information for a trade agreement with the Tuareg of the
Ajjer Plateau.

The two confederations of northern Tuareg – the Kel Ajjer and
the Kel Ahaggar – were deadly enemies. Of the two groups, the
Ajjer were the less numerous; at the time of Duveyrier's visit, wars
with the more powerful Kel Ahaggar had cost them rich grazing
land for their camels and goats. Under pressure to recognize the
authority of the Turkish *Vali* in Tripoli, they were anxious to
secure the goodwill of the French, and Ikhenoukhen, their *amenukal*, or chief, had treated Duveyrier as an honoured guest. Though
reputed to be already over eighty years old, Ikhenoukhen was still
able to ride and shoot. He was, in Duveyrier's eyes, 'a magnificent
and majestic old man'.[4] A decade later, this same 'majestic' old
man would give assurances to Alexine Tinne only days before she
was murdered by his nephew, Abu Bakr.

Ikhenoukhen assigned Duveyrier to the protection of a relative,
Sheikh 'Othman, a marabout, or holy man, of the Ifoghas clan,
who were respected as mediators, scholars and men of learning.
The young Frenchman stayed in Tuareg camps and spent hours
talking with the tribesmen round campfires. He became the first
European to witness the unique *ahal* ceremony, in which unmar-
ried Tuareg women gathered to choose prospective partners. He
had even, he hinted later, enjoyed liaisons with the women himself. Open, enthusiastic and romantic, Duveyrier saw in the
Tuareg only what he wanted to see: chivalrous warrior-poets
ready to rob the rich to help the poor and save damsels in distress.
He was taken in from the very beginning by their studied gestures
and their finely calculated aura of mystique.

While still in hospital in Algiers, Duveyrier was made Knight of the Légion d'honneur for his work, and received a personal letter of thanks from the Emperor Napoleon III. He returned to France to public adulation. Encouraged by what he had reported, a delegation headed by Captain Mircher was sent to Ghadames, in Tripolitania, to meet Ikhenoukhen and secure his signature on a treaty. Sadly, Mircher found that the 'magnificent' old Targui had melted away into the desert, leaving a gaggle of lesser nobles to sign a treaty they themselves considered meaningless.

That same year, Duveyrier published a book entitled *Exploration du Sahara: Les Touareg du Nord*, based on his diaries, which won immediate acclaim and the French Geographical Society's Gold Medal. Though a work of impressive scholarship, it was permeated by the same idyllic view of the Tuareg that had inspired him from the beginning. It convinced his readers that the veiled men were 'hospitable, generous, kind and peaceful', the noblest of noble savages, who would openly welcome the French to the Hoggar Mountains, provided they followed local customs.

The only problem was that Duveyrier had never visited the Hoggar himself. He knew of the Hoggar people and their mountain fastness only by hearsay.

6

A Deadly Killing Machine

The Hoggar had been a Tuareg sanctuary for a thousand years. Not long before William the Conqueror invaded England, camel-riders of a Berber tribe called the Hawwara had come loping across the horizons of the central Sahara, seeking a place of refuge. Their home was the Fezzan in Tripolitania, where they had lived since before the pharaohs ruled in Egypt. Their ancestors, wearing kilts of leather and distinctive pigtails, were depicted frequently in ancient Egyptian reliefs.

A millennium after the last pharaoh had been laid in his tomb, Hawwara land was overrun by a locust-swarm of Bedouin from Arabia, the Bani Sulaym and the Bani Hilal. These Arabs had been persuaded to pass through Egypt by its Muslim *khalifa* and to seek a new home in the west. They were fierce warriors and drove all before them, including the Hawwara Berbers. Fleeing from their own country, the Hawwara became known to the Arabs as *tawaraka*, outcasts or refugees, and the word entered Arabic as 'Tuareg'.[5]

The wanderings of these outcasts came to an end in the mountains of the central Sahara, for they found in these massifs the perfect sanctuary. The Arabs would never find them in the warrens of ravines, broken hills, chasms and tortuous valleys. The hitch was that the hills were already home to a stone-age people named the Isebeten, who subsisted by hunting, trapping, collecting wild berries and grasses, and herding goats.

The Isebeten possessed only stone tools, so, armed with their iron swords and spears, the Hawwara were easily able to master them. The Hawwara became the lords of the mountains, which they named Hawwar in their own honour. Over time Hawwar eventually became Haggar, or Hoggar, and the Hawwara became the Kel Ahaggar – People of the Hoggar Mountains. Their name for themselves was *Imuhaq* – the Ones Who Take. The ones from whom they had taken, the Isebeten, were obliged to pay tribute to their new masters, and the Imuhaq made certain that the Isebeten would never overthrow them by forbidding them camels and swords of their own. The vassals, permitted only to herd goats and sheep, became known in Tamahaq, the Tuareg tongue, as the Kel Ulli – the Goat People.

Faced with a familiar colonial dilemma of keeping in check subjects who were greater in number, the Imuhaq resorted to bluff. It was said that an Imuhaq warrior could go five days without water. He could cut a horse and its rider in half with a single blow of his sword. The *tawaraka*, who had arrived here as outcasts, fugitives, circulated legends about their toughness and ferocity so effectively that many still believe those stories today.

They deliberately cultivated an aloof and intimidating posture. They hid their faces behind their veils, and developed an elaborate semaphore of signals by adjusting their clothing in subtle ways. They dressed imposingly, in sweeping robes of purple, black and blue. Being men of only average height – usually no more than five foot seven – they learned to arrange their headcloths to make them look taller, a ploy that worked even on the Europeans who encountered them.[6] 'They are the finest race of men I ever saw,' wrote British traveller George Francis Lyon in 1818. 'Tall, straight and handsome, with a certain air of independence and pride, which is very imposing . . . their costume is very remarkable, and they cover their faces as high as the eyes in the manner of women on the sea-coast.'[7]

Unlike the Arabs, the Tuareg never walked if they could help it. Instead, they were so often to be seen dashing around on gangly-legged camels decorated like Christmas trees that they sometimes appeared to be part of the animals. Their 'imposing' appearance, weighed down with swords, shields, spears, daggers, clubs and muskets, together with their arrogant mode of speech and menacing body language, was the most effective weapon they possessed.

The arrival of the Imuhaq in the Hoggar Mountains caused ripples in the ecology of the Sahara that continued into the colonial era. Their coming destroyed the delicate balance the Isebeten had struck with nature. In times of drought and famine, the Tuareg had to look elsewhere for sustenance. They turned on each other, raiding each others' camps in the hot summer seasons when clans split into tiny groups to make best use of the sparse pasture. They also took to robbing outsiders, charging protection fees from all who passed through their lands, plundering traders and travellers. They began to dabble in trading themselves, using the salt – a priceless commodity in the Sudan – found in the Amadghor region on the eastern side of the hills. But their hearts were not really in commerce: they preferred to take. They raided the Sudan for slaves, filling up the mountains with blacks until they were as numerous as the Tuareg. They moved out north from their mountain lair to take control of the Tuat and Tidikelt, the vast string of oases along the margins of the Tademait Plateau.

Though nomadic, the Imuhaq were neither pastoralists nor cultivators. Their herds and flocks were tended by Kel Ulli or slaves, their gardens worked by Haratin, freed men who were traditionally paid one fifth of their produce. Any hardware they needed was produced by a caste of artisans, the Inhaden. The Imuhaq were a warrior caste, and over the centuries they had honed themselves into a deadly killing machine, using anything and everything at their command, from poison to ambush to a knife in the back. Unlike the Arabs who had chased them from the Fezzan, they were not a people of the open desert, accustomed to infinite horizons, but a hill-folk, used to close confines, narrow passages and dark defiles, and this was reflected in their character: while the Arabs were open, extrovert and hospitable, the Tuareg were conceited, closed, suspicious and xenophobic. They resented any intruder in what they considered their sacred land.

By the 1870s, the Kel Ahaggar were made up of three clans, known as 'drum-groups', because the chieftain of each clan possessed a war-drum as a symbol of his authority. The 'royal' drum-group was the Kel Ghela, from whom the paramount chief – the *amenukal* – was chosen. The others were the Taitoq and the Tegehe Mellet. All three groups had clans of Kel Ulli attached to them as vassals, who paid an annual tribute to the chiefs of the drum-groups in the form of goats, butter and grain. The Kel Ulli had originally been denied camels and weapons, but in the mid-nineteenth century there had been a power-shift. Many Kel Ulli were now armed and mounted, and capable of fighting alongside their masters.

The Kel Ahaggar considered themselves the aristocracy of the Tuareg. The Kel Ajjer, with whom Duveyrier had lived, were their poor relations. The Kel Ajjer had been amenable to Duveyrier's visit, because of their need for French support against the Turks. The gracious way Duveyrier had been treated, coupled with the idealism of youth and his lack of first-hand memories, had given him a wholly idealized view. In late 1877, when Duponchel began to unfold his updated plans for the Trans-Saharan Railway, *Exploration du Sahara* remained the only substantial account of Tuareg culture. The tragedy that was to follow can be laid squarely at Henri Duveyrier's feet.

7

'Less formidable than the "Redskins"'

In 1879, Duponchel published a 360-page tome, *Le Chemin de Fer Transsaharien*, or *The Trans-Saharan Railway*. It sparked off massive public debate. The Italian Geographical Society disparaged it, backed up by the German explorer Gerhard Rohlfs. A former French Foreign Legionnaire, and the most experienced desert traveller of his time, Rohlfs warned that any advance across the Sahara would come up against the Tuareg.

His comment provoked a wave of derision from Duponchel and his supporters. 'The hostility of the Tuareg is [a monstrous error],' declared a Duponchel man, M. Capitaine, editor of the paper *L'Exploration*, 'in fact, even supposing they are occasionally irritating, the Tuareg will never be numerous enough to cause us insurmountable difficulties.'[8]

'They are a people much divided,' agreed *La France Coloniale*, 'few in number, of a proverbial loyalty . . . and essentially honest . . . In the most pessimistic assessment, the Tuareg are less formidable than the "Redskins".'[9] None of these commentators realized that their views were wholly derived from Henri Duveyrier; his ideas had become received wisdom.[10] It was Duponchel himself who summed it up. 'A hundred uncivilized tribesmen armed with old-fashioned spears,' he wrote. 'What is that against the might of France?'[11]

Duponchel's report eventually landed on the desk of Charles de Freycinet, Minister of Public Works, an engineer by training and an astute politician. Freycinet saw big public works projects, especially in the colonies, as a way of bringing together a divided nation. He was a great believer in the development of French railways, and a natural ally of Duponchel; nevertheless he approached the proposal cautiously, handing the report over to be dissected by his engineering staff.

Meanwhile, public enthusiasm for the Trans-Saharan, so lacking when Duponchel had first announced the project four years earlier, had now reached a crescendo. In September 1878, Paris lawyer Gazeau de Vautibault, a passionate Trans-Saharan supporter, reintroduced the issue of the railway at the 3rd International Conference of Commercial Geography. The same delegates who had ridiculed Duponchel earlier now fell over themselves to pass a motion calling for immediate exploration of the areas concerned.

On the strength of this support, de Vautibault established the Trans-Saharan Company, with the object of organizing exploration projects in the Algerian Sahara, but the company's activities were nipped in the bud on 13 July 1879 when the President of the Third Republic, Jules Grévy, appended his signature to a document placed before him by de Freycinet. The document authorized the establishment of a 'high commission for the study of questions relative to the establishment of communications by railway, from Algeria . . . to the interior of the Sudan'. The High Commission was given a budget of two hundred thousand francs and was to meet at the headquarters of the Ministry of Public Works in Paris on 21 July.

8

Providence Had Given
Him Another Chance

After Duponchel disappeared towards the Atlas in a spiral of dust in early 1877, Paul Flatters returned to business as usual. The weeks passed and became months, and he heard nothing from Paris. His elation once again receded into the mists as he dealt with the realities of everyday life of the Cercle. Reports from the desert continued to look discouraging. Hardly had the dust settled in the tracks of Duponchel's diligence than he received a camel-courier from the south. The rider carried a message from a French explorer, Victor Largeau, who had been making vain attempts to reach the Hoggar Mountains for the past decade. In the Wadi Mya, south of Wargla, Largeau and his party had been accosted by an armed delegation bringing a message from the elders of the In Salah Oasis, and there was nothing subtle about it. 'No "Roumi" [European] will come to our place, or near our territory. Those who try will regret it.'[12]

Not two months later, a telegram arrived, informing Flatters that the German explorer Erwin von Bary had been found dead in the oasis of Ghat, apparently poisoned. Bary, a botanist, had been commissioned by the African Society of Germany and the Berlin Geographical Society to penetrate the Hoggar Mountains. A day before his death, he had written a letter in which he declared that his health was excellent. That same evening he had dined with the Ottoman governor of Ghat. The circumstances were suspicious.

In January 1879, Flatters was requested to escort an American journalist to the oasis of Wargla, on the extreme southern perimeter of his territory. Taking this as an opportunity for a desert patrol, he assembled a hundred *goumiers*, irregular horsemen and camel-men of the Shamba. The patrol covered a thousand kilometres, and Flatters found it invigorating. At Wargla he met Arabs who had just come from the Sudan, who told him that their people would be ready to take him to Timbuctoo through Tuareg country, provided that he had a large armed escort. He also met Louis Richard, head of the White Fathers' Mission in Tripoli, who had come to collect the remains of Fathers Paulmier, Bouchand and Menoret, murdered in 1876. Father Richard had reconstructed the crime from eyewitnesses, and was able to give Flatters a full account of their deaths.

Flatters returned to Laghouat after a thirty-eight-day absence to find a letter waiting for him. The news was bittersweet: he had been promoted lieutenant colonel and he was being recalled to France to take command of a regular unit, the 72nd Infantry Regiment of the Line. His dreams of an expedition to Timbuctoo, revived by the trek to Wargla, had been abruptly truncated. He was forty-seven years old and it seemed unlikely that he would ever return to the Sahara. He packed his few possessions, handed command over to his successor, Lieutenant Colonel Eugène Belin, and headed for France.

He found some compensation in his reunion with his family. His son, Etienne, was now eleven years old, and in need of a father. He moved Sarah and the boy to his new quarters in the regiment's depot at Amiens, but just a few weeks later another unexpected letter arrived. This time it came from the Minister of Works, Charles de Freycinet: Flatters learned with a frisson of excitement that he had been appointed a member of the High Commission for the Trans-Saharan Railway. He left for Paris on 27 June, convinced that Providence had, after all, given him another chance.

9

'Is there any point in being murdered peacefully?'

The inaugural meeting of the High Commission took place in the conference hall of the Ministry of Public Works in Paris. On the morning of 21 July, chairs squeaked as they slowly filled up with frock-coated delegates from the government, big business, the armed forces and the civil service. A buzz of excited voices filled the air until de Freycinet, a meek-looking, bearded man nicknamed 'the White Mouse' took his place on stage and banged his gavel to call the meeting to order. In a few terse words, he introduced the man who sat at his side: none other than the august Ferdinand de Lesseps, creator of the Suez Canal.

De Lesseps had little to say for himself. To Duponchel's surprise, he read out a letter from Henri Duveyrier, who had been elected to the High Commission but could not be present. Duveyrier immediately overturned Duponchel's idea of routing the railroad across the Tanezrouft. The Trans-Saharan should, he said, follow the traditional camel-road from Algiers to Timbuctoo through the Hoggar Mountains, passing the disused salt-workings at Amadghor. If it was to be built, he said, it ought to benefit the Tuareg through whose territory it ran. There could be no question of trying to subdue them by force. Any expedition into their territory must be non-aggressive.

Duponchel realized that Duveyrier was not interested in the railway; his only interest was in the Tuareg, and he remained obsessed by them, even after all these years. The project's only value to Duveyrier was simply as a means of assisting them. But Duveyrier was not an engineer, and it did not appear to have occurred to him that building a railway through the Hoggar Mountains would cost a great deal more than building it across the flat Tanezrouft plains. The thing that stuck in Duponchel's craw most was that Duveyrier evidently had the support of the great de Lesseps. He should have known better.

Duponchel was irritated to see that the focus of the commission was already beginning to shift away from railway construction to exploration. The mysterious Hoggar Mountains and their equally mysterious veiled inhabitants exerted a spell over some commission members that mere steam-and-steel technology could not match. Paul Flatters was one of them. He was perfectly willing to accept Duveyrier's proposal that the railway should pass through the Hoggar: this was the area that had drawn him from the beginning. What did bother him was Duveyrier's rhetoric about a 'non-aggressive' expedition. The old caravan route Duveyrier wanted to use had been closed for years because of the endless infighting between the Kel Ajjer and the Kel Ahaggar. Flatters believed that it could not be reopened without a well-armed military column. It had been proved over and over again in the past few years that isolated, unarmed travellers who set off hopefully towards the Hoggar would either be turned back, like Largeau, or murdered.

On that first meeting, the commission was divided into half a dozen subcommittees to examine particular aspects of the project. Flatters was attached to the subcommittee for exploration, charged with deciding how a survey expedition should be organized. This was Flatters' area of expertise. On the third meeting of the commission, on 17 October, he put forward the proposal he had already made to Governor-General Chanzy, in 1877, for a column of three hundred regular soldiers armed with the most modern breech-loading rifle, the 1874 model Fusil Gras.

His proposal was rejected out of hand. The committee opined that it would look to the natives like a military conquest, and Duveyrier had already convinced them that the reconnaissance must be non-aggressive. Seeing his last chance of glory slipping through his fingers, Flatters proposed a compromise. Instead of regular troops in uniform, he would take with him irregular *goumiers* raised from Arab tribes. They would be dressed in their traditional garb and their rifles would be packed in crates, and only broken out if needed for defence. Flatters would take with him five or six civilian experts – surveyors, engineers, geologists – and a handful of French officers, who would, like himself, wear civilian dress. The column would be non-threatening, but capable of packing a punch if the need arose.

De Freycinet recommended his compromise. Duveyrier gave it his blessing. Flatters stood up, thanked the committee, and said he thought such a non-military expedition had an excellent chance of success. 'It is not because I am a soldier that I believe I can succeed,' he said, 'but because I have been able to acquire a certain experience of the ways of the Sahara while working as Commandant of Laghouat.'[13] Flatters' sudden shift in opinion was startling, for he, more than anyone, knew the truth about Tuareg truculence, yet he was ready to accept the ascendancy of Duveyrier, a man who had not set foot in the Sahara for two decades. Flatters was by nature a man inclined to compromise. All his life he had sought the approbation of his peers, and it was not in his character to be obstinate. Later, it would be claimed that he was blind, stupid and ignorant, but this was not the case. Above all, he hungered for personal glory, and he was ready to accept the consensus if it got him where he needed to be, even though it might clash with his own experience. As for Duveyrier, there is no better example of the power of romantic ideas to mesmerize even the supposedly rational and intelligent. It was Duveyrier's word that ruled the High Commission and if Duveyrier wanted a 'peace-loving' expedition, that is what he would get.

Flatters might have lacked the personal integrity to point out that the emperor was wearing no clothes, but a colleague from the Arab Bureau, General Arnaudeau, did not. The general, former commander of a column at Wargla during the French conquest, made no bones about the threat posed by the Sanusiyya brotherhood. 'From the heights of Jabal Akhdar [Cyrenaica],' he said, 'the power of the mystical Senusi sect stretches throughout the Sahara, in the Tuat, at In Salah, in Ghat, among the Tuareg, among the Shamba, and in the Islamic Sudan . . . You want to go by peaceful means, you say? "Pacifism" isn't what's needed here. Is there any point in being murdered peacefully? You say that it's important not to frighten the natives, and maybe that's right, but at least you should have the strength to defend yourself. A hundred and fifty or two hundred soldiers, part French, part Algerian *tirailleurs*, or colonial infantry, armed with long-range rifles, could stop an attack by the strongest Saharan bands.'[14]

But Arnaudeau was a voice crying in the wilderness. The die was cast. On 17 November 1879, de Freycinet informed Flatters officially that he had been appointed to command a mission from Algiers to the Sudan, with a native escort. He was to open relations with the chiefs of the Tuareg and try to obtain their approval, but the *sine qua non* of the expedition was that it must remain 'essentially pacifist'.

Duponchel was furious. The commission had thrown out his proposed route across the flat plains of the Tanezrouft without even considering it. The Hoggar route might be interesting to explore, he thought, but it lacked any practical purpose in terms of building a railway. As for the reconnaissance mission, he had been left out in the cold. He did not dispute that Flatters had more experience but felt that he himself should have been made director of operations. 'My personal initiative,' he told the committee, 'the studies I have persevered with over five years, it seems to me, give me the incontestable right to claim this position . . . I feel that I have the ability to occupy it. I have asked for it . . . the Minister has refused me.'[15] Duponchel was not a man who could accept second place, especially in a project that had been his own hobby-horse. From this moment, he washed his hands of an enterprise that had inspired him for five years. 'I have never crossed the Sahara,' he commented bitterly. 'I have never seen the Sudan, and now I will probably never see it.'[16]

On 7 January 1880, Lieutenant Colonel Flatters and a hastily assembled team of officers and experts left from Marseilles on the steamer *The Immaculate Conception*, bound for Algiers.

10

'Danger does not show itself until it is too late'

Paul Flatters set off from Wargla, the last outpost in French Algeria, on 5 March, with three hundred camels, twenty-five Frenchmen, seventy *sokhrar*, or camel-men, twelve Shamba guides and a couple of Tuareg ex-prisoners who he thought might be useful to him. From the start, there were quarrels among the Arabs, and there was tension between them and the French. Things came to a head eight days after leaving Wargla, at Ain Ta'iba, where a young Arab Bureau officer, Second Lieutenant Le Chatelier, tried to retrieve some French water-skins the cameleers had taken. The Arabs immediately cocked their rifles and retired behind a dune. The Frenchmen did the same. Only Flatters' order relieving Le Chatelier of his command defused the situation.

Then, at the wells of al-Bayadh, a few days later, the Shamba guides declared they would go no further towards the Hoggar. The *sebkha*, or salt-plain, around the wells was deserted, and a reconnaissance showed no trace of the Tuareg, yet still the Arabs were uneasy. 'They knew,' wrote another young officer, Second Lieutenant Henri Brosselard of the 4th Infantry Regiment, 'that in Tuareg country, as in Arab country, danger does not show itself until it is too late, and that from now on it was going to be necessary to redouble their vigilance.'[17]

35

The guides told Flatters he must turn south-east into Kel Ajjer country, the area already explored by Duveyrier. Speechless with frustration, Flatters left the camp to stomp around alone in the desert. He was gone so long that the other Frenchmen had to send out parties to look for him. On 27 March, he reluctantly gave the order to leave the Hoggar route and turn south-east towards the oasis of Temassinin.

For one of Flatters' guides, Sghir bin Sheikh of the Shamba, this was déjà vu. Three years earlier he had come this way with the French explorer Louis Say, one of Victor Largeau's colleagues, who had set out to reach the Hoggar. Sghir had brought him as far as Temassinin, but had refused to go further because a band of Hoggar Tuareg had threatened to murder them. Sadly, Say had turned back the way he had come.

Despite this dubious recommendation, Sghir was valuable because he had good connections with the Tuareg. He had two wives – an Arab woman at Wargla, and an Ifoghas woman in Kel Ajjer territory – and he could slip between both societies as it suited him. Flatters instructed Sghir to carry a letter to the Kel Ajjer chief, Ikhenoukhen, reminding him of the treaty signed in Ghadames twenty years earlier and asking for permission to pass through his country.

It was sixteen days before Sghir returned, and by then Flatters had already resigned himself to taking the route towards Ghat, an oasis officially beyond the Algerian frontier, recently garrisoned by Turkish troops. When he finally turned up, Sghir did not bring consent from Ikhenoukhen. Instead, he brought thirty Tuareg warriors, who largely ignored the Frenchmen but appeared to be friendly with the Shamba. The following day the Tuareg guided the caravan to Lake Menghough, a pool about a square kilometre in area. This became Flatters' furthest point south.

More Tuareg tribesmen began to appear with their camels and families, pitching camp around the pool. It was if they had come to see a travelling show. Every day men, women and children flocked into the French camp, poking their noses into equipment and stores and demanding presents. Flatters became increasingly irritated. Sghir assured him that Ikhenoukhen had been delayed awaiting orders from the Turkish *Vali* in Tripoli. Flatters had no way of knowing if this was true, or if the *amenukal* was simply playing with him. He mentally gave Ikhenoukhen three days to answer: his supplies were running short, the number of Tuareg in the camp was growing daily and the risk of treachery increasing. The Arabs were too disorganized to fight should the column be attacked, because they had divided themselves into two factions and were bickering continuously. Flatters longed for a company of infantrymen.

By 20 April still no word had come from the *amenukal*. Flatters gave orders to strike camp and make for Ghat. He was aware that this might provoke a protest from the Ottomans, but he had no choice: Ghat was the only oasis in the area where he could renew his provisions. But the caravan had gone no more than four hundred metres when a host of Tuareg camel-riders appeared out of the desert and formed up threateningly across its line of march. Some of the French officers were for fighting, but Flatters demurred. The expedition was supposed to be 'non-aggressive', and in any case, he could not trust the discipline of the *sokhrar*.

Flatters ordered the column to make camp and for the rest of the day he and his countrymen mulled over the situation. Finally, it was agreed that they had no choice but to give up the attempt to reach Timbuctoo. At four o'clock on the morning of 21 April, the Trans-Saharan expedition turned tail and began to march back home.

11

'A temporary pause between two distinct phases'

It was an ignominious retreat. Adolphe Duponchel had scoffed at the idea of 'a hundred uncivilized tribesmen armed with old-fashioned spears' obstructing the might of France, but that was precisely what had happened. The French column had been superior in number and better armed, but the Kel Ajjer had turned them away without a shot being fired. Riding back towards Wargla, Flatters was torn by the same internal battle that had plagued him since his meeting with the High Commission. He had known all along that an uncompromising attitude was needed. The Tuareg were a warrior people who saw the world only in terms of the strong and the weak. On the other hand, he was committed to the commission, and determined not to disobey its orders.

The caravan arrived at the abandoned wells of Tabalbalet five days later in a blinding sandstorm. In the mess tent that evening, Flatters discussed the situation with his chief-of-staff, Captain Pierre René Masson. Both officers knew that they had failed in their mission; though they had followed the High Commission's directives to remain non-aggressive, they had wandered from the proposed route through the Hoggar Mountains. They had been defeated not by the Tuareg but by their faint-hearted Shamba guides, who had refused to take them the right way. Masson thought there was still a chance to salvage their battered honour, but it would mean getting guides from the Kel Ahaggar. The only way to do that, he said, was to write to Sheikh Yunis, better known as Aitaghel, the *amenukal* of the Kel Ahaggar confederation. If they got a favourable reply, the colonel could show it to the High Commission and get financing for a second expedition.

Masson had another suggestion to make. They had brought with them from Menghough three chiefs of the Ifoghas Tuareg. One of them, Sheikh Dubh ag Meza, had proved useful in providing information, and could certainly find his way to Aitaghel's camp. Why not send him off right away with the request?

Flatters had his doubts about this. Dubh was an Ifoghas, a clan belonging to the Kel Ajjer confederation, and thus an enemy of the Kel Ahaggar. Aitaghel might reject their plea simply because he did not like the messenger. Masson insisted it was their only chance, and Flatters let himself be persuaded. That night he wrote a letter asking Aitaghel to open the route through the Hoggar to the Sudan the following year. In the morning the letter was handed to Sheikh Dubh. Flatters instructed his messenger, Sghir bin Sheikh, to go along with the Targui and bring back the chief's reply as quickly as possible.

After the two men had departed, Flatters penned a dispatch to Charles de Freycinet. It was worded carefully, to give the impression that there had been no actual setback, announcing that his column had been given a stirring welcome by the Kel Ajjer. 'Various circumstances,' he said, had inclined him to return to Wargla and Laghouat, 'to revictual, to dispose temporarily of the equipment, and to receive your orders with respect to a reprise of operations in the autumn, on the direct route to the Sudan through the Hoggar.'[18] Flatters was desperate for a second chance. This was not the end of the operation, he wrote in his journal, it was not even a postponement, but 'a temporary pause between two distinct phases'.[19]

Flatters was so anxious to find out if Aitaghel had agreed to his request that he left the column before it reached Wargla, riding off ahead with a small party. When he reached the oasis, though, he was disappointed to discover that Sghir had not yet returned. He looked around for another courier and was introduced to Sheikh Bu Jamaa, a Shambi with a sound reputation as a guide, who was also an irregular soldier of the *makhazin* – the military reserve. Flatters scribbled a second request to Aitaghel and despatched Bu Jamaa to the *amenukal*'s camp, then rode fast to his old post at Laghouat, arriving on 2 June. After resting a day or so with his successor, Lieutenant Colonel Eugène Belin, he rode to Algiers and took the ferry to Marseilles.

He met the High Commission in Paris on 16 June.

12

'We will not open it'

Sghir bin Sheikh and Dubh ag Meza had sighted the camp of Aitaghel on 6 May. It was late afternoon, and the fifteen or twenty moufflon-hide tents cast shadows that made them look larger than they really were. The tents were pitched on a rocky escarpment above the bed of a wadi shaded with tamarisk and *tarha* trees. The riders could see dark figures working around them. The smoke of several cooking fires rose straight up into the unblemished sky like fine-drawn pencil-lines.

Beyond the tents lay the landscape of the Hoggar, brooding and sinister: chimneys of rock, gouged by wind and sand into gargoyle shapes, dominating a maze of serpentine valleys, hemmed in by sheer ravines and impenetrable expanses of loose scree. To strangers the mountains were a place of terror, desolate, dark and dreary, a living purgatory where evil spirits lurked.

Dubh and Sghir couched their camels at a discreet distance from the camp and were ushered into the presence of the chief moments later. Aitaghel received them gracefully, making the customary inquiries about their family and herds. All three men adjusted their veils to their most formal configuration and sat down facing each other. There were no rugs or mats. They sat cross-legged under the awning of Aitaghel's tent on a carpet of fresh, clean sand that had been brought up from the wadi.

A message from the French was an event, and many of Aitaghel's entourage gathered round to hear what was said. Naked
boys with coxcomb haircuts peered out curiously from inside the
tent. They were shooed away by beautiful, unveiled women with
braided black hair. A slave kindled a fire, placed a kettle on a
three-stone fireplace and began to make tea.

Dubh handed Aitaghel the letter from Flatters and explained
that it was a request to allow a French-led caravan to pass through
the Hoggar Mountains during the coming winter. He may have
added that the mission was being sent to survey a route for what
the French called an 'iron road' across the Sahara. Whether
Aitaghel understood the significance of the 'iron road' is doubtful.
The chief did grasp that Christians were proposing to cross the
Hoggar Mountains, where no Christian had been before, and
establish a new trade route with the Sudan. If such a route were
established, it would end Tuareg perquisites, including the *ghefara*, the toll they extracted from any caravan passing through
their lands.

Aitaghel had held the title of *amenukal*, drum-chief of the Kel
Ahaggar, for only four years, but he had already acquired a
reputation as a courageous warrior and a man of good sense. He
had been chosen by the council to succeed the previous chief, al-
Haj Ahmad, who had been killed during a war with the Kel Ajjer.
The war had almost destroyed both groups, the advantage tipping
first to one side, then to the other, so that no one knew in the end
who had really won. Hundreds of tribesmen had been killed, and
hundreds of camels had changed hands.

During the war, Aitaghel had led a raiding-party eight hundred
strong, and his scouts had found the Kel Ajjer near Ghat Oasis.
Warned of their approach, the Kel Ajjer chief, Ikhenoukhen –
Duveyrier's 'majestic' old man – had moved his people, tents,
goats, camels, donkeys and all, up the slopes of a nearby mountain
named Ejmidhan. Unable to take the mountain by frontal assault,
Aitaghel had surrounded it and waited. For ten days the Kel

Ahaggar had waited, and each night Ikhenoukhen's watchmen had seen the enemy campfires twinkling below them. Then, at midnight on the tenth day, with campfires lit as usual, Aitaghel had led a party of a hundred men up a secret path he had found, to the top of the jebel. The Kel Ahaggar scaled the slopes so silently that Kel Ajjer sentinels did not hear so much as the scuff of a rock.

Sunrise revealed Aitaghel's party as they swarmed into the enemy camp. In the ferocious clash of sword and spear that followed, forty of Ikhenoukhen's men were killed and many more injured. Among the dead were two of Ikhenoukhen's sons. Aitaghel and his war-party returned triumphant, with scores of enemy camels in tow. That action sealed Aitaghel's reputation, but it did not end the war.

After assuming the title of *amenukal*, Aitaghel decided that both tribes had lost enough men, and he opened peace negotiations with the Kel Ajjer. The treaty had been agreed on three years earlier, at Ikhenoukhen's camp near Ghat.

The sun went down in a bat's wing of furled vapour, sending brilliant orange and scarlet tracers across the jagged horizon. A slave passed round sweet tea in tiny glasses, and the Tuareg drank it under their indigo veils. More warriors squatted around Aitaghel's tent to join the discussion.

Aitaghel was not a hasty man. He was aware that the Christians in the north were an energetic and powerful people. He did not welcome the idea of taking on new enemies after the recent devastating war with the Kel Ajjer. Yet his position as *amenukal* was insecure. Though the chief must be chosen from the Kel Ghela, the noble family of the confederation, and must be of direct descent from a previous *amenukal* through his mother, there was no accepted system of consensus.

Aitaghel's main rival was Khyar ag Hegir, the stepson of the previous *amenukal*, al-Haj Ahmad. Khyar had been schooled in diplomacy by his stepfather, and he advocated conciliation with the Christians. Many of the Kel Ahaggar agreed with him. Now

Khyar adjusted his veil, indicating that he wanted to speak. There was silence – Khyar was a well-respected man. In a steady voice, he advised the *amenukal* to tread with caution where the Christians were concerned. They were capable of joining forces with Ikhenoukhen. Everyone remembered how the Kel Ajjer chief had sought help from the Turks during the war, and with what consequences. The Kel Ajjer, backed up by four hundred Fezzan Arabs armed and paid by the Ottoman Bey of Murzuk, had routed the Kel Ahaggar five days out of Ghat. They had killed scores of warriors and taken everything – camels, goats, sheep and slaves. If he could do that with the Turks, the old man was perfectly capable of doing the same with the Christians.

Aitaghel listened closely to Khyar's argument. Privately he agreed that it made sense. The Kel Ahaggar had been weakened by the war, and there was more profit to be made in alliances than in enmity. Yet Aitaghel knew that he was walking a tightrope. If he came down on the side of conciliation, it would suggest that he was bowing to Khyar's authority. Many of the warriors would take this as a sign that the true chief of the Kel Ahaggar was Khyar. At the same time, appeasement would alienate his supporters, especially his nephew Atissi ag Shikkadh, a warrior renowned for his courage, cunning and ruthlessness. Atissi was the leader of the 'hawk' faction among the Kel Ahaggar, and the embodiment of their most chauvinistic qualities. It was Atissi who spoke next, reminding the *amenukal* that the Hoggar Mountains were the sacred refuge of the Kel Ahaggar. No Christian had ever entered the area and escaped alive. He contended that it should stay that way.

After sunset, the chiefs of the two other drum-groups, Sidi al-Keraji of the Taitoq and Shikkadh of the Tegehe Mellet – both close relatives of Aitaghel's – arrived to discuss the matter. The talks continued deep into the night, turning first one way, then the other. It became clear to Aitaghel, as he listened, that the other chiefs were with Atissi and staunchly against any Christian incursion into their lands. Before the sun came up, the three men had agreed on their answer to 'Sheikh' Flatters.

Aitaghel sent for his scribe and had him pen a letter, which was signed by all three members of the council. It was written in condescending style, and its tone was uncompromising: 'We have received your letter, we have read it and understood it,' he wrote. 'You have asked us to open the road to the south to you. *We will not open it.*'

13

Colonel Boum

In his two meetings with the High Commission that June, Flatters put the best possible spin on the fiasco at Lake Menghough. He stressed to the committee the lessons that had been learned and the experience gained. It was true that he had broken no new ground, but his maps were more accurate than Duveyrier's, and his experts had garnered a mass of scientific data in the fields of botany, geology, prehistory and geophysics. To those who suggested that he had been thwarted by the Tuareg, Flatters replied, disingenuously, that he could not have proceeded further in the direction he had been going, for to do so would have meant reaching Ghat, a post now garrisoned by two hundred Turkish janissaries. This could have resulted in an ugly diplomatic incident. He conveniently forgot that before the Kel Ajjer had blocked his advance, he had given just that order, to make for Ghat.

Summing up, Flatters claimed to be satisfied that he had surveyed the route of the railway for three hundred kilometres south of Wargla. The second expedition he now proposed – or rather, the second 'phase' – would be no more than a logical extension of the first. It would traverse the unexplored country of the Hoggar Mountains, and continue south through the Ayr Mountains to the Niger River and Timbuctoo.

Luckily, Flatters was preaching to the converted. Charles de

Freycinet was no longer in office. He had been replaced by a newcomer, Henri Varroy, who was so impressed by Flatters' feat that he recommended him for promotion. Many of the armchair explorers on the commission had been more interested from the start in the vicarious thrill of exploring the forbidden Hoggar Mountains than in the mundane task of building a railway. But there were even more compelling reasons for their assent. The Trans-Saharan was sponsored by the Ministry of Public Works, whose officers were aware that another government body, the Ministry of Marine Affairs, was far advanced in its own plans to lay a railway running inland from Dakar on the Atlantic coast to Timbuctoo. They could not stand the thought of being pipped at the post by their rivals.

Seeing that the wind was blowing his way, Flatters requested that the new mission should be of military character. The Shamba *goumiers* had proved to be undisciplined and had lacked cohesion. He wanted the second expedition to be accompanied by at least fifty trained *tirailleurs*. The commission debated this for a while and came up with a new compromise: Flatters could have his fifty *tirailleurs*, but they must be disguised as civilian camel-men. They would wear native dress rather than uniforms but would carry their Fusils Gras rifles openly. In this way, the commission was convinced, they would appear to be ordinary travellers, since everyone who travelled in the Sahara was armed. Flatters abstained from pointing out that most Saharan caravaneers or nomads carried swords, spears and daggers, and perhaps an ancient flintlock or two. His state-of-the-art rifles would be as much a giveaway as having the word 'soldier' tattooed across every forehead.

Flatters was instructed once again to lead a non-aggressive expedition. His orders were to avoid straying east into Ottoman country, but to stick as far as possible to a route passing through Wargla, Amadghor and the Hoggar Mountains. Adolphe Dupon-chel, still bitter at the rejection of his proposed route across the

Tanezrouft, could not resist highlighting the folly of this under-taking. The expedition, he believed, had no chance of producing worthwhile results: the railroad could not be laid through the Hoggar. The fact that Flatters had allowed himself to be turned back had simply made the situation worse. Every brigand in the Sahara would now regard a foreign expedition as easy prey. 'If failure might have been doubted last year,' Duponchel wrote, 'it is absolutely certain now.'[20]

Flatters made no comment. He had got what he wanted, what he had prayed for all the way back from Lake Menghough: a chance to redeem the failure of the first mission. Far from reprimanding him, the commission had accepted his version of events. Though Varroy's request that he be promoted to full colonel had been turned down, it was only because he lacked the seniority. Instead, he had been awarded a civilian medal: Officer of State Education.

Flatters might have pulled the wool over the commission's eyes, but he had not deceived everyone. Another embittered enthusiast, the lawyer Gazeau de Vautibault, had not forgotten how de Freycinet had whipped the rug from under his Trans-Saharan Company the previous year. De Vautibault, a devotee of private enterprise, christened Flatters 'Colonel Boum' and mocked the government's futile efforts on the first mission. 'He committed himself to go as far as Timbuctoo,' de Vautibault wrote, 'at the head of a hundred chosen men, at a cost of eight hundred thousand francs, in twelve months – well! Colonel Boum's mission returned without glory. It didn't get far: it was fleeced, deviated from its route, and finally (always finally) was forced to return without having passed points already known to previous explorers.'[21] Flatters was stung by this and other disparaging reports that appeared in the national press. He was determined that, whatever the cost, he would not be forced to return a second time.

14

'Encouraging letters from the chiefs'

The letter of refusal sent by the Kel Ahaggar council in early May had still not reached Flatters. At the time he was addressing the High Commission in June, it was in the possession of Sghir bin Sheikh, who was near Tabalbalet and well on the way to starving to death.

Sghir had ridden fast from Aitaghel's camp, hoping to catch up with Flatters before he reached Wargla. Near Tabalbalet he was picking his way down the rocky path, crossing the ridge where the well was situated, when his camel was startled by a jackal that appeared suddenly out of a clump of bushes. The camel shied, throwing him, and fled. Sghir hit the ground so hard that the breath was knocked out of him and he lost consciousness; when he came round, there was no sign of the camel. He cursed himself for travelling alone in the Sahara, which was against all his instincts. If he had not been near to the wells, death would have been certain.

Sghir considered his options. He had been injured in the fall, but even if he were completely fit, walking across the desert without a camel and without a water-skin would be suicide. His best bet was to remain where he was, trusting in God that a caravan would come by sooner or later and pick him up. He spent the first two days lying in the shade of a thornbush. There was no sign of his camel; the beast seemed to have been swallowed up by the desert. Once he had recovered from the initial shock, he decided to concentrate on getting food and water.

Lacking a vessel of any sort, the Shambi was obliged to painfully climb down into the well every time he needed to drink. He would soak his *shesh* in the water and suck the moisture from the cloth, until he found some colocynth melons growing nearby, desert succulents of the squash family, with gourds as large as oranges. The pulp was bitter and caused stomach-cramps, but Sghir squeezed it out with his fingers and swallowed it greedily. He ate the flowers and chewed the water-filled shoots, then scraped out the seeds. Finally, he fashioned crude cups from the soft shells with his dagger.

For days, Sghir waited patiently for a caravan to appear. He ate locusts and beetles, caught mice, lizards and desert rats. He ate the beetles and lizards raw. The mice and rats he gutted and roasted in their skins on hot stones. He made fire by striking flint on steel, letting the precious spark fall on a piece of cotton he had torn from his headcloth and beaten into a fibrous mass with a stone.

Occasionally he managed to club a desert hare or dig a fennec fox out of its burrow and strangle it. These animals had little meat on them, but Sghir skinned them carefully, ate a little and hung the rest on a bush to dry. When there was nothing else, he picked the berries off trees and ate the pods of acacias. Finally he was reduced to cutting the wild grass the Tuareg called *afezu*, rubbing the ears on a prehistoric saddle-quern he found in the desert. He ate the *afezu* flour raw. Days passed and became weeks, and still no caravan appeared.

Sghir was beginning to lose hope. When he counted off the days he realized he had been there an entire month. He was emaciated, and his strength was beginning to ebb fast; in a few days he would no longer be able even to fetch water.

Then a miracle happened: he awoke one day to find a party of

Ifoghas Tuareg riding across the well-field on their camels. They had found his runaway camel grazing on their desert pastures. Though Sghir was an Arab, he had married the daughter of ʿAbd al-Hakim, an Ifoghas marabout. The Ifoghas scouts had recognized his camel and had come to look for him.

They took the starved man back to their tents, where he spent weeks recovering from his ordeal. Months passed before he was fit enough to travel, and he finally handed Aitaghel's letter to Lieutenant Colonel Eugène Belin, commandant at Laghouat, on 15 September, more than four months after it had been written. By the time it reached Flatters in France, he had already received two other letters from the Kel Ahaggar chief.

Flatters was perfectly aware that Aitaghel's first letter was missing, because Aitaghel had referred to it in his second. Now, laying out the three letters in chronological order, Flatters tried to divine their underlying content. In the first, dated 7 May, Aitaghel had stated unequivocally that he would not open the route. In the second, dated 27 July, the chief told him to ignore what he had written in the first. He claimed that the request had been brought by a person in whom he had no confidence – presumably Sheikh Dubh ag Meza, whom, as Flatters had predicted, he regarded as an enemy. In this second letter, Aitaghel wrote that he was ready to open up the route, but suggested that the colonel should postpone the expedition until April 1881, when he would have more time to receive it. 'This is very difficult,' he concluded, 'and nothing would push me to do it except the promise of a great deal of money.'[22]

In the third letter, dated 2 September, the *amenukal* had adjusted his position yet again. In this, he warned Flatters that the approaches to the Sudan were riddled with war and disease, and that the *negroes* had recently wiped out a caravan from Tripoli that was said to have been made up of Christians. 'It would be better,' Aitaghel added, 'to stay at home.'[23] What mystified Flatters even further was that while the first letter had been signed by the three-man council of the Hoggar, the other two had come from

Aitaghel alone. Did this mean that the majority of the Kel Ahaggar wanted to keep him out, and that in declaring he would open the route, Aitaghel was acting independently?

The waters were muddied further by a letter from Ikhenoukhen, the Kel Ajjer chief, sent through the French Consul-General in Tripoli, M. Féraud. The Kel Ajjer had turned Flatters back at Lake Menghough, but Ikhenoukhen claimed to have arrived at the lake after Flatters had departed, having missed him by only a few days. He swore everlasting friendship and said that the colonel could rely on a safe passage through his territory.

All in all, the messages were incomprehensible. Aitaghel had refused to open the route, then agreed to open it, then advised Flatters to stay at home. Ikhenoukhen had let him down in April, but now offered him safe passage through Ajjer territory, where he no longer wished to go. There were wheels within wheels here, and Flatters knew from experience that this must reflect the fact that neither of the Tuareg chiefs had absolute power over his people; both were subject to the whims of other powerful factions within their tribes.

The letters gave Flatters an almost unlimited range of interpretation and, presented with this mass of conflicting information, he chose to believe what suited him. By shading out the threads he didn't like, he was able to convince himself that he had received 'encouraging letters from the chiefs of both the Kel Ajjer and the Kel Ahaggar', that Tuareg country was open to him, and that he could pass in complete security wherever he wanted to go. Aitaghel's letter of refusal had come too late to change anything, and in any case, the chief had told him in writing to ignore it. He decided not to mention it to the High Commission at all.

15

'It's possible I might be killed out there'

At first light on 4 December 1880, the second Trans-Saharan expedition assembled outside the oasis of Wargla. The two hundred and eighty camels were led up, couched and loaded by Arab cameleers and Algerian *tirailleurs*. The Arabs were wild-looking men in *gandourahs* (long white shirts), white burnooses and *sheshes* held in place by cotton bands. All of them carried rifles. The *tirailleurs* were dressed Arab-fashion and were distinguishable from the cameleers only by their Fusils Gras rifles and the newness of their clothes.

The camels were the big-bodied beasts raised by the Shamba in the open plains and ergs, the sand seas of their homeland. They were long on stamina, but used to the level going of the plains. They snarled and rumbled as the Arabs fitted pack-saddles, scooped away dirt to draw ropes under their bellies and lashed sacks, boxes and bags on their backs. The animals leapt to their feet, casting their loads, gnashing shark-size canines, vomiting green cud. The camel-men jerked them down again, arguing excitedly with each other, yelling and cursing in the half-eaten syllables of their Arabic drawl. Camels lolled on their side and thrashed bone-crushing limbs, spraying soft pellets of dung everywhere. The camel-men hauled them back to their knees. They grasped them by the tender lips and nostrils and stood on their folded legs until they kept still enough to load.

Slowly, out of the pandemonium, the piles of baggage began to diminish. There were food supplies for four months – biscuits, flour, rice, couscous, dates, preserved meat, preserved vegetables, dried fish, wine, meat stock, brandy, chocolate, coffee, tea, sugar and salt. There was water enough for eight days, fifty thousand cartridges, instruments, photographic equipment, tents, beds, tables, lamps, pots, pans, shovels, axes, buckets, ropes, and a thousand other items. From among the serried ranks, the loaded animals rose grumbling to their feet.

To Captain Pierre Masson and Lieutenant Joseph Henri de Dianous de la Perrotine, the scene was familiar. They were both Algerian veterans, and the only regular officers under Flatters' command. Masson, who came from Rambouillet and had been educated at Versailles, was thirty-four years old, and had graduated in the top ten of his intake at St Cyr. Considered a brilliant officer, he had been earmarked early for the general staff. As ADC to General Trecourt, commandant at Constantine, he had fought Arab rebels at al-ʿAmri, where he had been wounded and awarded the *Légion d'honneur*. Flatters had first met him at Amiens, and had headhunted him as the mission's adjutant. They had got on well during the first expedition to Lake Menghough.

Henri de Dianous was a few months older than Masson, though junior in rank. He was a newcomer to the expedition, but he had served under Flatters at Laghouat and knew the colonel well. Fluent in Arabic as well as Berber, Dianous was a soldier's soldier, who had joined the 82nd Infantry Regiment as a private, and had made sergeant before being selected for officers' training school at St Cyr. He came from Seregnan in Provence, the third of an impoverished baron's fifteen children; the family had been established in the area since the sixteenth century. Affable and sympathetic, he was much liked and respected by the Arabs and highly thought of by his superiors. He had been thrilled when Flatters had selected him for the mission. 'He had such an air of contentment,' said his aunt, an Algiers resident who had seen him before his departure, 'full of ideas for the present and plans for the future.' De Dianous had also been realistic enough to admit the dangers, telling her, 'It's possible I might be killed out there, but don't say anything to the family who would be worried on my account.'[24]

Flatters had also recruited two French sergeants and one private soldier. Sergeants Pobeguin and Dennery were in charge of logistics, while the private, Louis Brame of the 72nd Infantry Regiment, was Flatters' batman. Sergeant Joseph Pobeguin, a twenty-seven-year-old Breton from Cleguerec, was a tall, blond-haired NCO known for his professionalism and his candidly martial manner. Like de Dianous, he was a man who could be depended on in a fight. The third of four children, he had joined the Armée d'Afrique in 1873 and served in the 3rd Spahis, a colonial cavalry unit. In his time as commander of the fort at ʿAin Touta, near Biskra, he had developed a passion for the desert, and he had leapt at the chance of accompanying the second Flatters mission.

Now, standing among the *sokhrar* issuing orders, he felt conspicuous in his half-Arab, half-European attire – a Scottish tam o'shanter, velvet trousers, a woollen waistcoat and three burnooses, yellow, white and red.

Very little is known of the other NCO, Sergeant Dennery, not even his first name. All that has been recorded is that he had previously served in a regular cavalry unit, the 3rd Chasseurs à Cheval.

By seven-thirty that morning the caravan had assumed some semblance of order, and Paul Flatters rode out of the oasis on his grey mare. He, Masson and de Dianous went over the saddlery and equipment with a fine-tooth comb. Badly fitted saddles would rub and produce swellings that could easily turn into ulcers and eventually kill the camel. Poorly balanced loads would mean stoppages.

The single most important item was the water, carried in

water-skins. Though it was the cool season in the Sahara, every man would require at least five litres a day. Water-skins had been used in the Sahara since time immemorial – they can be seen in rock-paintings from the Neolithic era. They were ideally suited for camels, could be repaired easily by using a twig or a piece of camel-dung, and could be rolled up and packed away when not in use. They even kept the water cool. Their main drawback was that they lost liquid by evaporation, especially in a hot wind. On the first mission, Flatters had tried to solve this problem by using steel drums as water containers, but these had been so awkward that he left them behind this time.

After the baggage-camels had been given the once-over, the officers reviewed the guides, *tirailleurs* and camel-men. They were all mounted on *meharis*, or riding-beasts. Apart from two friendly Ifoghas Tuareg, all the guides were Shamba, past masters of the caravan trade through the central Sahara to the Algerian coast. The Shamba were merchants, desert guides and pastoral nomads, a restless people, constantly on the move. They wandered with their black tents as far east as the Tripolitanian border, and as far west as the Moroccan Atlas Mountains, always returning to the Mzab Valley for the date harvest in autumn. They were famous for their tracking skills. It was said that a Shambi could guide a caravan five hundred kilometres across featureless erg and place it within three metres of a single well. Only the Shamba could live in the great sand seas of Algeria, where a man could journey for three weeks and never see a tree or a rock or a blade of grass.

The Shamba were traditional enemies of the Hoggar Tuareg, but when not at war with them, they lived on terms of uneasy truce. The Tuareg regarded the Shamba as the descendants of bitches; the Shamba thought the Tuareg bloodthirsty pagans. Yet these Arabs were no strangers to slaughter themselves. A Shamba war-party mounted on camels and horses would fall on an enemy camp at sunrise, approaching from several directions and attacking without warning. They would open fire as soon as they were in range.

'These *razzias* (forays) most of the time, turn into shocking carnages,' wrote desert veteran General Eugène Daumas. 'The men, caught unawares, are almost all put to death; it is enough to despoil the women of their garments. If time permits, the victors carry off the tents, lead away the Negroes, the horses, the herds. The women and children are abandoned.'[25]

Flatters' thirty-one *sokhrar* were drawn from two tribes, the Shamba and the Awlad Na'il, and had been recruited from five hundred volunteers in Laghouat. They were mostly ex-Armée d'Afrique, or veterans of the first expedition. They looked like jockeys, perched up on the camels' backs on their double-pronged saddles, lightly armed with rifles, daggers and sticks. The forty-five *tirailleurs* rode their animals more awkwardly. They were clad in *gandourahs*, baggy trousers, burnooses, *sheshes* and ten-inch-high rawhide boots. They were all volunteers from the 1st and 3rd Régiments Tirailleurs d'Algérie, stationed at Laghouat. The 3rd RTA was recruited almost exclusively from the Awlad Na'il, Berber-speaking nomads from the hills north of the Saharan Atlas, whose womenfolk danced for their dowries with such abandon in the streets of Boukhrari. The 1st RTA was made up of settled Arabs from the *tell*.

The *tirailleurs* were physically fit, well disciplined and tough. They had all gone through a three-month course in drill, physical training, small arms, infantry tactics, attack and defence, patrol and reconnaissance, and bayonet fighting. They had survived gruelling desert route-marches, of up to thirty kilometres, in full kit, and were skilled in the use of their 1874-model Fusil Gras breech-loaders. Designed by General (then Captain) Basile Gras, the rifle was basically the old 11 mm Chassepot model with a more efficient cartridge, combining a percussion cap in the centre of the base with an elliptical bullet. The cartridge fitted snugly into the breech-block and was ejected by a lever. The Gras rifle could fire six rounds to every one fired by a muzzle-loader, and in the hands of a marksman like Sergeant Joseph Pobeguin, it could hit a target at a thousand metres. The *tirailleurs* were trained to fire both independently and in volleys, with devastating effect on both cavalry and infantry in close formation.

Satisfied that the column was at last in order, Flatters gave the signal to march. The first section of fifty camels Left the oasis in single file, then fanned out into open order to cross the rocky plateau, descending into the *sebkha*, the salt plain, whose gleaming surface raised a haze veiling the mysteries of the unexplored Sahara.

16

No Obvious Connection
With the Divine Porte

The second departure of the Flatters column had not gone unnoticed by the world's press. In the Italian newspapers especially
there had been an outcry against a 'secret French agenda in the
Sahara'. The French government had been accused of a conspiracy
against Ottoman interests, and fingers had been pointed at Paul
Flatters, Father Louis Richard of the White Fathers' Mission,
and the French Consul-General in Tripoli, M. Féraud. These
reports were read with great interest at the Yildiz Palace in
Constantinople, site of the Divine Porte.

The Ottoman Sultan, ʿAbdul Hamid II, knew of the French plan
to build a railway across the desert, and the Sanusiyya Brotherhood had a permanent ambassador at his court. Although there is
no documentary evidence, it is widely believed that, some time in
the winter of 1880, the Sultan discussed the Flatters expedition
with the Sanusi ambassador.

ʿAbdul Hamid was known as Abdul the Damned, or the Red
Sultan. He was thirty-eight years old and had become Padishah of
the Ottoman Empire four years earlier, after deposing his elder
brother Murad V and incarcerating him for life. Terrified that
someone would do the same to him, the Sultan had constructed a
labyrinth of bolt-holes and tunnels under the palace, and had

secreted hundreds of pistols around the place in case of assass-
ination attempts. His outbursts of rage were proverbial and
courtiers quaked when called into his presence. His food was
tasted by poison-snoopers, his cigarettes puffed first by servants;
even his clothes were tried on first by his valet, in case they might
have been smeared with noxious stuffs.

ʿAbdul Hamid's ancestors had dominated the Middle East and
North Africa since the fifteenth century, but now the Empire was
sick. The French had kicked out the Dey of Algiers fifty years
earlier, and the British and French now held controlling financial
interests in Egypt – the jewel in the crown of the Ottoman Empire.
Britain and France were officially Turkish allies and in the 1850s
had fought to defend Ottoman interests in the Crimea, but these
allies had deserted him in the Russo-Turkish war of 1877–8, and
the Russians had regained all the losses they had sustained two
decades before. The Sultan knew he could no longer expect help
from the European powers, and after the Russian victory he had
suspended the Constitution and dissolved Parliament.

Since then he had rarely left the confines of his rambling palace.
Here in the Yildiz he sat like a spider at the centre of a web whose
strands stretched out thousands of kilometres, across mountain,
sea and desert, in the form of telegraph wires, secret police and spy
networks, to the farthest-flung outposts of his tottering domain.

The trans-Saharan trade was a gold mine. Since 1850, the Turks
had held the monopoly on trading caravans in the eastern Sahara.
The caravan routes from the Sudan through Murzuk and Ghadames, intersecting at the key oasis of Ghat, carried goods valued
at more than ten million French francs a year. The chief com-
modities were slaves, ostrich feathers and ivory. Although the
trade in human beings had officially been banned in 1856, some
five thousand slaves survived the desert crossing every year, and
about half of these ended up in Constantinople, where they were
sold for two and a half times what they made in Ghadames, and
many times what they were bought for in the Sudan. Ostrich

feathers were even more profitable, thanks to the French Empress Eugénie, who had made them highly fashionable throughout Europe. On the Paris market a single white feather could fetch as much as five hundred francs. The trade in ivory was also booming; it was much sought after in Europe and the United States, where it was used for piano keys, knife handles and billiard balls. Annual exports of ostrich feathers and ivory alone were worth about seven million francs.

The Sultan knew the Sanusiyya controlled the caravan routes, collecting taxes and import duty and exerting considerable influence over the nomads of the eastern Sahara. Although its chief, Sayid al-Mahdi as-Sanusi, had never gone out of his way to accept the emblems of Ottoman sovereignty, the Sultan tolerated the Brotherhood because it was useful. Many Ottoman officials were themselves members of the Sanusiyya, a situation of which he approved. Now abandoned by the Christian powers, he could see the advantage in playing the pan-Islamic card. As hereditary *khalifa* of Islam, the official successor of the Prophet Mohammad, he had the right to call the faithful to jihad. There was little to be gained by alienating committed Muslims such as the Sanusiyya, as long as they presented no challenge to the Ottoman Empire.

During their meeting at the Yildiz, the Sanusi agent may have pointed out that if the French built a railway across the Sahara, the revenues now flowing into Ottoman coffers would soon be enriching Christians instead. Ikhenoukhen of the Kel Ajjer Tuareg had been invested with the scarlet robe of an Ottoman *kaimikam*, but he had never been a staunch ally of the Porte. It was true that he had allowed the Turkish *Vali* in Tripoli, Ahmed Rasim Pasha, to move troops to Ghat in 1875, but that was only because he had needed Ottoman help against the Kel Ahaggar. Recently he had written to the French offering them free passage through his territory. Clearly, he could not be relied on.

The antagonism between the two Tuareg confederations could be played upon to the Ottomans' advantage. The Turks could use the Kel Ahaggar as a counterweight against Ikhenoukhen. The Hoggar folk lay on the direct route from Algiers to Timbuctoo, and had much to lose from a French-controlled trade route across their territory, especially if it were to take the form of a railway.

The Kel Ahaggar were not officially Ottoman subjects – they lived outside the frontiers of the vilayet of Tripoli. They were Muslims, though, and thus the spiritual, if not temporal, subjects of the Sultan in his role as *khalifa*. The ambassador might have suggested that the Sanusiyya dispatch an agent to confer with Aitaghel, to remind him of his duty to carry out the jihad.

In Salah would be an ideal meeting place, for it lay on a direct route from Ghadames, and its merchants had close ties with those of Tripolitania. The people of In Salah were staunchly anti-French, and had declared allegiance to the Sultan of Morocco; a few years ago they had issued a blunt warning to the French explorer Victor Largeau. There was as yet no Sanusiyya Lodge at In Salah, but there was one at Ghadames, and its sheikh, Thani, was among the Brotherhood's best agents.

We cannot know for certain that this conversation took place, but if it did, it is likely that nothing was said about halting French plans to build a railway. Certainly, the Sanusi agent knew that if any accident should befall the Flatters mission, it must have no obvious connection with either the Brotherhood or the Divine Porte.

17

The Devil's Mirror

The morning had been cold, but by noon the sun was unsheathed in its full brilliance. The *sokhrar* drew their headcloths across their faces and pulled their burnooses tight. Wargla and its forests of palm trees was already out of sight. The column that had seemed so huge in the narrow confines of the oasis was reduced to a sprawl of tiny insects on the mighty canvas of the salt lake. Each of the six sections was self-sufficient in food and water, and each had an escort of *tirailleurs*. At point for the first section the seven guides rode easy and loose on their lanky animals. At their head was Mohammad bin Raja of the Zawa, one of the Shamba clans from the deep south, and riding with him were Sheikh Bu Jamaa, who had taken the message to Aitaghel for Flatters in May, and Mohammad Bul-Ghiz, a sombre, silent Arab of great energy and physical strength. Beside him rode Sghir bin Sheikh, now recovered from his ordeal and long isolation at Tabalbalet.

Sghir had met Flatters on his arrival in Algiers. He had explained the reason for his delay in delivering the letter and Flatters, though initially exasperated, had long since forgiven him – it was impossible to remain angry with Sghir, who was a persuasive talker and a humorous raconteur. Sghir had brought with him to Algiers ʿAla, his more reserved young brother, his Tuareg father-in-law ʿAbd al-Hakim, and another nine Ifoghas guides,

63

sent by Ikhenoukhen as a sign of his recently avowed friend-
ship. Flatters had accepted only two of the Ifoghas – ʿAbd al-
Hakim and another, named Hamma – but he had been grateful for
Ikhenoukhen's gift.

As for Aitaghel, Flatters continued to find his attitude a puzzle.
On the way from Laghouat, another message had arrived from
Consul-General Féraud in Tripoli. The news was that Aitaghel had
ridden to Ghat and met with Ikhenoukhen. It was common knowledge, Féraud said, that the Kel Ahaggar chief was fiercely opposed
to Flatters' expedition. He had apparently given his old enemy a
tongue-lashing for encouraging the French.[26]

The six sections of camels spread out over the glistening plain,
moving in dense bunches. The Arabs did not string the camels
head to tail in Tuareg fashion; their style of marching was to allow
each animal to walk freely, while the cameleers drove them from
behind. Unlike the Tuareg, who always rode, the Arabs rode and
walked alternately. They would slip down lightly from the camel's
back, tying up the head-ropes and letting their *meharis* drift along
with the baggage-animals. When mounting, they did not bother to
couch their animals, but simply brought their heads down, stepped
on the curve of their necks and pirouetted gracefully into the
saddle.

Paul Flatters envied the vigour of his camel-men. Sciatica had
plagued him on and off for years and it had flared up badly while
on his way from Laghouat. Now he was unable to walk for more
than half an hour, as the sciatica sent fiery bolts of pain that began
in his lower back shooting down the sciatic nerves in both his legs.
Walking was agony, but the pain was at least bearable while he
was riding a horse.

In Wargla he had consulted Surgeon Major Robert Guiard, the
expedition's medical officer, who had been with him on the first
mission. Guiard, the twenty-nine-year-old son of a Parisian university professor, was a graduate of the Strasbourg School of
Military Medicine, and had served as medical officer with the

87th Infantry Regiment of the Line and the 2nd Zouaves. He was highly rated, both as an excellent doctor and a man of integrity and energy, and his qualifications for the expedition included his interest in botany – on the first mission he had collected no fewer than a hundred and thirty new specimens of plants. Besides being expedition medic, he was also responsible for zoo-logical and anthropological studies, and was the mission's official photographer.

In Wargla, Dr Guiard had examined Flatters and told him that he had probably ruptured a vertebra, maybe the result of years in the saddle. Ideally, he needed a long period of bed-rest. This would have meant delaying the mission, which was already perilously late, so Flatters chose instead to have the doctor administer a stiff shot of morphine four times a day. The morphine didn't do much to relieve the pain, so Flatters resorted to the old Arab remedy: the cauterizing iron. Each morning Guiard burned fifty points with a red-hot iron along the sciatic nerve, as far down as the knee. This freed up the ache enough for him to walk for an hour.

Flatters had posted one or two members of the expedition to supervise each section. Apart from Masson, de Dianous, Dr Guiard and Sergeants Dennery and Pobeguin, there were three civilian experts. The most distinguished of them was Émile Beringer, a myopic forty-year-old engineer from Strasbourg, who had worked alongside Ferdinand de Lesseps two decades earlier on the con-struction of the Suez Canal. The bespectacled Beringer had some military experience too: he had volunteered as an auxiliary lieuten-ant in the 25th Corps during the Franco-Prussian war. Afterwards he had done notable work as a railway engineer both in Brazil and at home in France. Now attached to the Ministry of Works, he was respected as an original thinker and a man with a unique know-ledge of his field. Beringer had accompanied Flatters on the first mission; now he retained responsibility for map-making and astronomical, geodesic and meteorological observations.

Jules Roche, the mission's geologist, had also taken part in the first expedition. He was fourteen years younger than Émile Beringer, the son of a coach-maker from Eyguières in the Rhone Valley. A brilliant mathematician, he had studied in Tarascon and Marseilles. As an engineer in the Corps of Mines, he had worked in Austria, Hungary, Italy, Spain and Algeria, and had acquired a taste for travel. Roche was a modest, self-deprecating man with a sympathetic manner and a generous nature. Fired with the prospect of solving the mysteries of the Sahara, he had volunteered enthusiastically for the first expedition, but had harboured doubts about the second. 'It's possible you won't see me again,' he had told his brother on the quayside at Marseilles. 'The escort is too small, but I gave my word and I have to go.'[27] Roche's instructions were to produce a geological report, and to assist Beringer with the cartography.

The third civilian expert was Joseph Santin, a civil engineer by training, who had been brought along to help Beringer and Roche. Finally, there was Paul Marjolet, who had joined the expedition at Wargla. Marjolet was not listed on the mission's official roster and remains, like Sergeant Dennery, a dark horse; he was, in different accounts, a private soldier, an assistant engineer or a professional cook. The Flatters Mission's French contingent numbered eleven men in all.

The caravan, plagued by the inevitable teething problems, made only fifteen kilometres that day. Shifting loads, loose ropes and leaking water-skins meant it advanced in fits and starts. As the hours passed, the excited chatter that had marked the start gave way to silence as each man drifted into his own thoughts. Soon there was no sound but the rhythmic creak of the saddles and the slosh of water in the skins. Far away on the southern horizon dust-devils whirled across the caravan's line of march. To the left and right, hog's-back ridges rose from the velveteen surface, their crests whittled by erosion into the grotesque shapes of shark heads, crouching dwarfs and squinted steeples. Jules Roche, the geologist, gazed around him, fascinated, trying to read the syntax of the desert surface, and to understand the forces that had been at work here over the eons. The saline flats they were crossing, he concluded, were a sea-without-water – they could only be the residue of a great inland lake that had existed here in past ages, but had long ago dried up. The cliffs and ridges around them had once been the shores of that phantom ocean. The forests of palms they had left behind them at Wargla grew where the water-table lay nearest the surface. The oasis was the last vestige of a once well-watered land. Points on the polished surface of the *sebkha* winked at him like sleepy eyes. In places he could see the distinct ripple of water where there was only salt crust – depressions the Arabs called 'The Devil's Mirror'.

In the early afternoon the caravan descended into the bed of the Wadi Mya, a dry watercourse snaking like a great serpent down from the plateau of Tademait to the south. Roche speculated that the wadi was all that remained of an ancient river that had once flowed into the Wargla 'sea'. No European had ever ventured here before, but it had been suggested as an ideal route for the railway. The wadi neatly skirted the edge of the Great Eastern Erg, a honeycomb of rippling dunes stretching away towards the sunrise. Engineer Émile Beringer, who had made a study of the dunes on the first mission, surmised that the erg was itself the bed of a sea that had vanished long ago. The climate had changed, the sun had turned the water into vapour and the wind had whipped up the sandy silt-beds into the strange formations surrounding them.

Flatters ordered the expedition to halt and make camp on the right bank of the wadi. Away to the east, acres of wind-graded *serir*, gravel-covered plains, dropped down towards the erg. The dunes lay across the entire eastern horizon, pinkish and insubstantial, like low cloud hanging in the heat. To the west lay the naked rock scabs of the Bu Sharib Plateau. The camp was pitched on precise military lines, with the camels couched in echelon on the perimeter, and the tents of the expedition members in the centre, grouped around a larger mess tent. The stores were piled between

the expedition quarters and the tents of the *tirailleurs*, who posted
sentries on all four sides of the square. The soldiers who were not
on duty sat together smoking pipes or cigarettes of an absinthe-
scented desert herb called *shih*, rolled in scraps of paper. The
sokhrar dumped their personal kit anywhere, and slept on the
ground wrapped in their burnooses next to the camels. After dark
they sat huddled shoulder to shoulder round smoky fires, cooking
bread in the sand under the ashes, drinking tea, patching water-
skins, stitching saddle-bags, and talking endlessly. The seven
guides camped on their own, some distance ahead of the square.

The Frenchmen slept in two-man tents of green cloth, each
furnished with a folding table, collapsible beds, a chest for their
personal effects, water-filters, lamps and candle-holders. Sergeant
Joseph Pobeguin, whose tent was the last in the file, decided to
take no chances, despite the pacifist nature of the mission. He lay
down to rest with his two rifles and his revolver loaded and ready,
his dagger on the table and his sword in hand. 'Advice to amateurs!' he wrote in a letter home. 'If they come they will find
themselves faced with someone who is *not* one-armed, and has
good big eyes.'[28]

18

'The country we are crossing is real desert'

The caravan soon found its rhythm. The Arabs would be up before first light, moving among the camels, releasing them from their knee-hobbles to browse along the fringes of the wadi. By the time they had finished, flames would be leaping up in three-stone fireplaces, kettles and pans balanced over them. While they warmed their hands at the fire, the *muqaddam* Sidi ʿAbd al-Qadir, a holy man of the Tijaniyya Sufi Brotherhood, would chant the call to prayers.

One of the most powerful Sufi fraternities in North Africa, the Tijaniyya's base was at ʿAin Mahdi, not far from Laghouat. To the fury of its Sanusiyya counterparts in the eastern Sahara, the Tijaniyya had allied itself with the Christian colonial power. Its sheikh, Sidʾ Ahmad al-Tijani, was married to a Frenchwoman, Aurélie Picard. Flatters had included the *muqaddam* in the expedition in the belief that his marabout status would impress the Tuareg. In fact, the Brotherhood's Islamic credentials had long since been considered compromised by its pro-French stance.

When the dawn showed as a brand of orange fire across the eastern skyline, the Arabs would drive the camels in towards the piles of baggage, couch them and begin to load. Tents were struck, beds and tables folded, lamps stowed away in chests as the party shifted from settled to mobile mode. It took the *sokhrar* only forty-five minutes to load, and before it was fully light the caravan would be on its way.

Paul Flatters rode at the head of the column on his grey mare, usually with Pierre Masson astride one of the two other horses. Often, Flatters would pause to take notes on the nature of the country. Behind him, on a camel, rode engineer Joseph Santin, whose job on the march was to make a time-and-compass traverse of the route. Joseph Pobeguin kept his eyes skinned for dorcas gazelles and desert hares. He had charge of the expedition's four salukis, greyhound-like hunting dogs bred for their wide paws, which made them capable of running fast on soft sand. A dorcas gazelle could outrun a saluki, but the dogs could take a hare from a standing start at five hundred metres. When a saluki caught one, it would bring it back to Pobeguin to be skinned and cooked at the halt. The sergeant became quite attached to his dogs.

Roche, Beringer and Dr Guiard would leave the main party during the morning, riding off with the Shamba guides to take measurements or collect specimens of rocks or plants. They would rejoin the caravan in camp during the early afternoon. After a few days it became obvious to Émile Beringer that the wadi was unsuitable as a route for the Trans-Saharan Railway. It proceeded in a series of switchback curves, changing direction continually. In places it was squeezed between the sides of deep ravines, or blocked entirely with massive sand-drifts, forcing the caravan to scramble up escarpments, stumble through *hammadas* of large boulders, cross chalky plateaux and toil up and down endless corrugations. It was exhausting work, and the column rarely made more than twenty kilometres a day. 'The country we are crossing is real desert,' wrote Joseph Pobeguin on the fourth day. 'Not a village, not a tent, only sand, nothing but sand and stones.'[29]

There had been no rain for two years and the wadi was dry. The skeletons of tamarisk and acacia trees could be seen along the margins, but they were all dead, their branches brittle and desic-cated, bleached pale like bony fingers. There were patches of esparto grass for the camels, but all the *geltas*, or natural rainwater cisterns, they passed along the way were empty. Eight days before Christmas, they reached the well at Hassi Inifel. They had marched for the past week without watering the caravan.

The *hassi* was a major crossroads on the routes from Wargla, In Salah, al-Golea and Ghadames. It lay six hundred and fifty kilo-metres south of Laghouat. The column was now deep in the Sahara, and for the last two hundred kilometres it had been travelling through terra incognita. Flatters was elated by the achievement, despite the fact that the survey had so far been a flop as far as the railway was concerned. He admitted frankly in a letter to the Governor-General that the route he had taken on the first mission had been far more suitable for the Trans-Saharan. Duponchel's prediction was already coming home to roost.

This first phase of the trek into the unknown had proved tougher than even Flatters had imagined. The going had been hard, even for camels, and the nights had been shockingly cold, with the thermometer plunging to minus 4 or 5 degrees Celsius. In the mornings the water-skins were frozen blocks.

To cap it all, the French team had been plagued with health problems and the medical officer, Robert Guiard, had been con-stantly in demand. Pierre Masson had gone down with fever, probably malaria, and Louis Brame had contracted malaria too – he had been so ill that Flatters had actually considered sending him back. Henri de Dianous had developed a bad infection in the eye; but for Guiard's care, he might have lost it. As for Flatters himself, his sciatica had not let up and he was still taking four morphine shots a day from Guiard, as well as the cauterizing-iron regime.

As the camp was being pitched, Émile Beringer looked about him and shivered. It was the most desolate place he had ever seen. Near the well lay the mud-brick tomb of Sidi ʿAbd al-Hakim, an Arab saint who had been buried here eighty years earlier. The wadi

was no more than a narrow gutter cut through a scree of black
boulders undulating into the distance, without a single flash of
green. Where the two opposing slopes met, there was a slim ribbon
of pasture, but apart from that and the pale shapes of several
dunes on the horizon, there was nothing at all to attract the eye.

Things looked even grimmer when Flatters and Masson peered
into the well. It was six metres deep, but it contained only a trickle
of water. It was obvious that it wouldn't yield enough for the
entire caravan. The *sokhrar* and *tirailleurs* tied up their baggy
trousers and began to dig a second well with shovels, ropes and
leather buckets. It was back-breaking work. The men laboured in
shifts in the narrow shaft, scraping sand and soil into the buckets.
Others hauled the spoil up on the ropes and used it to mould
watering-basins. When the diggers finally got down to the water,
they rigged up a makeshift wooden frame and pulley, raising the
water and splashing it into the troughs they'd made for the camels
to drink from.

The beasts pressed around the mud basins, snapping and tus-
sling. The Arabs chanted age-old watering songs as more vessels
came up. The camels gulped, the piston-like muscles in their great
necks convulsing, their flanks swelling out as their bellies filled.
Every two minutes or so, they would toss their heads and shake the
drops from their blubbery lips. These big desert camels were capable of quaffing a hundred to a hundred and thirty litres a session,
at a rate of six or eight litres a minute, but the water supply was so
poor that many drank only half their fill; Beringer complained that
his camel had drunk only sixty-five litres. The beasts had to be
driven from the troughs to make way for the next section. This
went on deep into the night, and Flatters realized that they would
have to remain here for at least three days if they were to fill all the
skins and water all two hundred and eighty camels.

The sun set in a scythe of crimson, searing away the flawless
blue of the sky. Dark came quickly and lamps flared up behind the
veils of the tents, their fragile light the only cheering prospect in

the vast and eerie void. Paul Flatters sat in his tent listening to the rhythmic chanting from the wells, glad of a few minutes' respite. On one hand, the expedition was going well. The experts had done an excellent job. Beringer and Roche had produced detailed tables on water, vegetation and topography that would soon be incorporated into an accurate map. On the other hand, the shortage of water was an unexpected blow. Flatters had intended to head south-east from Hassi Inifel, but his guides warned him that, because of the two-year drought, there would be no water and little pasture that way. They advised him strongly to quit the wadi and head due south along its tributary, the Wadi In Sokki, towards the Tademait Plateau, where water and pasture would be more abundant.

Flatters agreed only reluctantly. The Wadi In Sokki would take his column dangerously near to In Salah, and he couldn't help remembering the uncompromising message the oasis inhabitants had delivered to Victor Largeau three years earlier: 'Any Roumi who comes near our land will regret it.'[30]

What worried him most was that he had heard nothing from Aitaghel. It was true that the caravan wouldn't be in Tuareg country for another seven or eight days, but Flatters had been expecting a message from the *amenukal* – even a personal visit. Beneath his air of confidence, he was still troubled by the conflicting messages he had received: he wanted to be reassured that his optimistic interpretation was correct. Since none of the guides he had with him, Shamba or Ifoghas, knew the way through the Hoggar Mountains, his success was totally dependent on the goodwill of the Tuareg chief.

19

At Home in the Empty Spaces

Weeks earlier, before the mission had left Wargla, two Tuareg warriors had arrived at Aitaghel's camp near Tazruk on exhausted camels. The sons of a Targui called Khatkhat, they belonged to the Kel Ahem Mellen, a small noble clan living on the Muydir Plateau, north of the Hoggar Mountains They had just made a remarkable dash – almost a thousand kilometres in a week – to bring news of the Christian caravan's departure.

The warriors had been on a mission to Biskra to demand restitution from some Arabs for a Tuareg camel they had stolen. On the way back they had sojourned near Laghouat with some Shamba who owed them *ghefara*, the toll they charged outsiders for travelling through their lands. It was from the Shamba that they heard rumours of the Flatters expedition.

One day during the third week in November they slipped away from the Shamba *douar*, or tent-village, in the freezing hour before dawn. Riding at a fast trot, halting only occasionally to let the camels graze, to draw water, drink tea and eat dates, they were able to cover more than a hundred kilometres a day. They themselves did not reckon the distance in kilometres or miles; their world was not one that could be measured so precisely. It was a flat world, and if one travelled far enough in a straight line, one was certain to fall over the edge. Journeys were gauged only by the number of days it took to get there by camel. The stars were lights in the sky put there by God, and all of them changed place except the North Star. The sun was there to give light, and its shadows showed the way. The moon existed only to illuminate the night. The past was a cycle of tales about their ancestors, who lived and walked close to them unseen and whose voices were still there, in the mountains and the *serir*. For them, time itself was not a linear progression from past to future but an eternal cycle, a parade of dawns, sunsets and seasons that might differ slightly in detail but would ultimately return to the beginning.

The riders felt perfectly at home in the great empty spaces of the Sahara. They did not feel cut off from the landscape but part of it. They never lost their way. Navigating by the shadow of the sun during the day and the North Star at night, they also looked out for the small details others might miss: a small depression in the surface here, the way the sand formed along a dune crest there, changes in the size and shape of gravel on the *serir*, the presence of a certain type of plant. They were illiterate, but they had excellent memories. They could pick a single thorn tree out of a forest of thousands, and needed only to glimpse a stranger for a moment to memorize every detail of his appearance.

They pushed the camels as far as they could after sunset, until the beasts shied from the cold, then they halted and made a fire. One of them mixed flour and water into a dough, which he moulded into a round loaf. When the fire had burned down, he scraped the embers away and placed the dough carefully in the sand, then raked the embers back over it. Twenty minutes later he fished out a warm, hard loaf of bread, which they ate with dried dates and ghee. After they had eaten and drunk tea, they lay down on the freezing ground, wrapped up in their burnooses. It was too cold to sleep, so they dozed fitfully most of the night, getting up frequently to rekindle the fire.

Riding day and night, they pushed themselves and their camels on until the animals were almost dropping with fatigue. At last, they sighted the sawtooth peaks and buttes of the Hoggar Mountains. Travelling more slowly now, they worked their way from camp to camp, sharing bread and salt with the Imuhaq, demanding food from Kel Ulli and Haratin. As they passed deeper into the mountains, they noted that the tents of the Kel Ghela were mostly empty. This was strange: it was the cool season and not the traditional time of year for large-scale raids. When they finally arrived at Aitaghel's tents, they found that the *amenukal* had departed, gone to the Tuat Oasis to settle a dispute with the local people. He had taken with him three hundred warriors of the Kel Ghela and Tegehe Mellet drum-groups.

The warriors asked to talk with Atissi ag Shikkadh, Aitaghel's nephew, the truculent anti-French leader of the Kel Ahaggar's hard-line faction. He was related to them on his mother's side, and was more than ready to give them a hearing. Atissi agreed that the news was serious and that the chief should be informed. The following day he saddled his best camel and rode out with a small escort of warriors, hoping to catch up with the *amenukal* and his party before he reached the Tuat.

20

'Protect them against hostile elements'

If there was a central axis on the caravan routes across the Sahara, it was In Salah. It was almost exactly midway between Algiers and Timbuctoo, and it was also the midpoint on the east–west caravan routes that joined the Tafilelt Oasis in Morocco with Ghadames and Cairo. The Tuat and its western extension, the Tidikelt, were a continuous forest of palm groves – the Street of Palms – growing at angles along two sides of the Tademait Plateau. The 'Street' stretched the best part of a thousand kilometres, and contained four hundred villages and several million trees. In Salah itself was not a town like Laghouat and Wargla. It consisted of four distinct fortified villages, or *ksur*, each with its own citadel. The *ksur* were built of flame-coloured or purple terracotta, and stood within a stone's throw of waves of dunes, screened by a dense jungle of palm groves.

When the three hundred Tuareg camel-riders first came in sight of the *ksur*, they appeared to be no more than a dark mirage on the distant skyline, a subtle thickening of the heat-haze. From ten kilometres away the column looked shapeless and immobile. It was more than an hour before any movement could be discerned, then the mass of men and camels seemed suddenly to spring into focus. Individual riders could be made out, scouts riding ahead of the main body, then the columns themselves, moving forward inexorably over the dark *serir*.

Aitaghel rode in the van of the column with his nephew Atissi, who had caught up with him a few days earlier. The *amenukal* had not been surprised to hear that the Flatters caravan was on its way; like Flatters, Atissi was puzzled as to his uncle's true attitude. He had been present when Aitaghel had written that he would not open the road through the Hoggar. Since then, he appeared to have relented, yet he had still taken the trouble to remonstrate with Ikhenoukhen for offering to help the French.

The Kel Ahaggar dominated the Tuat and often behaved atrociously in the oasis. They strutted around in their finest robes with their veils pulled tight and their swords in leather baldrics slung over their shoulders, helping themselves to goods without paying for them. A hungry Targui would barge into the house of a complete stranger and demand to be fed. If he were refused, he would throw back the sleeve of his *gandourah* and clutch the hilt of his dagger. Mostly they traded peacefully, but they were not above raiding villages and taking what they wanted by force. The *ksurians'* only sanction was to close their markets. This hit the Kel Ahaggar hard, as they were entirely dependent on the Tuat and Tidikelt for their grain, dates and other food supplies. Unless they wished to fight a continuous war with the *ksurians*, they would be obliged to reach an agreement, and it was ostensibly to do so that Aitaghel had come here.

The *amenukal*'s first task had been to visit the town of Awlef, to the west of In Salah, to hammer out a solution to the dispute. Now that was accomplished, he was visiting In Salah to meet the sheikh of the council, 'Abd al-Qadir bin Bajuda, who doubled as sheikh of the Awlad Ba Hammu, a powerful tribe of Arab nomads who lived around the Tuat. The Ba Hammu had adopted Tuareg culture, but because they wore white veils rather than black, they were often referred to as the 'White Tuareg'.

Bin Bajuda was the man who had penned the warning to Victor

Largeau three years earlier. It is likely that a shadowy third party was present at the meeting: Thani, the Sanusiyya agent from Ghadames, who had made the journey here specially to meet the Kel Ahaggar chief.

Aitaghel told them that the French mission was approaching and that it would be passing through the area within days. Bin Bajuda replied that the In Salah elders were fiercely opposed to the Christians crossing their land or passing through the Hoggar Mountains. Their convictions had not changed since they had delivered the ultimatum to Largeau in 1877. The In Salah merchants were in constant touch with their counterparts in Ghadames. They, like the Sanusiyya and the Ottomans, had no intention of handing over their profits to the French. 'I know you like money,' bin Bajuda told Aitaghel, 'and that is the reason you favour the passage of the Christians in our country where no Christians have ever been. I tell you, as far as I'm concerned, if the expedition comes within a day's march of In Salah I will fight it.'[31]

Thani might have told Aitaghel that he had been sent under the authority of the Ottoman governor of Ghadames, Abu Aysha.[32] The governor had been surprised to hear through a prominent Ghadames merchant, Tahir al-Hassidi, that Aitaghel had promised to open the route to the French. Thani may also have reminded the *amenukal* of the White Fathers, the Christian holy men determined to turn Muslims into apostates. Despite the murder of their emissaries four years ago, they showed no sign of giving up their mission. The Sanusi agent undoubtedly added that any action against the Christians would be a meritorious act of jihad and would earn Aitaghel the gratitude of both God and the Padishah Sultan in Constantinople. It is unlikely that Thani gave Aitaghel explicit instructions, but the *amenukal* sent a letter to Abu Aysha later, making it clear that the Kel Ahaggar had been asked to guard the caravan routes through their mountains, and 'protect them against hostile elements'.[33]

21

'Proudly and boldly as befits people who know their business'

Shortly after Flatters' caravan turned due south along the Wadi In Sokki, on 19 December, his guides came across the tracks of a hundred camels going north-west towards al-Golea. They had met no one since leaving Wargla, and the sudden discovery was disquieting. Sghir bin Sheikh and his brother, ʿAla, slipped down from their camels and examined the tracks carefully. They quickly agreed that they were seven or perhaps eight days old, and Sghir thought they belonged to marauders returning from a raid, bringing with them stolen camels.

This was not wild speculation. The Shamba were renowned for their tracking skills, for they could read the desert like a book. They prided themselves on *guwat al-mulahadha* – the power of observation – and never missed any detail, no matter how small. Often, their lives depended on it.

The Shamba learned to read camel-tracks as infants, for each animal's sign was as distinct as a fingerprint. A camel's flat footpads were crisscrossed with a pattern of folds and wrinkles that was unique. In a fresh print, this pattern was clearly visible, but it diminished progressively as the days passed. The clarity of the tracks was also affected by wind and rain, so a first-class tracker needed a good memory for recent changes in the weather. He could tell whether the camel was male or female, hobbled or free, stray or laden, tired or fresh, one-eyed or lame, thirsty or hungry. From examining its dung he could tell what it had been eating and deduce where it had come from. A detailed knowledge of the surroundings would tell him where it was going, and possibly even to which tribe it belonged. The Shamba knew the tracks of all their own camels by sight. The very best trackers could remember the tracks of every camel they had ever seen.

The mission followed the raiders' trail for two days. On the second morning, they were overtaken by some Shamba from Wargla who were on their way to In Salah. They had brought a telegram from Consul-General Féraud in Tripoli, warning Flatters that he should be on his guard against a band of marauders led by a bandit named al-Haj 'Ali Gaga. Flatters began to worry that the tracks they were following belonged to that same al-Haj 'Ali and his band. He was beginning to think that all the desert tribes of the south were rising up against him.

As the Wargla men would be returning home after their visit to In Salah, Flatters asked them to take the mission's mail. They agreed, but for twice the normal fee. Flatters then made a serious mistake, possibly the worst mistake of his life. Perhaps he was afraid that bin Bajuda would confiscate the letters he had handed over to the Wargla men and pass them on to the British Consul. He knew that In Salah folk bowed to the Sultan of Morocco, whose power was guaranteed by the British government. Whatever the reason, he decided against being conciliatory; instead, he sent bin Bajuda an intimidating message. He informed the Wargla men that he intended to enter In Salah. 'If I am not well received there,' he went on, 'in a manner befitting an envoy of France, the good natives may some day see before their houses an armed column coming to settle accounts.'[34]

For an instant, Pierre Masson's eyes widened. He knew Flatters had no intention of entering In Salah, and he had just blown the mission's cover. The threat of an 'armed column' following him gave exactly the impression the High Commission had wanted to avoid. The whole point of disguising the *tirailleurs* as camel-men was to convince the natives that the Flatters mission was peaceful, and *not* the vanguard of an invasion force. The soldiers were meant to show their real colours only if attacked. Flatters had not only made an empty threat – for there was no column following him – but he had also given the people of In Salah and their Tuareg allies a good reason to attack him. If the Tuareg believed that a stronger column was to follow, their best strategy would be to wipe out the Flatters Mission and scare the French government away.

Flatters later explained that his idea had been simply to knock bin Bajuda off balance. If the sheikh decided to resist, he would have to call up his fighters, and while he was doing so, the French column would simply slip off unnoticed in another direction. Flatters did not yet know that more than half the fighting strength of the Kel Ghela and the Tegehe Mellet were already massed at In Salah.

Masson thought Flatters' explanation unsatisfactory. Far from being a carefully considered strategy, it had all the hallmarks of a half-baked threat blurted out in frustrated chauvinism. 'I really do want to make a peaceful exploration,' Flatters wrote a few days later, 'but one must not forget that we represent France. The In Salah people come into our country when they like: it is only right that we can pass through theirs . . . the devil take me if I don't pass proudly and boldly as befits people who know their business.'[35]

The visit of the Wargla Arabs heralded meetings with other travellers. On the fourth day out of Hassi Inifel, Flatters' guides encountered five Shamba on their way from In Salah. The two parties halted, dismounted and shook hands, repeating phrases over and over like a mantra. Some of the newcomers belonged to the Zawa, the same clan as the guide Mohammad bin Raja, who was pleased to find among them one of his cousins.

When the greetings were over, bin Raja's cousin asked for the news. 'The news is good,' the guide replied. This was ritual – the news was always good, even if there had been a raid, a massacre, or dozens had died from drought. The Arabs then squatted down together, and bin Raja went through everything they had come across since leaving Wargla – the tracks of the raiders, the pasture, the animals, the state of the wells. Nothing was left out, and the other party listened intently. For these Arabs, every detail was important. It was from such exhaustive accounts that they built up an accurate picture of their surroundings; such knowledge might be crucial to their survival, if not now, then in days to come.

In turn, bin Raja's cousin related all they had seen since their departure from In Salah. He then told them the real news: Aitaghel was in the Tuat with a band of three hundred warriors. He had come to solve a dispute with the *ksurians* of Awlef; it had been settled amicably. When Flatters and Masson arrived, the new-comers rose to greet them, and the news was repeated. 'Everything is at peace in the Tuat,' bin Raja's cousin added, 'and your caravan can travel freely and in all confidence. Aitaghel has made it plain that he has given you leave to cross the country of the Kel Ahaggar, and everyone is in agreement with him.' Flatters was delighted. It seemed that his optimism had been justified. Aitaghel had mentioned in one of his letters that he would be at In Salah that winter, and he had kept his word.

After Flatters and Masson had gone, bin Raja's cousin took the guide off to squat in the shade of a thorn bush and, after exchanging family gossip, he told bin Raja the real situation at In Salah. Bin Bajuda and the elders were up in arms against the French column, and were prepared to resist its passage. Though his cousin did not know the true intentions of the Tuareg chief, bin Raja himself suspected that all was not well. If Aitaghel really intended to frank the mission through his country, why had he not come to greet them? If his letters were sincere, that would have been the obvious thing to do.

At camp that evening, bin Raja visited Flatters' tent and, sitting in the lamplight, passed on what his cousin had said. He also mooted his suspicions about Aitaghel. 'He wants to betray you,' he said. 'Don't go to the Hoggar. Go to Ghat instead.'

Flatters shook his head and said he was certain the Tuareg chief would keep his word. 'What is more,' he added, 'those who want to oppose my plans by attacking me will find they have met their match. For the others I will do only good.'[36]

22

They Had Taken the French Caravan for Marauders

Three days after Christmas Flatters led the caravan up the escarpment out of the Wadi In Sokki, where an ancient camel-track, the
Mejebed Ilgu, led over a limb of the Tademait Plateau. It was a
path of slim grooves meandering through a wilderness of rock,
where thousands of camels had passed over hundreds of years,
kicking the loose scree out until a clear path remained. The
grooves did not run in straight lines but oscillated gently left and
right, plunging steeply into wadis, occasionally passing cairns of
stones, piles of camel-bones, and places where camels had knelt
down, leaving imprints in the gravelly earth.

In hard desert like this, prints could stay for centuries. In certain
places in the Sahara there still remained the marks of Roman
chariot wheels. Looking at these old camps was like staring
through a window in time, thought Jules Roche, the mission's
geologist. You could rarely do the same in Europe, where most of
history's leftovers were swiftly buried in humus and new layers of
earth. Here, it was as if the people who had made the camps had
gone away only a few hours earlier, when it might have been
hundreds of years. But that was only yesterday compared with

some of the things he had found. These were flint arrowheads and edged scraping- and cutting-stones that he reckoned dated from the Old Stone Age, hundreds of thousands of years ago. It was a thrill to think his hand might have been the first to touch them since their makers'. When he asked the Shamba and Ifoghas about them, they shrugged and told him that such stones as this dropped out of the sky.

The Mejebed had probably existed since before the Tuareg arrived in the Hoggar. Local legend had it that it was named after Ilgu, a twelfth-century chief of the Zenata, Berber-speaking nomads distantly related to the Tuareg, who had lived here from the earliest times. Ilgu's men, it was said, had sacked Ghadames, but had been tracked down by the formidable Bani Hilal Arabs – the same tribe who had driven out the Hawwara from the Fezzan. The Arabs had caught the Zenata here on the Mejebed and slaughtered them. Raid, counter-raid, slaughter – it seemed to Paul Flatters that life in the Sahara was an endless cycle. This was, of course, the way it had always been to the Shamba and the Tuareg. Tribes rose and fell, but the life of the desert went on eternally.

Jules Roche had reason to doubt that interpretation: his evidence suggested a much bigger cycle. First of all, he was certain that the Sahara had once been greener than it was now. Water had played a major role in shaping the features around him. At one time there had been more rain. Rivers as big as the Nile had traversed what was now hyper-arid desert, flowing into inland seas larger than the lakes of Europe. If this *were* so, then the Sahara had in the past been forest and savanna, teeming with big game animals like elephant, rhino, buffalo, lion and leopard.

These insights, revealed in cosy discussions in the mess tent round the dinner table, would normally have been of great interest to Paul Flatters, but these days he was irritable and preoccupied. First there was the problem of the camels. They were heavily laden, and ideally they should be watered every three or four days, so the route had to stitch a path from water to water. This had already meant one major deviation, to In Sokki, and now he was travelling almost due east instead of south. Most of the wells had been filled in by floods and had to be dug out, a difficult and time-consuming task. The watering itself took hours, and almost always the wells yielded too little for the camels to drink properly. In the cool season, the animals could go for months without water, provided they were devouring the desert grasses known to the Shamba as 'ushub. They could last for up to four years after a rain, but grew only in patches, often separated by hundreds of kilometres. When the caravan came across such a pasture, there was no choice but to halt and let the camels graze, no matter how long they had been travelling and how awkward the stop. At a push a thirsty camel could carry on for weeks, but a hungry camel would drop dead in days.

They had found more pasture and water for the camels in the Wadi In Sokki than in the Wadi Mya, but it had not been enough, and the camels were weak and exhausted. Occasionally they set up a communal keening that sent a shiver down Jules Roche's spine. The beasts had begun to waste away, their humps flopping, ribs showing through the hide on their flanks. Of the original two hundred and eighty, thirty were dead. Some had keeled over; others had just sat down and refused to get up, regarding their handlers with baleful eyes. The *sokhrar* shouted, kicked and beat them with sticks, then gathered round and tried to haul them up by force. When that failed, they even lit fires under their bellies. Some animals managed to stagger to their feet only when their baggage and saddles were removed, and they hobbled on painfully after the caravan. Most stayed where they were. No power on earth could shift them.

If the camel died of natural causes, its meat was not *hilal* for the Arabs, so if there was still time, one of the camel-men would slip out his razor-sharp dagger and stab the dying beast in the jugular vein at the base of the neck, drawing the blade across its throat. Then the men went to work on the flesh – the hump, the neck, the lights, the large muscles of the thighs. Four *sokhrar* could butcher a camel expertly in twenty minutes. They ate the jelly-like stuff of the hump and the liver raw, spiced by the sour juice from the camel's gall-bladder, 'the desert lemon'. They cut the rest of the meat into strips and hung it up to dry in the shade of thorn-scrub at the rest halt.

Even more exasperating than the lack of water and dying camels was the silence from Aitaghel, as far as Flatters was concerned. He had rested at In Sokki well for three days, watering the camels and awaiting word from the Tuareg chief. At the suggestion of Sghir bin Sheikh, he had taken on another Shambi guide, a man called 'Ali bin Mahdallah, who had visited the camp the day before Christmas Eve. It was clear that 'Ali knew his way around these hills alone, but what Sghir did not tell Flatters was that he was a fugitive: the previous year he had robbed and attempted to kill a merchant from the Mzab.

On 27 December Flatters had called to his tent Sheikh Bu Jamaa of Wargla, his native assistant and courier. He handed the Arab a sealed letter and instructed him to take it to Aitaghel at In Salah. The letter officially announced the arrival of the French caravan, and asked the *amenukal* to meet him at Tioukenine, a well tucked into a narrow ravine on the route from In Salah to the Hoggar Mountains. He asked the chief to bring him guides of the Kel Ahaggar, as his Shamba and Ifoghas could only take him as far as the outskirts of the Hoggar range. He also gave Bu Jamaa a burnoose, two revolvers and half a dozen silk handkerchiefs as presents for the chief.

On 31 December, the caravan left the Mejebed and began to descend the Wadi Awlugi, a ravine cut through sheer rock walls into the sweeping valley of Hassi Messeggem. For their guide, Mohammad bin Raja, this was coming home. The Messeggem Valley was his clan's territory; his family's tents were pitched down on the *serir*. On the morning of New Year's Day 1881, the column broke out of the ravine through a cleft in the jagged rock, silted up with the interlocking plinths of fish-scale dunes. Beyond this rock doorway lay a *sebkha* shimmering with reflected light, and on the other side of it lay the well. Roche observed that the plain was no more than a wide valley between the Tademait and Tinighert Plateaux, with the lazily boiling sands of the great erg just visible to the north.

By eight a.m. they had neared the wells. The camels, sensing that they were approaching water, picked up the pace, their pads slapping on the hard surface. The sky was a brooding grey, almost the same flint colour as the plain, marbled by whorls and rosettes of cloud. There was a sharp smell of dust on the air. The sun hung suspended in a hammock of cirrus before them, its beams bursting out like the points of a many-limbed star. As they marched, camels and men left elastic shadows stretching across the plain.

Flatters pondered where to make camp. Too near the well would mean messing up everything with camel-dung; too far would mean endless comings and goings with camels and water-vessels. He selected a campsite, and gave the order to unload. The *sokhrar* were already slipping out of their saddles, tugging head-ropes, bringing the camels to their knees. The animals bleated, roared and snapped as the camel-men dumped baggage in piles on the hard earth, unpicked knots and lifted saddles. While the tents were going up, Flatters and Masson rode to the *hassi* with guides bin Raja and Sghir bin Sheikh. The two Shamba peeked over the rim: it was half-filled with sand and mud. Bin Raja told Flatters this was a result of a flood two years before. Beneath the silt the water was abundant here, and usually to be found at a depth of 'five men' – an Arab measurement derived from the average height of a man with his arms raised above his head. Flatters calculated this to be around eleven metres, which meant they had some five and a half or six metres of earth to dig out.

As soon as camp was pitched, Masson, de Dianous and the two sergeants, Dennery and Pobeguin, organized the *sokhrar* and *tirailleurs* into sections of ten. The cameleers tucked up their *gandourahs* or stripped down to their baggy trousers and set to work. Shovels struck earth, buckets of spoil were hauled up, men shouted, cursed and bawled out orders. The work was not only hard, it was also hazardous. One *tirailleur*, ʿAbd al-Qadir bin Bahariyya, fell when the walls collapsed and broke his arm. Every two hours, the shift changed. It took almost twenty hours to get down to the water, and when Flatters tasted it he found it was brackish. He made a sour face, but said nothing; they had no choice but to accept it. In this unknown desert, water was life. It was a sad country, Flatters thought. He couldn't help smiling as he remembered how the High Commission imagined the Tademait Plateau: lush, wooded hills, thick cypress forests, cool streams cascading through dappled glens. The reality was a starkness of rock, rock and more rock, with occasional folds of dunes and, in the valley itself, a few stunted camel-thorn shrubs.

As soon as the diggers struck water, the tedious round of watering the camels began. That evening, bin Raja returned from reconnaissance to report that there was rich grazing not far away – *ʿushub* still flourishing, despite the two-year drought. The column remained at Hassi Messeggem for five days while the camels made the best of the pasture. The guides, led by bin Raja, toured the nearest Shamba *douars* looking for camels to replace the dead beasts. One afternoon the sentries spotted a caravan approaching: twenty-seven baggage-camels with eight mounted Tuareg armed to the teeth. Joseph Pobeguin watched them coming warily, his trusty Fusil Gras at the ready. Then a curious thing happened. The eight riders suddenly abandoned the baggage-train and shot off towards the horizon on their *meharis*, leaving a trail of dust. Pobeguin laughed at this un-Tuareg-like behaviour. Evidently the 'Lords of the Desert' had taken the French caravan for marauders. Flatters sent his guides to chase them, and after a while they came trotting back with three of the runaways in tow.

The men greeted the French officers hesitantly, and after some prodding the colonel discovered that the caravan leader was Mulay Ahmad, a relative of bin Bajuda, the hostile sheikh of In Salah, though most of the caravan belonged to Mohammad bin Zaid, a Ghadames merchant, who was also travelling with it. The caravan-eers were not Tuareg, but Arabs of the Tuat, returning from Ghadames with a cargo of European cottons, tea, sugar and trinkets. They had passed this way two months earlier with gold-dust, ostrich feathers and slaves bound for Tripoli. The desert was so troubled by reports and rumours of bandits that they had dressed themselves Tuareg-style. They claimed to have mistaken the mission for a raiding party, but they might have recognized the caravan for what it was and feared reprisals for their slave-trading activities.

Mulay and bin Zaid were delighted to find that Flatters' men had reopened the well and, feeling embarrassed at their pusillanimous behaviour, put on a show of friendliness. They assured Flatters that Aitaghel would still be at In Salah, and that they could see no earthly reason why he should not come to greet the French mission. This was music to Flatters' ears. Taking them at their word, he assumed this meant that the In Salah people were well disposed towards him, and that the warning bin Raja's cousin had delivered at In Sokki was false.

Over tea, Mulay waxed rhetorical about the benefits that would derive from the opening up of the old trade-route to Algiers, but not even Flatters was taken in by this hyperbole. What advantage would a slave-merchant gain from using a route on which slavery was banned? When the Trans-Saharan Railway was built, he wrote to his wife that night, this unspeakable trade in human beings would be finished once and for all.

Despite the proximity of In Salah, and the assurances of the Arabs, Aitaghel did not arrive. Neither did Sheikh Bu Jamaa. Instead there came a lone camel-rider, who scouted around the camp but did not explain satisfactorily why he was there. It was evident to everyone that he was a spy. On 6 January, Flatters decided that he could delay no longer. He ordered the caravan to load up and move out at first light next day, hoping desperately that Aitaghel and Bu Jamaa would be waiting for him at Tioukenine.

23

'Will the fish . . . bring us bad luck?'

There was a frost that morning, and the men woke shivering with cold. The water in the skins was frozen solid. As the camels panted up the narrow defile on to the Tinighert Plateau, their breath came like puffs of smoke. The sun did not rise, but peered suddenly through a rip in the sky, its fire diluted watery-orange by veils of cloud. The clouds looked heavy enough for rain and the Arabs eyed them hopefully. There had been a light shower a few days earlier at Hassi Messeggem, but after the first rush of droplets it had petered out. Today, the rain-heads retreated as the sun grew bolder, bursting out in a cascade of beams like a slowly rotating fan. The beams burned away the cloud into filaments of fleece, and at once the heat began to fall on men and beasts like hot oil.

The camels clinked through the angular boulders of the *hammada*, burned and burnished since time immemorial. From a height of five hundred metres the Frenchmen looked out over a chaos of canyons, faults and gullies, jumbled up and rising out of each other in confusion as far as the eye could see. The sun illuminated veins of shadow in mauve and magenta among the chains of ridges. An iridescent haze rose up between them, giving them the look of prehistoric monsters basking in steam. Below the caravan lay two sheer lines of cliff, like gigantic steps whose edges had been melted down into massive organ-pipes, sculpted into twisted columns and the trunks of fossilized trees. Below that lay the *serir* of Ajemor, like the floor of an immense hall carpeted in ochre, brown and sienna, cut by radiating wadis like spread fingers. To Jules Roche, it felt as if they were standing on the edge of the world.

For thirteen days the caravan pushed on through the labyrinth, plodding across moonscape screes, pitching down the sides of gullies and scrambling up escarpments. The camels, accustomed to the open plains and sand-seas of their native soil, stumbled and fell. They cast their loads, held up the column, winced and gasped as the sharp stones of the *hammada* pierced their soft footpads, went lame and limped along painfully. Sometimes the column passed through furrows so narrow that the camels had to walk in Indian file. Eventually they sloped down into the basin of Wadi Melah, where the walls of Tinighert had been chiselled into forests of slanted and skewed pillars. From the Wadi Melah they descended into the Igharghar, a colossal groove between the Tinighert and the Tassili-n-Ajjer, with walls in places as sheer and smooth as if they had been bored out by a glacier. Reaching the wadi-bed, the column turned south across the *serir*, in places forty kilometres from wall to wall, a roadway of wind-graded limestone turned black by a patina of iron and manganese. The Igharghar marked the edge of the Tassili-n-Ajjer – the domain of Ikhenoukhen – and the Flatters caravan began to tramp along under its walls. The guides adjusted its head directly towards the inselberg, the prominent steep-sided hill the Shamba called Garet al-Junun, the Hill of Demons, which was the outer bastion of the Hoggar range.

The caravan was a moving village, yet it seemed no more than a dark scarab on the majestic backdrop of the Sahara. Days passed with no sign of human life other than themselves. Where the ancient footpaths gave out, there was no evidence that human beings had ever been here. It was only at or near the wells that they encountered other travellers. At Hassi al-Hajaj, a place with an evil reputation, known as the haunt of bandits and cut-throats, they bumped into an old acquaintance from the first mission, Sliman al-Hartani, caretaker of the mosque at Temassinin, who was on his way home from In Salah with two slaves. Sliman had no good news to impart; he confirmed to bin Raja that the people of In Salah were violently opposed to Flatters' expedition.

Bin Raja asked to see Flatters, and told him once again that he ought to turn back. Could he not see that Aitaghel's absence foreboded only evil? Flatters tried to dismiss this new message as another wild rumour, answering that his absence was probably just the *amenukal*'s way of bargaining. No doubt he was getting ready to push up the price of his help. Secretly, Flatters was less sanguine. For one thing, he was unable to make the rendezvous with Bu Jamaa at Tioukenine. As it turned out, the well was a long way off his line of march, in the Immidir Plateau. To approach it across the barren Igharghar *serir* would be too much for the thirsty caravan. Instead, he sent bin Raja and Hamma of the Ifoghas to meet his courier there. He hoped they would bring back Aitaghel and the Tuareg guides he had requested.

The scouts returned six days later and couched their weary camels by Flatters' tent. Bin Raja was given permission to enter, and ducked under the flap without a word. His weathered face was rimed with dust. He told the colonel that they had found the well, but no sign of Bu Jamaa or the Kel Ahaggar – not even fresh tracks. They had left a signal indicating the caravan's direction – a rebus design made from a bagful of Wargla dates that Bu Jamaa, born and bred in Wargla, would be sure to recognize.

When bin Raja left Flatters' tent that night he joined Sghir bin Sheikh and the Ifoghas at their fire. He accepted the glasses of tea Sghir handed him. Bin Raja had been brought up on the edge of Tuareg country and he knew his enemy. He did not feel quite at ease with Sghir, whose tendency to slip into Tuareg dress and language and his ability to hobnob with his Ifoghas in-laws gave him the air of a shape-shifter. Bin Raja admitted to Sghir that he had never expected to find Aitaghel at Tioukenine but had gone along for Flatters' sake. He suspected the Kel Ahaggar chief of duplicity, and felt that the French, and the colonel in particular, were turning a blind eye to the threat that lay in wait for them. They were preoccupied with collecting stones and plants, but did not see what was under their noses.

'I have warned the colonel three times,' bin Raja said. 'Once at In Sokki, again at Hassi al-Hajaj, and once here. Each time he assured me that the *amenukal* would keep his word. Now I wash my hands of it: I am going no farther than Amgid.'[37] Sghir said nothing and stared into the fire.

The absence of the courier was a blow to Flatters. Bu Jamaa had left the column at In Sokki, only five days' ride from In Salah. Flatters had expected him back within two weeks, but three had now passed and there had been no word from him. Now, he was wondering if the Shambi had reached In Salah at all. Perhaps he had been refused entry – even attacked, robbed or murdered on the way. The main thing was that they were only three days away from Amgid, the last point on the route known to his Shamba guides. Should Aitaghel fail to reach him there, it would be almost impossible for them to go on.

The end wall of the Tassili escarpment went on and on, pale grey at midday, blazing gold at sunset. Amgid was located in a fissure that opened like a gate in the *falaise*, a narrow ravine between sheer cliffs, its sandy bed littered with boulders that had broken off from the mother-lode and tumbled down thousands of metres. Some of them were covered in prehistoric graffiti – engravings of giraffes and elephants – as well as more recent scrawlings in rune-like *tifinagh*, the written language of the Tuareg. To the west of the fissure's opening lay the butt-end of the huge jelly-mould dune called Amgid Erg that stretched a day's journey along the Igharghar Valley.

When the caravan entered the gorge on 18 January, Flatters' worst fears were confirmed: the place was deserted. He had

expected at the very least to find Kel Ahaggar tents pitched beneath the towering parapets. After examining tracks around the
watering-place, bin Raja declared that no one had been here in
months. The water point was not a well, but a series of *geltas* up to
twenty metres across, fed by a small stream that ran down through
a cleft. The stream snaked across the gravel through patches of
esparto grass and wild thyme. It was the first running water the
expedition had seen in the Sahara, but it did not cheer Flatters.
There were yellow-eyed fish in the water – *Clarias lazarea*, the
same type they had found in Lake Menghough – and the colonel
was reminded of his nemesis there last April. 'It seems a bad sign,'
he wrote to his wife. 'Will the fish inadvertently bring us bad
luck?'[38]

The situation here was starting to look alarmingly similar to the
Menghough débâcle. The mission was on roughly the same lati-
tude as it had reached that April, and on the same wadi, the
Igharghar, though much further to the west, on the opposite side
of the Tassili-n-Ajjer. Then, as now, Flatters had been thwarted by
the absence of a Tuareg chief and the lack of local guides to frank
him through.

After the tents had gone up that evening, he assembled the
guides and inquired about the way ahead. The Shamba knew the
Hoggar only by hearsay – there was no one here old enough to
remember the old caravan route through the Amadghor salt-workings. Bin Raja and the Ifoghas had heard tell that the salt-pans
stood in an immense gravel plain that went on for five days,
without grazing or water. Even the Tuareg avoided it.

After dark, Flatters sat at his table with his head in his hands,
deep in thought, until Louis Brame presented him with a stiff
cognac. He knocked back the brandy and asked Brame to call
Masson and de Dianous. After the two officers had sat down and
been given drinks, Flatters told them that if Bu Jamaa did not
arrive with Tuareg guides in five days, they would have to give
up the mission. That would mean heading back up the Wadi

Igharghar and making for Ghat. Masson protested that Flatters had already told the High Commission he had been unable to visit Ghat on his previous trek for fear of causing a diplomatic incident. If they ended up there this time, it would be awkward. They had done a thousand kilometres from Wargla through country as little known to Europeans as the Arctic. Everything had been going well, but after all Flatters' years of preparation, after all his compromises and his kowtowing to Duveyrier, it had come to this.

Masson thought he had never seen his colonel so tense. The mask had dropped, the bonhomie had deserted him. 'This bitch of a country,' he fumed, 'it is not accessible the way we want to go.'[39] He was still convinced that Aitaghel would not voluntarily break his word; if it were true that the people of In Salah were opposed to the mission, it was possible they had prevented the *amenukal* from visiting him. The mission had been on Tuareg land for ten days already, and had heard or seen nothing of him. On the other hand, he pointed out, it had not been attacked, stopped, or pillaged – some indication, surely, that Aitaghel was not ill-disposed towards them.

Whatever happened, Flatters was determined not to give up this time. He couldn't endure more derision of the 'Colonel Boum' variety. This, he told the others, was not the end. It meant only that they had to avoid the Amadghor *serir* they had been ordered to cross. 'The route of the railway can still be established on the plain that has blocked our passage here,' he said, 'if we can only manage to reach the other side of it by zigzagging through the mountains.'[40]

If they were to go that way, the Ifoghas guides, 'Abd al Hakim and Hamma, would be able to take the caravan as far as Kel Ajjer country. Beyond that they would need men who knew the route south. Next day he called Sghir bin Sheikh, his brother and his father-in-law, and asked them to ride through the Igharghar and circle round the Tassili-n-Ajjer to locate Ikhenoukhen's camp.

Sghir was to give the old *amenukal* a present of money and ask for new guides.

Émile Beringer had noticed Flatters' tension. He and Roche had seen the colonel like this on the way to Menghough, when he had stamped about alone in the desert. Over breakfast, Beringer tentatively suggested that as they would be remaining for some days, he, Roche and Santin should use the time in making surveys to the south. Flatters perked up slightly. He not only agreed, but also announced that he would accompany them, with Joseph Pobeguin and five *tirailleurs*. Masson thought it was a bad idea, given the uncertainty of their current circumstances, but his was not to reason why. The same day, Flatters' survey party saddled up and rode south towards Garet al-Junun.

Within twenty kilometres, they found that the great wall of Amgid turned sharply to the east, giving way to the *serir*, an enormous gravel plain stretching on endlessly southwards. It was liberating to be free of the rock maze and back in open desert. The going was easy for the animals. A day's march further on, the Hill of Demons loomed out of the sand-mist like a monument. To the Tuareg it was sacred; to the Shamba it was the haunt of evil spirits. The scouting party left the Wadi Igharghar and headed down a branch, the Wadi Tajert, towards a lone knoll the Shamba called Khanfussa, or The Beetle. They camped on the slopes, and in the morning Pobeguin spotted two camel-riders approaching. At least one of them was a Targui. He ordered the *tirailleurs* to take up defensive positions and watched through narrowed eyes as the riders drifted nearer. It was only when they couched their camels a few metres away that Flatters recognized Sheikh Bu Jamaa.

24

'The sky will fall on my *shesh* before I let you run the slightest risk'

Bu Jamaa had found Aitaghel and had brought a letter from him. While he and his Targui companion, a man called Sidi Moham- mad ag Mumin, squatted down to drink water, Flatters read the letter, noticing that it was scrawled on the reverse side of the one he had sent. It was written in Arabic and he saw at a glance that it was favourable. The Tuareg chief had given him permission to cross Kel Ahaggar territory to the Sudan. Aitaghel wrote that he could not meet Flatters in person, as he was riding back to his tents in the Hoggar. He felt he had been away from home too long and needed rest. But he had sent a guide: 'I send you my uncle, Shikkadh, a good man and another me, who will lead you. You wish to go to the Sudan; pass through my territory; you need not have any fears; but as for giving you recommendations [with regard to guides beyond Kel Ahaggar territory] I cannot, because I am not well in with those people.'[41]

Flatters was euphoric. He had been right all the time, and everyone else had been wrong: Duponchel, Rohlfs, Féraud, Arnau- deau and the rest – even his guide, Mohammad bin Raja. Aitaghel had never had any intention of letting him down, as he had always maintained. The Tuareg were men of their word, and Duveyrier was vindicated. The final problem had been solved. He was going to become the first European ever to cross the Hoggar Mountains.

When Flatters asked Bu Jamaa why he had delayed, the Shambi told him that by the time he had reached In Salah, the *amenukal* had already departed, with a huge caravan of five hundred camels. He had been obliged to track him down and had caught up with him after five days at a place called Wadi Menyet. He had had to hang around there another week before Aitaghel had decided to send Shikkadh. On the way back from Aitaghel's camp he had met up with his present companion, Sidi Mohammad, who had agreed to guide him to Amgid.

Flatters was so excited at the news from Aitaghel that he accepted the chief's poor excuse for not coming in person. He did not inquire why, since they were going in the same direction, the chief couldn't have killed two birds with one stone by travelling with the French column. Such quibbles were forgotten in another flash of good news. It had rained recently on the Amadghor *serir*, which meant that there would be water and pasture in plenty. The arid plain was not going to present the formidable obstacle that Flatters had feared.

The new guide, Shikkadh – unknown to Flatters, the chief of the Tegehe Mellet drum-group – was holed up in the Igharghar, seventy kilometres north of Amgid, awaiting word from Bu Jamaa. Flatters asked Sidi Mohammad to return to Masson's camp with orders that the rest of the column be moved to Khan-fussa, then to ride as quickly as he could to Shikkadh and bring him back.

Masson and de Dianous led the caravan into Flatters' camp three days later. As the tents were being erected, a group of Tuareg warriors arrived. The salukis barked. All heads turned to see the long-awaited guides, proud and upright on their lean camels, their black, blue and purple robes trailing, eyes flashing behind the narrow slits of their veils, swords slung across saddles, spear-tips glinting in the sun.

Bu Jamaa introduced Flatters to Shikkadh, a tall, lean Targui, who took careful note of everything around him with steady eyes. When he let his veil dip, Flatters saw that he was an old man with deeply tanned skin, a goatee beard and a gap between his teeth. He wore blue robes and a Tunisian skullcap with an enormous tassel dangling from it, held in place by a black scarf. He shook hands and assured Flatters he was here as a friend. 'The sky will fall on my *shesh* before I let you run the slightest risk,' he declared.[42] Flatters liked him at once, and pronounced him 'a good old chap'. Shikkadh was not really Aitaghel's uncle, but his brother-in-law – he was married to the *amenukal*'s elder sister. His son, Atissi, was the truculent leader of the hard-line element in Aitaghel's camp. He had brought with him another guide, named Ahmad, and a handful of vassals of the Issekermaren clan, who had come to sell camels.

There was an almost palpable sense of excitement in the camp after the arrival of Shikkadh. Everyone had been aware that the help of Aitaghel and the Kel Ahaggar would be the key factor in the mission's success. The crucial stage was the twenty-eight-day hike from Amgid to In Azawa, a remote clutch of wells that marked the southern frontier of the Hoggar. Beyond In Azawa they would be in country already explored by men like Barth and von Bary, but until then they were on a different planet. 'The crisis is happily over,' wrote Émile Beringer, 'and I now trust we will arrive in the Sudan, because once at In Azawa it will be shorter to push south than to re-cross the desert.'[43]

In the evening, Flatters and Shikkadh talked further. Shikkadh said he would accompany the column until another guide arrived, and he emphasized that the caravan must take the direct route to In Azawa through the western edge of the Hoggar. It must not deviate from the route and would not be allowed to visit Kel Ahaggar camps. This suggested to Flatters that Aitaghel suspected his motives. If that were true, then why was the chief allowing him through the Hoggar at all? Flatters mulled it over, and came up with a logical answer. The *amenukal* did not really want Flatters in his territory, but was determined to prevent him from passing through Ikhenoukhen's. If he blocked the road, Aitaghel knew that the mission would take the route through Ajjer, and that the considerable profits would go to his rival. From Aitaghel's point of view, Flatters reasoned, it was better to let the caravan pass through the Hoggar as quickly as possible and make sure his people collected the reward. As for Shikkadh's conditions, he did not like the idea of being confined to one particular line, but it was better than having to turn back.

The following morning he dismissed most of the guides who had brought him this far. It felt like a family splitting up. The *sokhrar* in particular grumbled about the loss of bin Raja, but Flatters put this down to their traditional distrust of the Tuareg. The guide had served him well, but he had outlived his usefulness. He thanked bin Raja and told him to go back to his *douar* at Hassi Messeggem. He called for his last Ifoghas guide, Hamma, and told him to catch up with Sghir and his party, who were already on their way to Ikhenoukhen's camp beyond the Tassili. He instructed Hamma to tell Sghir he no longer needed the Kel Ajjer guides. Sghir and the Ifoghas were dismissed with honour, and should return to their own tents.

That done, Flatters put his trust in his new acquaintance, the 'good old chap' Shikkadh, to guide him through the Hoggar Mountains, to everlasting glory. The Flatters caravan had crossed twelve hundred kilometres of unknown desert since Wargla. 'I think for the moment,' he wrote presently, 'I can consider it a success.'[44]

25

'Travelling with the Tuareg, in the country of the Hoggar Tuareg'

The Hill of Demons was the summit of Wudan, the bookend of a chain of hills extending north like a probing finger, a hundred and fifty kilometres out of the Hoggar massif. This limb, known to the Tuareg as Tefedest, rose to 2300 metres, and marked the western boundary of the Amadghor Plain, an almost uniformly flat waste of wind-graded gravels and salt-saturated earth stretching south from the walls of the Tassili-n-Ajjer. The plain was without water and boasted little vegetation. It was bounded on the eastern side by two lone jebels, Wunan and Tukmatine, and by the small sand-sea of Tihodaine, a dense drift of sand dunes as white as snow. To the south, the edge of the *serir* was indicated by another lone hill called Tin Kukur, that had for centuries been a landmark for salt-caravans heading south from the salines at Tisemt on the western edge of the plain.

In past years the Tuareg had shipped salt-blocks from Tisemt on caravans numbering thousands of camels, and the approach to Tin Kukur was cut by scores of meandering ruts, rubbed shiny by camels' feet over countless years. Up to a generation earlier, men had come to Tisemt to work on the salt-pans, and in good years wandering merchants from all parts of the Sahara had set up their wares there, holding an improvised trade-fair. Now the salines were abandoned, and the fair had not been held for decades. One of Henri Duveyrier's ambitions had been to reopen this market, and to make Tisemt the crossroads of the new trade routes across the Sahara. The High Commission had viewed this site as the possible junction of the railway, a place that would one day grow into a great city.

The caravan left at first light on 26 January, its six sections fanning once again into open order. The camels stepped out, glad to be away from the confines of the hills. The hugeness of the *serir* soon reduced them to an ebony necklace, and from a distance the whole caravan had the appearance of a tiny boat cast adrift on a boundless sea. The day was still and hot, with not a flaw in the limpid blueness of the sky. The camels' feet crunched on the *serir*, leaving patterns of prints where veins of yellow sand seeped through the ash-like surface. Riding ahead with the new guides, Jules Roche gazed around him keenly. He had grown accustomed to the Sahara's language, written in the features of its hills, plains and sand-seas. At his back lay the long *falaise* of the Tassili escarpment, running east as far as the oasis of Janet. To his right he could see the volcanic protuberances of the Ejere Hills, and far to the south-east the peaks of Wunan and Tukmatine. At his side, Émile Beringer was also absorbing the sights with an expert's eye. 'We are in granite, gneiss, and basalt,' he wrote, 'and the land-scape has become a bit less monotonous than in the preceding Cretaceous and Devonian plateaux . . . it's hot at midday, but not too hot – from 25 to 30 degrees Celsius – the mornings are cool.'[45]

The *tirailleurs* were less sanguine about casting off into the wilderness. They glanced distractedly at the Hill of Demons to the south-west, and watched the Amgid Gorge getting smaller behind them, like a slowly closing door. Joseph Pobeguin, with the four faithful salukis trotting at his camel's heels, overheard one trooper saying that he had recognized the voice of a jinn whispering across the emptiness, which meant they would all be dead within a month. Pobeguin rejected the superstition but understood the sentiment. There was an eeriness to this *serir*, a sense that they were being followed by others just out of their vision. As the sun rose higher, the quartz particles in the surface formed mirages like water-pools, or blinking eyes. In a place like this, it was easy to believe in *junun*.

After three days the caravan made the well at Inzelman-Tikhsin, where a volcanic stump of heat-mauled gneiss poked out of the surface. Here, Shikkadh suddenly announced that he was leaving. Flatters was surprised. He reminded the old man he had vowed to remain until other guides arrived. Shikkadh pointed a gnarled finger at Ahmad, the Targui he had brought with him, and at Sidi Mohammad ag Mumin, the man Sheikh Bu Jamaa had met by chance on his way from In Salah. They would guide the column from here, he said. Shikkadh demanded a reward for his three days of service. Flatters handed over five hundred francs, a burnoose, a silk scarf, a silk gown and a *shesh*. He also gave the guide presents for Aitaghel, for Sidi al-Keraji, chief of the Taitoq drum-group, and for Shikkadh's son, Atissi. This amounted to another thousand francs, a silk headcloth, a belt and another *shesh*.

Shikkadh stuffed the money and garments into a gazelle-skin bag and rode off into the *serir*, but instead of heading south towards the Hoggar, he rode north, back towards Amgid, saying that he had pitched his tent in the Wadi Igharghar. With him went Flatters' last Shambi guide, Qaddur bin Muissat, carrying dispatches and documents bound for Wargla and Laghouat. Among them was Flatters's *journal de route*, and a letter to his wife, Sarah. 'What we have done is an important achievement,' he had written, 'more than twelve hundred kilometres from Wargla, where no European foot has ever trod. [We are] travelling with the Tuareg, and in the country of the Hoggar Tuareg, to which no one has ever been given access as far as this . . . If things continue to go well we will reach the sea in Sokoto and the mouth of the Niger. The original instructions given by M. le Freycinet do not extend that far, and we would have fulfilled them to the letter without even reaching In Azawa. We are eighty kilometres from the most extreme point noted [i.e. the Amadghor saline] and we will be there in three days. I expect to be at In Azawa in twenty-five days, without incident.'[46]

The letter is curiously reminiscent of the one Alexander Gordon Laing had written, not far west of here, fifty-five years earlier, just after he had been joined by a band of Tuareg guides.

PART TWO
AN OCEAN
OF LIES

1

Many Tracks Led in but None Came out

Flatters was irritated by Shikkadh's abrupt departure. He had known that the old Targui wouldn't be staying long but had expected him to remain at least until an official replacement from Aitaghel arrived. The guides that had been dumped on him did not inspire him with confidence. From the moment Shikkadh departed they seemed increasingly restless, and finally, four days out of Inzelman-Tikhsin, they claimed to be lost.

Flatters was furious. This was the first time on the expedition that his guides had lost their way. He had been brought as far as Amgid by Shamba, who had been out of their home territory but had never put a foot wrong. Now the Kel Ahaggar maintained they were stumped, in their own country, and he did not believe it. He guessed it was a ploy of some kind, but exactly what he couldn't decide. When he asked the guides questions, he never got direct answers, unlike his Shamba, who immediately had come back with names, places, distances and detailed descriptions of the way ahead.

When Flatters checked his compass he saw that the guides were veering constantly to the south-east, which was no good to him. The one fixed point he had to visit on this trek was the Tisemt saline, and that was further south-west; he guessed that the Tuareg were deliberately taking him away from it. When he asked specifically about this, they began to prevaricate, until he pointed out the salty crust underfoot. They were already on the *sebkha*, he said, and that meant that the salt-pans couldn't be far away. They capitulated, and asked him to halt the caravan while they went in search of Tisemt.[47]

The guides returned at last light, appearing first as black commas floating across the unreal sheen of the *sebkha*, with the sun drifting down through layers of fire-gold and canary-yellow, leaving streamers of burning dust in the sky behind them. They couched their camels by Flatters' tent and reported that they had located the saline. From their information Flatters calculated that it was about fifteen kilometres away. At dinner in the mess-tent that night, over meat stew and red wine, he announced to the team that they would visit Tisemt next morning. The caravan would remain where it was and the camels would make use of the little grazing. He instructed Sergeant Joseph Pobeguin to take command of the camp.

At dawn, Flatters' party set off for the salt-pan. It was not easy to find. Its silvery surface was indistinguishable from the *sebkha*, and it was only when they were on top of it that Flatters realized they had arrived. Jules Roche was fascinated. The whole vast plain of Amadghor now had a logic to it. He was aware that salt was produced naturally where the uptake-rate of water-vapour was high. When the rainfall here had been about a third more than it was now, he thought, water had flowed down from the massifs around into the Amadghor Plain. The great lake that had once covered the plain had dried up slowly as the rainfall had declined, and the stages in its death were still evident on the surface. The water level had retreated to the area now marked by the *sebkha*. Finally, it had retreated again, until all that remained was a pool where the pan was now situated – a pool that would not have been much different from the one they had seen in April at Menghough. Then that too had eventually dried up, leaving the thick salt deposits as a souvenir.

The guide Sidi Mohammad told Flatters that in his father's and grandfather's day the salt had been worked regularly and shipped out to the Sudan, but no caravans had visited the place for decades, because constant attacks by pillagers had made the operation too risky.

Flatters led the party back to the camp at sunset. He was happy that he had surveyed the point specified in his orders, but wondered how this God-forsaken place could ever become an important junction on the Trans-Saharan Railway, let alone the great city envisaged by some in the High Commission. In any case, he was delighted to be able to say that he and his team were the first Europeans ever to have set eyes on it.

Not long after they set off, his mood was wrecked by the discovery of fresh camel tracks heading in the same direction, at least three hundred beasts. Sidi Mohammad suggested that they probably belonged to a local caravan that had come to cut salt and had then headed off towards the hills. This contradicted what he had said earlier, about the salt-pans being disused, and the inconsistency disturbed Flatters. He did not need his Shamba guides to tell him that these camels had not been tied head to tail in the style of a Tuareg caravan but were walking loose, like a raiding-party.[48]

Next day the mission tramped towards the Hoggar. The guides told Flatters that it would take five days to cross the plain, and as there was no water and little grazing, they would make forced marches. The weather had turned since they had come down from the plateaux. Gone were the skies full of fleece and the edge of rain in the air; now the heat wafted across the emptiness like a furnace blast, leeching the liquid from the water-skins, dehydrating the men and torturing the camels. Animals began to stagger and slump down, laying their heads on the hot gravel bed. This time there was no stopping to butcher them; they were just abandoned. Their baggage was shifted to the remaining camels, until they in turn succumbed to overloading and heat. The pace was unrelenting, and for the first time the caravan became strung out over a long distance. The laggards were left so far behind that they had to overnight alone and did not catch up till the following day.

The third day after Tisemt was the worst. The water had been finished the previous night, and the heat lay on their backs like a heavy blanket. From the early morning the men's mouths felt like sandpaper. Within hours their lips had cracked and their tongues had become so bloated and covered in mucus that they could not swallow, or talk. By midday even those who had remained on camel-back were bent over with kidney-pain. Their eyes dried up, and it felt as if they were sinking into their heads. Robert Guiard, the mission's doctor, calculated that if they did not get water soon they would be comatose by sunset and by next morning probably dead. Neither Roche nor Beringer felt up to making their usual meticulous observations. The Arabs suggested slaughtering some of the camels and drinking the water from their stomachs, a tactic they used in emergencies. Flatters would not hear of it.

All day the peaks of the Hoggar winked along the horizon. On the left, the guides pointed out Telertheba, outlying the Anahaf Massif. This crest of schists and quartzite marked the western end of Kel Ahaggar country and the eastern boundary of the Kel Ajjer. Somewhere under the shadow of the two-thousand-metre-high peak lay the wadi of In Sekan, where there was a *gelta*. After a discussion, Flatters rode off to search for it, taking Sheikh Bu Jamaa, the Tuareg guides, and a few *tirailleurs* leading a string of camels carrying empty water-skins.

The *gelta* lay at the end of a narrow defile between toppling grey basalt walls. When Flatters' small party got there, they found the water less than plentiful. The guides filled up little bowls and offered the water first to Flatters, advising him not to drink too much too quickly. When they had all drunk, they brought up the camels and couched them. Squatting on their haunches and leaning over the basin, they began to fill up the water-skins, scraping their bowls along the rock bed. Soon a dozen skins were laid out on the sand like bloated brown cucumbers. They loaded them on to the camels one by one and headed back towards the caravan.

That night the mission regrouped. They were almost off the Amadghor *serir* and the mysterious Hoggar stood before them: a volcanic wasteland of fang-tooth peaks, loose shale and warped canyons. The Arabs cast fearful glances in that direction, whispering about *junun* and demons, and about Ra'ul, the ghostly Drummer of Death.

In Flatters' dreams that night the mouth of the Hoggar gaped open like the lion's den in Aesop's fable – many tracks led in but none came out.

They did not enter the Hoggar the next day. The guides found a rich seam of *had*, a desert sedge like a small, dense bush as high as a man's calf, that the camels craved. Men and beasts rested. The French observed what they could of the eroded granite plateaux where no other Europeans had ever ventured. Far to the west, hidden in sand-mist, lay the heart of the fortress, the great buttress of Atakor, with its peak, Tahat, rising to over three thousand metres. It was here that the Tuareg placed Assekrem, the End of the World. On the eastern slopes of the Atakor lay the tiny hamlet of Ideles, with its orchards, palms and gardens. Duveyrier had marked Ideles on the map, based on hearsay, but it was not on Flatters' line of march. Instead, his caravan would be bypassing the heartland of the Hoggar, marching south from In Sekan, under the wall of a volcanic mount called Serkhout and along a series of wadis that would lead directly to In Azawa. That small collection of wells in the middle of nowhere, only a matter of days away, now glowed radiantly in Flatters' mind like the promised land.

2

'Let it come down'

The next morning, Flatters spotted four Tuareg camel-riders approaching the camp. More beggars, he thought. His only visitor the previous day had been a Targui who had come to ask for presents. As he watched them couch their beasts by the *sokhrar* camp, he noticed something familiar about one of them, but it was only when the Targui approached him and dropped his veil that he recognized Sghir bin Sheikh.

Flatters was amazed to see him. He had sent orders with Hamma that Sghir was to return to his *douar*, as he was no longer needed. The Shambi had ignored the order. He had come, he said, with his brother, to demonstrate his zeal, and he had brought with him two Kel Ahaggar guides, Khebbe and Baba, whom he had run into on the way. Flatters did not need Khebbe and Baba,[49] nor did he need Sghir; he distinctly remembered that, during the first part of the trek, the Shambi had assured him that he did not know the route through the Hoggar Mountains. Suddenly, Sghir seemed to know the place much better than he had originally pretended. He had left Amgid on 18 January dressed as an Arab, and now, three weeks later, he had returned in the black veil and dark robe of the Tuareg. He had even dropped the modest Arab style and adopted the menacing body language of the Kel Ahaggar.

Flatters did not quite like the new Sghir, but he didn't send him away. He accepted him, his brother ʿAla, and the guides he had brought with him, even though the four meant extra mouths to feed.

The following day the caravan plodded into the Hoggar. The men fell silent as the blistered walls of granite and basalt closed in around them, blocking out the great vistas of the *serir*. Flatters drank in the landscape; its desolate beauty was made the more poignant by the knowledge that his were among the very first European eyes to see it. The first thing he noted was that it bore little resemblance to the scene imagined by some scholars back in Paris. There, it was widely accepted that the summits of these hills were covered in snow for four or five months a year. He recalled the address of a Senator, Foucher de Careil, during a conference on the Sahara: 'We know that in the heart of the Sahara,' de Careil had announced, 'there is the mountain massif of Hoggar or Ahaggar which conceals on its flanks mysterious oases, fertile valleys where many cattle graze, in the midst of a flora similar to our own, on the slopes of mountains that recall those of Switzerland.'[50]

There were no snow-capped peaks, no lush flora, no fertile valleys; instead there was a graveyard of volcanoes looking like a backdrop from a Gothic nightmare, a landscape of delirium. The mountains grew out of a triad of interlocking plateaux. They averaged two thousand metres in height and covered an area about a quarter the size of France. The massif was a geological dumping ground of screes and boulder-strewn *hammadas*, a rubble of black volcanic shell in a billion shards. Long reefs of cliff stretched into the distance, sheer rock faces grooved and fluted, excoriated as if by giant claws. Soft lava cones pitched at disquieting angles over acres of black clinkstone, their sides punctured with cracks and blisters, looking like gigantic termitaries. Apart from a few grass-hut hamlets like Ideles and Tazruk, inhabited by sharecroppers, the only relief in this moonscape of stone was the wadis of white sand that cut through it, where tamarisk, acacia and hardy grasses flourished beneath the soaring vertical faces of deep ravines.

The caravan meandered between walls that seemed intent on crushing them like great grindstones. As they progressed, signs of human life proliferated: ancient camel-tracks like wandering tram-lines, the spoor of goats and sheep, the debris of old camps, nests of boulders used as corrals for kids. The guides were navigating on Serkhout, a volcanic extrusion segmented like a vast caterpillar, whose lava shell gleamed like polished metal. The going underfoot was soft sand interspersed with boulders. In the afternoon the wadi narrowed as it passed through thickets of tamarisk, whose foliage broke up the light into whorls and dapples, like a long expanse of leopard-skin. As soon as Flatters had ordered the halt, the place filled up with Tuareg visitors, clamouring for presents and vying to unload worn-out camels on the expedition. They eyed the mission's baggage with interest, inquired if the boxes con-tained gold and tried to finger the *tirailleurs*' Fusils Gras. Flatters was once more reminded of the scene at Lake Menghough. He did, however, part with four hundred francs for a camel. That night the animals were left to browse amongst the tamarisk. In the morning the *sokhrar* reported to Pobeguin that two of them had vanished. This was not an accident. The tracks showed clearly that someone had unfastened their hobbles and driven them off. This was the first time any camels had been stolen.

For Flatters, this was yet another blow to his tranquillity. Only days earlier, at Amgid, he had pointed out that they had suffered no hostile act from the Tuareg. Now that had changed, and he hoped desperately this was not the opening shot of a concentrated campaign. That day the caravan halted at Agendis, a *gelta* lying two hundred paces above a narrow wadi beneath a pinnacle 1800 metres high. In the afternoon there was another development. An old Targui appeared riding an emaciated pony, declaring that he had been sent by Aitaghel to guide them to In Azawa. As they watched him ride in, the Arabs had to suppress their guffaws. The

horse's ribs showed through its flesh and the Targui rode on a sack
for a saddle, using for a bridle a piece of string. The old man
dismounted at Flatters' tent and introduced himself. His name was
al-ʿAlam, he said, and he had actually left Aitaghel's camp on the
same day as Shikkadh. He had fallen far behind because his mount
was unable to keep up with Shikkadh's camel.

The pony-rider had an important announcement to make: an
official delegation from Aitaghel would be arriving the next day.
He then mounted his horse and rode off into the hills, returning
after dark with a flock of eight sheep and seven goats, tended by a
boy and a slave.

In the morning he asked to see Flatters again and told him the
delegation was near. He demanded the sum of two thousand five
hundred francs to lead the caravan to In Azawa, payable at once.
The fee was exorbitant; Flatters' *tirailleurs* were being paid only
one franc a day for their trouble, but this unimpressive old man on
his bony nag was expecting for a job of two weeks the equivalent
of seven years' pay.

Reluctantly the colonel shelled out a thousand, telling al-ʿAlam
that he would get the rest when the mission arrived safely at the In
Azawa wells. The guide stuffed the money into his burnoose and
informed Flatters he was going to deposit it somewhere safe.
Flatters agreed, but sent Sghir bin Sheikh to escort him back.

The caravan remained where it was, awaiting the delegation. At
noon, thirty Kel Ghela warriors in dark robes and veils appeared
out of the hills on their camels, approaching as silently as phan-
toms. As they couched their beasts by the camp, Joseph Pobeguin,
ever alert, noticed that all of them were heavily armed. This was a
tacit warning, he thought, for messengers of peace did not arrive
dressed for war.

On the face of it, the Kel Ghela seemed friendly. They greeted
the Frenchmen and welcomed them to the Hoggar Mountains. The
leader of the band introduced himself as Atissi, son of the previous
guide, Shikkadh, and the nephew of Chief Aitaghel.

Atissi was about thirty-three years old, a pocket Hercules of a man, feared for his physical strength and bullying nature. He had brought with him an older Targui named Wangadi, another nephew of Aitaghel's, who was not only as deaf as a post but also enormously fat. With them was a man called 'Abda, the chief of a section of Kel Ulli who were riding with the noble Kel Ghela. To French eyes the vassals and nobles were indistinguishable.

'Where is Aitaghel?' was the first question Flatters asked.

'He is tired after his stay in In Salah,' Atissi told him, 'but he welcomes you.' Atissi went on at great length, explaining how pleased he was to see Flatters and his men and repeating that the French were welcome in the Hoggar. The Frenchmen began to feel at ease as the first impression given by the Tuareg's martial entrance was dispelled. Then Atissi let slip something that changed the mood abruptly. 'I am happy to escort you to Ideles,' he said.

For a moment Flatters didn't know how to respond. Aitaghel knew perfectly well that his caravan was heading for In Azawa, the doorway to Timbuctoo and the Sudan. Not only was Ideles way off his course, but this offer contradicted what Shikkadh had said: that the mission would not be allowed to visit any Tuareg settlements. Flatters was suspicious, but remained poker-faced. 'I am grateful for your kind words,' he said, 'but we cannot go to Ideles as it is far from our way.'

Atissi knew that he had made a faux pas. Later, he tried to regain Flatters' confidence by throwing his arms round him fraternally and slapping him on the back. Flatters was aware this was not Tuareg style and was not impressed. That evening there was a great feast. The *sokhrar* went to work slaughtering, butchering and cooking the fifteen goats and sheep. After they had eaten, the Tuareg wandered uninvited around the camp, rummaging through the baggage, asking endless questions about what the mission was carrying, and what the boxes contained. They demanded presents. They wanted Fusils Gras and cartridges, and Atissi wanted one of the horses. Flatters said he would give them gifts, but refused to part with rifles, ammunition or mounts. He promised Atissi that he would get one of the mares when the caravan arrived at In Azawa.

Next day, when Flatters began doling out money and clothing, the visit degenerated into a circus. The Tuareg began to show their real character, griping that their presents were too cheap, or that someone else had been given more. One Targui threw the money at Flatters' feet and spat in disgust. Atissi and a fellow noble had a violent dispute over the relative value of their presents and ended up grabbing each other by the throat. This was the final straw. Flatters, who thought he had been more than generous, lost his temper and declared that the coffers were closed. 'I don't know what power you think you hold over me,' he said in Arabic, 'but let it come down!'

Moments later Atissi announced they were leaving, and the thirty warriors scurried to their camels. Without explanation they took with them Ahmad and Baba, two of Flatters' guides. They also went off with two of the mission's camels. Some *sokhrar* followed in hot pursuit and found the camels tied to a bush. When they began to lead them back, two or three Tuareg warriors rushed them, but ran away when the camel-men let rip with their revolvers. These were the first shots fired in anger since the mission had left Laghouat.

3

'If you don't go back now, you're lost'

At first light, the wall of Jebel Serkhout loomed over them like an impenetrable barrier. The ancient drainage system here had been obscured by lava flows, so that the country north of the massif was another maze of wadis, *hammadas* and canyons. The remaining guides, Sidi Mohammad, the man Bu Jamaa had brought, and Khebbe, who had arrived with Sghir, directed the mission due east across the grain of the run-off system. Their object was to reach the series of north–south-oriented wadis – including Takalous, Tidaqqaten, and Ti-n-Tarabin – that would lead them directly to In Azawa.

The going was terrible. Every wadi was a dead end, and every defile seemed to lead to another. Dreary, dark towers of basalt leered down at them, remnants of devils' castles warped by a holocaust, trunks of burned and blasted giant trees. Fields of volcanic clinker lay underfoot like the waste-heaps from some cosmic boiler. Cliffs rose above them, their sides shattered into immense angular boulders. Jebel Serkhout looked like a bloated python, its skin stretched taut over the faces of monstrous creatures it had swallowed, which were now trying to force themselves out of its belly. Flatters felt as if he were on the dark side of the moon, beyond the bounds of the known world, in a chilling, blasted waste where there was no help nor sustenance. No rescue mission could reach them here.

At the halt, al-ʿAlam and Sghir returned with another Targui called Aitaghel – no relation to the *amenukal* – who brought with him a letter that purported to be from 'the council of the Kel Ahaggar', but evidently came from Atissi. The letter reaffirmed the good intentions of the Kel Ahaggar and asserted that they would do their best to ensure a safe passage through to the Sudan. The real message, however, was that Flatters should hand over the mare he had promised Atissi to the bearer of the letter, as the Targui could not wait until he had reached In Azawa.

The sun set over the landscape of fangs and giants' claws in dagger slashes of crimson that ripped open the belly of the ashen sky. Darkness fell over the camp like a cloak, and Flatters had Louis Brame light his lamp. He could not sleep, and spent most of the night pacing to and fro. The night air was ominously still, lit occasionally by sudden shocking flashes of lightning the Arabs called 'scorpions'. His nocturnal tramping was interrupted by the cameleers who had brought back the stolen camels. They reported that on their way to rejoin the column they had come across the fresh tracks of a party of at least fifty Tuareg camel-riders follow-ing the line of the mission's advance. Flatters shrugged it off in public, but he had de Dianous double the guard.

More claws of forked lightning cleft the screen of darkness, and from the hidden depths of the mountains came the boom of dry thunder. On the other side of the camp, Sghir bin Sheikh, still wearing Tuareg dress, was sitting by the fire among the *sokhrar*, trying to persuade them to abandon the mission. As he spoke, lightning flashes illuminated his face momentarily, revealing eyes peering intensely through the slit in his veil. When the cameleers asked what he was afraid of, he told them that he had a blood-feud with the Awlimmiden, the Tuareg of the Sudan. 'I once killed two of them,' he said. 'If we try to get through, they'll slaughter us all.'

The camel-men asked why Sghir had returned to bring them bad luck when the colonel had given him orders to go home – and why had he come back dressed in that ludicrous veil? Only dishonest men hid their faces. Sghir grew frustrated. 'If you don't go back now, you're lost,' he raged. 'Personally, I'm going to save myself. I'm going over there to demand leave from the colonel. It's just hard luck for you!'[51]

Shortly afterwards, Sghir made his way to Flatters' tent and asked to be allowed to leave the column. Flatters frowned, wanting to know why he had changed his mind so suddenly, especially after returning to the mission against orders. Sghir repeated his story about the blood-feud with the Awlimmiden. Flatters considered it for a moment. 'In Azawa is only another ten days,' he said. 'When we get there, you and anyone else who chooses will be allowed to go home. Until then, we all stay together.'

That night, for the first time since leaving Wargla, it poured with rain.

4

A Jigsaw Piecing Itself Together in His Head

Though the actual route of the Flatters Mission over the next two days is unknown, most likely the guides took the caravan around the foot of Serkhout Mountain and into one of the big wadis running directly south towards the Sudan – Tidaqqaten, probably, because this wadi debouched into Tin-Tarabin, the great 'trunk wadi' where In Azawa itself was situated. The going was deceptively good. The wadi was wide, and in places lush with tamarisk and acacia. In Azawa lay only ten days away now – but though Flatters could almost taste the success, still he could not quite rid himself of a sense of oppression, nothing overt, just a feeling of tension among the *sokhrar* and *tirailleurs* . . . and a jigsaw piecing itself together slowly in his subconscious from a hundred small events: the theft of the camels; Atissi's graceless behaviour; his suggestion they should go to Ideles; the continued non-appearance of Aitaghel; the unexpected return of Sghir dressed as a Targui; Bu Jamaa's long absence; the behaviour of the guides on the Amadghor Plain; the report of a large band of Tuareg shadowing them . . .

The days passed, following the now-familiar routine: up before dawn, the camels ready to go at first light. Masson and Flatters rode off in the advance party with the guides. The caravan followed, the beasts walking freely in their sections, the camel-men pushing them along from behind, the *tirailleurs* either walking or riding their camels. The Arabs jogged along with their sticks across their shoulders, chanting the ancient herding songs that had come with their ancestors from Syria, whistling and grunting cries of encouragement to the camels. All around them rose escarpments littered with boulders, slabs and flakes of stone. In places there were the remains of villages, stone rings where huts had stood on promontories above the wadi-bed, once occupied by the Isebeten, the aboriginal folk of these hills. In the distance the camel-men glimpsed the strange peaks of the Hoggar, tilted towers looking as if they were about to fall, huge massifs pierced with natural tunnels and arches right through the centre, flat buttress peaks like the citadels of enormous *ksur*. The easier progress should have made the camel-men happier, but there was a brooding presence to the place, a closed-in feeling that made them ill at ease.

On 15 February, they made good time, covering about thirty kilometres. That night, as they pitched camp in a sandy depression, they were visited by two 'masks' – the term the French now used between themselves for the Tuareg. The 'masks' offered to sell them sheep. Flatters agreed, and the Tuareg asked if they could stay the night and bring the beasts the following day. After dark, the two men wandered the camp, talking to everyone, their keen eyes missing nothing. Later, they sat by the fire with Sghir, al-ʿAlam and the other Tuareg guides, drinking endless tea and chatting in Tamahaq. By dawn next morning, they had vanished.

5

'If you meet any Tuareg . . . they won't harm you'

The caravan set off at first light as usual, and continued heading south down the wadi. The camels had not been watered since Agendis, and the water-skins were hanging flabbily against their flanks. The guides told Flatters that they would be passing a well that morning, one that would yield water enough for the whole caravan. The sunrise came as a slight thickening of apricot behind the hills to their left, then an upheaval of colours – pumpkin, chrome and raw sienna, charring away the edge of darkness, breaking up the night into dabs of turquoise, woad and aniline-blue. The cloud turned white, melted into gossamer and floated away on a sky bloated with heat.

By ten o'clock, when they had already travelled some fifteen kilometres, the guides suddenly halted and fell into a discussion. Flatters approached and asked why they had stopped. Al-ʿAlam, still astride his bony nag, tweaked his veil until it drooped; the gap looked like a grinning mouth. He told the colonel that they had missed their way and marched right past the well they had intended to water at – in fact, it lay in another wadi completely, one called In Wahawen.

Flatters turned crimson. This was the second time the Kel Ahaggar claimed to have lost the way in their own country. The colonel knew well the qualities of desert nomads: in the area where they had been born and bred, they could literally find the way blindfold. They were familiar with every hillock, every nook and cranny. He realized this was a pretext, but dismissed it as a bargaining chip – another deliberate ploy to increase the time, raise the stakes, or claim bigger rewards.

Al-ʿAlam pointed to a knoll with skirts covered in loose scree. 'The well is to our right, a little way in the rear,' he said. Rather than taking the whole caravan back, he suggested, they should drop the baggage and make camp here. They could take the camels to the well unladen except for the empty water-skins. They would need some of the Arabs to help dig out the well, to fill the skins and water the camels, but the well wasn't deep and wouldn't need much work.

Flatters shook his head. He had planned to make camp near the well – tonight he wanted to hold a 'farewell dinner' with the local Tuareg. Al-ʿAlam told him they would find no pasture near the well, but here in Tidaqqaten there was plenty. It would be a waste of time and energy to lug everything to the watering-place and back, which sounded like good sense. Flatters was well aware that it was tactically unsound to split the caravan, but there were several precedents. At Amgid he and a small party had left the mission for several days, and he had left it again to visit Tisemt, and to fetch water from In Sekan. The mission had been marching for seventy-five days now, and except for the two relatively minor incidents of stolen camels, he had not seen any behaviour that was overtly aggressive.

For a moment the fate of the mission hung in the balance while he considered it. The horses fidgeted and snaffled grass; the camels nibbled at the tiny leaves of the acacia trees. The main part of the caravan continued to advance up the wadi behind them, leaving a veil of dust that layered the aquamarine sky. Flatters was uneasy after the events of the past few days, but he had nothing concrete to focus on. Al-ʿAlam pointed out tersely that the colonel was employing him as guide, and therefore must accept his advice. The tipping-point was that Flatters did not want to disturb the camel-men and *tirailleurs*, who had already been stirred up by Sghir bin Sheikh. On the first mission he had been forced to change route because the Shamba had refused to go any nearer the Hoggar. He was so near success now – In Azawa was only eight days from here – and the last thing he needed was a *sokhrar* mutiny. The guides watched him, hawk-eyed. Finally, he gave the order to halt.

The successive sections began to couch the camels and pile provisions and equipment. The tents started to go up. The empty water-skins were loaded up for watering. At about eleven o'clock, Flatters was ready to set off to the well. He did not see Sghir telling his brother, ʿAla, and the Shambi guide ʿAli bin Mahdallah, to mount up and follow the watering party, but he did notice that Sheikh Bu Jamaa was missing. When he asked about him, Pobe-guin said that the sheikh and Mohammad bin Bul-Ghiz had gone off with the salukis to hunt gazelle. Flatters stopped ʿAla bin Sheikh and told him to go and look for them.

The Arabs reported that twenty camels were ready for watering and the guides wanted to move off. The rest of the animals would follow when they were ready. Flatters gave Henri de Dianous com-mand of the camp, telling him that he expected to be back within a few hours – certainly before sunset. Robert Guiard, Émile Beringer and Jules Roche jumped on their camels to accompany the watering party, and Paul Flatters and Pierre Masson mounted their horses. The five guides set off, al-ʿAlam on his horse, with Sidi Moham-mad, Khebbe, the messenger Aitaghel, and Sghir bin Sheikh forming a close huddle on their camels, about fifty metres in front. Flatters and Masson followed, with the three other Frenchmen behind them. After them came the first twenty baggage-camels carrying the empty water-skins, driven by four Arabs, and escorted

by seven *tirailleurs* under the command of Private First Class
Mas'ud bin Sa'id.

Once the rest of the camels were unloaded, they were marshalled into groups of thirty. The second group left the camp
about half an hour later, under the command of Private ʿAli bin
al-Massai of the 3rd RTA. They were two kilometres behind the
advance party. As they trekked out, ʿAla came back with Bu
Jamaa, who had shot a gazelle and was jogging up the wadi
carrying the carcase, the four salukis yapping at his heels. Bu
Jamaa ditched the gazelle, mounted his camel and hurried after
Flatters.

The way led out of the wadi, over the rock-strewn escarpment
where narrow tracks wove between the hills. The camels were
often obliged to walk in single file. The animals dipped down into
narrow arroyos, clanked over screes, stumbled across convex
undulations the texture and colour of elephant-hide. The journey
seemed to take for ever.

Many accounts claim that Bu Jamaa, wary because of the long
distance, rode after Flatters to warn him that he had been betrayed
– but Flatters told him the Shamba had ruined his mission the
previous year and they were not going to ruin this one. Though
this incident continues to be cited, there are good reasons to sup-
pose that it never happened: the distance was not great, and it is
most likely that Flatters arrived at the well without suspecting that
anything was amiss.[52]

The final approach to Tajnut Tan-Kuffar, known then simply by
the generic name *tajnut*, meaning a shallow well, was along a
constricted dry-wash with bulging brownstone corries on one side
and a rubble shelf on the other. The *tajnut* lay in the bed of In
Wahawen, just south of the point where two branch wadis met,
opening into an arena more than a kilometre wide with a sheer
cliff rising straight out of the sandy bed on the western side. The
rock face was breached by fissures where water had carved out a
path over countless ages. It was capped by shale-covered peaks the

colour of weathered copper. On the eastern side the wall was a broken line of pudding-shaped buttes, approached over a steadily rising convex obscured by gullies and hillocks. To the north the land was gouged and furrowed, an endless groundswell of corrugations as far as the eye could see. The flat bed of the wadi was scattered with tamarisk trees, some of them old, with fluted boughs warped into nests of serpents, in places forming impenetrable copses. The well stood slightly above the place where the wadi lurched to the west. There was an old flood-zone of dried and cracked clay at the foot of the rock walls.

The *tajnut* was about six kilometres from the camp. The two French officers arrived there after about two hours' ride and dismounted to examine it. They were surprised to find it was no more than a hole, with a few mud watering-basins around it. It was full of detritus from the rain three days earlier and, though it was not blocked with sand, would need some time to clean out. Guiard, Roche and Beringer couched their camels and began to look around with interest. The guides dropped from their saddles. They raised their animals and squatted to hobble them by the forelegs, sending them shambling off to browse among the trees on the western side of the wadi.

A quarter of an hour later the first section of the caravan stalked out of the ravines, making for the well. While the *tirailleurs* barracked the camels and began to help unload the water-skins, two of the cameleers, Sheikh bin Ahmad and Baraka bin ʿIsa, took the horses. Masson stopped them, saying their skills were more urgently needed in clearing the well. The horses were handed over to al-ʿAlam and Sghir bin Sheikh.

As the *sokhrar* went to work, Sergeant Dennery arrived on his *mehari*. Flatters asked for Pobeguin and was told he had stayed behind. He took out six hundred francs, stuffed them into a skin bag, and handed it to Masʿud, the senior *tirailleur*. He told him to take three soldiers and go with the guide Sidi Mohammad and a camel-man, Qidir, to the nearest Tuareg camp. He was to buy two dozen sheep for the feast that night. 'If you meet any Tuareg on the way,' Flatters said, 'don't worry about them – they won't harm you.'

This was just as well, for though Mas'ud was armed with a loaded revolver, the other three *tirailleurs* had no ammunition for their rifles, the result of Flatters' standing order to stop the soldiers' tendency to blast wildly at any animal that moved. Mas'ud knew he should have instructed them to load their rifles before leaving the camp, but in their haste, he had forgotten.

The four *tirailleurs*, with the camel-man on foot, followed the guide Sidi Mohammad, mounted on his camel. They trekked north along the wadi to the place it divided, taking the right-hand, narrower, fork to the north-east. Out of sight of the wells, where the dry-wash curved through tamarisk groves, they suddenly ran into twenty armed Tuareg loping up the wadi on their *meharis*. The warriors' black robes belled out by the motion of the camels; they were carrying fighting spears with barbed points, shields, swords and rifles. Among the band Mas'ud recognized Wangadi, the enormously fat, deaf-mute cousin of Aitaghel, whom he had seen with Atissi at Agendis five days earlier.

The Tuareg riders took no notice of the *tirailleurs*, and Mas'ud assumed it was a delegation visiting Flatters – no doubt they would be guests at the party that night. Though the colonel had told him not to worry about any Tuareg he encountered, a little further on he witnessed a sight that startled him. Round the bend in the wadi they came across no less than three hundred Tuareg warriors, all heavily armed, standing by their couched camels. The Tuareg watched the soldiers silently as they passed. Mas'ud could not read anything more than the usual menace in their body language, but the sight of them sent shivers up his spine. He was reminded of a vast gathering of vultures.

Mas'ud told the camel-man, Qidir, that they ought to report this gathering to Flatters. The Arab scratched his beard. 'They're here to ask for presents,' he said. 'The Tuareg are nothing but beggars.'

Just then Mas'ud saw seven warriors trotting towards them on foot, toting spears and rifles. The warriors rudely ignored the *tirailleurs* and greeted Sidi Mohammad, starting a long conversation in Tamahaq. The discussion went on interminably. At last, Mas'ud reminded the guide that they had to buy sheep and get back to the well as soon as possible. 'Be patient,' Sidi Mohammad said, but a second later he jumped off his camel and swiftly snatched the bag containing the money from Mas'ud's grasp. Before the *tirailleur* could go for his revolver, the group of Tuareg were poking their razor-sharp spears in his direction, and Mas'ud noticed with consternation that dozens more of them were moving in. He held his hands up and in moments the Tuareg warriors had relieved the group of all their weapons.

6

Then the Demons Were upon Them

Two kilometres to the south, Flatters and Masson were supervising the four camel-men who were clearing out the well. Dennery had gone off on his *mehari* to meet the next section of camels, leaving the three remaining *tirailleurs* with the colonel. Glancing to the north, where Mas'ud and his men had just disappeared, Flatters could see the figures of Jules Roche and, trailing some metres behind him, Robert Guiard. Both men had their eyes fixed on the wadi-bed, seeking out specimens. Émile Beringer was sitting in the shade of some tamarisks by a cleft in the rock wall, about five hundred metres to his west. Not far from him, the guides al-ʿAlam and Aitaghel were attending to the horses, watched by Sghir, ʿAli bin Mahdallah, the *muqaddam* and Bu Jamaa.

It was a little after two p.m. and the air was very still. The couched camels flicked their tails lazily at the hordes of flies. The heat reverberated from the rocks. The sky was azulene-blue, and clear as a bell. Suddenly, two crisp gunshots rang out from the north. Jules Roche was the first to see the attack. As the shots slapped the silent air, he lifted his head to gape at more than three hundred Tuareg camel-riders bearing down on him, swords drawn and spears glittering, screaming out cries in Tamahaq. The camels' feet made a slithering sound as they ran. Roche fumbled for his revolver. Before he could draw it he was encircled by madly bellowing camels and ferocious veiled men. As he sought desperately to duck between them, the geologist was gutted with spear-thrusts, and cut across the head and shoulders with swords. Roche collapsed, his blood gushing from a severed artery and spattering the sand.

A little behind him, Dr Robert Guiard stood for a second, rooted to the spot. Then he drew his revolver, levelled it at the nearest camel-riders and fired. He snapped out six shots in rapid succession, until the hammer clicked on an empty chamber. He groped for a fresh clip, but in that moment he was engulfed. Sword blades snicked, shearing the tendons of his shoulders. A barbed spear sliced into his throat, severing the windpipe, ripping flesh as it was jerked back out. Guiard dropped his pistol and clutched at his throat, gagging for air as blood spurted, splashing the nearest camels. As he staggered, a Targui struck his head with a horizontal blow of such force that it almost shaved off the crown. More spears plunged into his chest and legs. By the time his body hit the ground he was already dead.

A little to the north, round the bend in the wadi, Mas'ud and his detachment had heard the two shots and seen the mass of Tuareg charge down the wadi in a roil of dust. An instant later there was an ear-splitting crack as a Targui shot one of Mas'ud's comrades dead, his head disintegrating in a mess of blood, flesh and brains. The warriors grabbed a second *tirailleur* and plunged their daggers into his chest. Mas'ud ran for his life, reaching the nearest rocky butte in one piece. He began to scale the rocks, pulling himself up hand over hand.

By the well, Flatters and Masson had stiffened at the sound of the first shots. As they spun round, they saw a spine-chilling sight: the wave of Tuareg riders crashing along the wadi-bed towards them, hardened fighters clad in their distinctive black, blue and purple robes that billowed behind them, the gaps in their veils giving them a menacing, reptilian look. The sun flashed on the barbed heads of their spears and the blades of their unsheathed swords. The camels snarled as the riders pulled on the head-ropes, their serpentine necks snaking back like dragons' heads, the sound of their feet susurrating on the sand, punctuated with shrill screeches of death from the Tuareg warriors. Puffs of white smoke appeared intermittently as muskets and rifles cracked among the dense ranks.

Flatters' eyes went wide. In that instant he finally understood his fatal mistake in bowing to the whims of the High Commission and in believing so fervently in Henri Duveyrier's romantic reports. The Tuareg had lied and lied. His entire experience had been for naught; his mission had been doomed from the start.

He cast around desperately for his horse, but it was nowhere to be seen. He drew his pistol. Masson did the same, and the two officers looked around, checking what support they might have – and realized that Sheikh bin Ahmad, Baraka bin 'Isa and the two remaining camel-men had already scrambled out of the well. They were running for their lives – without their weapons. Two of the *tirailleurs* had deserted them and were scuttling off, their feet kicking up little spurts of dust. A third soldier of the 1st RTA was standing his ground, and was taking careful aim with his Fusil Gras. He fired, the report almost deafening the two officers and, in the few seconds before the wave of warriors hit them, Masson and Flatters stepped forward, lifting their revolvers purposefully. With steady hands they blasted away at the oncoming horde as sharp-pointed spears whistled past them, burying themselves into the sand. Flatters shot a Targui warrior at almost point-blank range, barely able to see the wine-coloured blotch that appeared suddenly on the rider's dark robes. The man dropped his sword and toppled off his camel, crashing to the ground at the colonel's feet.

A round from Masson smashed into the body of a second Targui, smacking through his shield and boring a bloody hole in his abdomen. As the warrior tumbled out of the saddle, Flatters put a bullet into the sword-arm of a third rider. The Targui howled and let his weapon go. Then the demons were upon them.

Flatters tried to defend himself, but his pistol was empty and a sword-blade swiftly cut it from his hand. Camels snapped at him as a razor-sharp blade scythed a groove in his shoulder and three or four nine-foot-long spears thudded into his chest. Flatters twisted in agony, blinded by his own gore. The last thing he saw was Masson, trying to reload his weapon, already half-crazed from a deep wound in his shoulder. A spear-head pierced Masson's left cheek and emerged the other side in a shower of mangled flesh. The captain gurgled, retched blood and teeth and screamed as another spear thwacked into his leg. He staggered and fell. Instantly the Tuareg jumped from their saddles and hurled themselves on the fallen Frenchmen like furies, hacking with their swords, stabbing with their spears and knives.

As Masson struggled to get to his feet, his assailants slashed through both his shoulders, severing his arms completely, and chopped off both his legs at the knee. They surrounded the *tirailleur* who had made a stand with the officers and dis-embowelled him with their barbed spears, plunging them into his body again and again. As he lurched backwards, coughing up blood, a black-robed warrior bounded forward and slit his throat from ear to ear. The soldier let his rifle slip from his hands and heaved over in his death throes. The Tuareg leapt on him, beside themselves with battle fever, cutting at his head, doling out furious spear-thrusts to the rest of his body.

A hundred metres further south, the masked riders had already caught up with the fleeing *tirailleurs* and *sokhrar* and were pig-sticking them from camel-back, using their spears fiercely. To their right, under the rock wall, Émile Beringer was lying nose-down under a tamarisk on a mat of blood-soaked sand, murdered by the guide Aitaghel, who, as soon as he had heard the first shots, yelled, 'It's the Awlimmiden! Save yourselves!' He abandoned Flatters' horse and hurtled towards the engineer with his sword in one hand and a spear in the other. Beringer had removed his glasses and was cleaning them with a handkerchief; half-blind without them, he

saw only a fuzzy shape coming at him. He jumped up, but he was
too late: an instant later Aitaghel had buried the head of his spear
deep in the engineer's side. Blood pulsed from the wound and as
Beringer clutched at it in shock, the treacherous guide ripped open
his guts with a vicious cross-cut of his blade.

Before Aitaghel had even reached Beringer, Sghir bin Sheikh and
al-ʿAlam had bounded on to the officers' horses and galloped off to
join the enemy. ʿAli bin Mahdallah followed them, and though Bu
Jamaa later claimed that he fired shots at the enemy before running
to his camel, eyewitness accounts place him firmly with the traitors. The *muqaddam* jumped on his *mehari* and escaped.[53]

When the first shots were fired Sergeant Dennery was on his way
to meet the second section of camels, just emerging into the wadi
to the south. This group of thirty-two camels was commanded by
Private ʿAli bin Massai and escorted by eight *tirailleurs*. The third
and fourth groups, with another fifteen *tirailleurs*, were not far
behind. Dennery wheeled round to see the Tuareg behind him,
rolling up the wadi-bed on their *meharis*. He could clearly see the
bodies of the men they had just slaughtered, but the well itself was
veiled in a nebula of dust.

Dennery lifted his Fusil Gras and skidded out of the saddle,
couching the animal and using it as a shield. He drew a bead on
one of the nearest camels, not more than two hundred metres
away, and squeezed the trigger. The 11 mm round burned air and
thumped into the beast's big body; it crashed into the wadi-bed in
a cascade of dust, sending its rider sprawling. Dennery already had
another round in the chamber. He fired again, this time at the rider
now scrambling to his feet and a scarlet aura seemed to halo the
warrior's head as the deadly elliptical bullet smacked home. The
Targui sprawled over a second time. Dennery reloaded grimly,
firing again and again, bringing down more camels and riders,
until his hand closed on an empty bandolier and he realized his
ammunition had run out.

The Tuareg charge had been momentarily checked by the fire

from the lone shooter, but now they closed in on him abruptly. As the first warrior approached, the sergeant rose and swung at him with his rifle-butt. The Targui hung low from his saddle, his sword at the ready. Dennery glimpsed a maniacal grin in the eyes peering through the veil, then the fighter brought the sword across in a scything movement, knocking the weapon from his hands and almost amputating the NCO's arm. Dennery was spun around by the blow, showering the sand with blood. He glimpsed more leering demon masks above him as barbed spear-heads punched into his legs and chest. His world turned black.

Dennery's brave one-man stand had given the *tirailleurs* time to group themselves on a rise on the eastern side of the wadi. The alarm was screamed out to the advancing sections. 'We heard shots,' said ʿAmar bin Hawa, 'and a few minutes later they became more numerous. At the cry, "The colonel is under attack!" we set off running at the double. About ten minutes later, at the top of a little hill, we saw about four hundred Tuareg coming towards us, riding their camels at the trot.'[54]

Private ʿAli bin al-Massai mustered twenty-one *tirailleurs* into a crooked rank. 'Load weapons!' he bellowed, and there came the rattle of bolts being shot backwards and forwards. As he screamed, 'Fire!' gouts of flame and smoke spewed from the rocks and rounds singed the air, buzzing like flies. Tuareg camels screeched in agony and went down. For the first time, the black riders faltered. The attack broke off. Masked men pivoted from their mounts and jerked them down, then, kneeling behind the beasts, they began to return fire. Coifs of smoke leapt from their rifles as rounds whined and pinged across the stones, the roar of musketry echoing back from the rock wall.

The robed figures divided into two groups and began to crawl towards the caravaneers from left and right. The *tirailleurs* broke into independent fire, trying to pick them off one by one.

The *sokhrar* had marshalled sixty camels and were trying to turn them back towards the camp, but, sensing they were near water, the beasts refused to be herded and instead broke ranks and stampeded in the direction of the wells. As scores of Tuareg raced to capture them, six Shamba formed a wedge, blasting at them with their rifles, but it was just moments before their bullets were spent. The Tuareg leapt on their ancient enemies, their swords slashing and stabbing, spears piercing and gashing. The Shamba fought back with their now-useless rifles, but their blows fell harmlessly against the tough hide of Tuareg shields until, throwing down their empty weapons, the Arabs fought back with daggers, sticks, and even sharp stones, until their bodies were immersed in a torrent of dark-robed figures, leaping and hewing in an orgy of bloodlust. The Tuareg severed the heads, hands and legs of the fallen, then moved on.

The defence had lost all cohesion; they had tried to save the vital camels, but almost all of those had now fallen into enemy hands. The few *tirailleurs* who had been able to make a stand were outnumbered, scores to one, and they were quickly shot or stabbed to death. ʿAli bin al-Massai had vanished, and of the twenty-one infantrymen he had mustered moments earlier half were already dead or badly wounded. Those *sokhrar* who had not fallen had scattered among the rocks in an attempt to escape. Almost encircled by the Tuareg, the surviving *tirailleurs* knew they had to make a last effort to break out. The infantrymen rose up from their places on the little hill and rushed, bellowing, at the enemy, shooting from the hip. Rounds slapped through shields, sending the masked warriors reeling long enough for the *tirailleurs* to burst through the enemy lines. The Tuareg gave chase as they sprinted for the camp, catching the slowest two, spearing them in the back and cutting their throats. The rest outran them, and they did not stop running until they reached the camp in Tidaqqaten, six kilometres away.

7

'We can't do anything
for the colonel now'

When the first blood-smeared, tattered, breathless *tirailleur* lurched into the camp, gasping out news of the massacre, Henri de Dianous refused to believe it. The four other Frenchmen – Joseph Pobeguin, Joseph Santin, Louis Brame and Paul Marjolet – agreed that such a thing was impossible, until, only minutes later, the first-comer was joined by five or six more soldiers and a couple of Arabs, some wounded, some crazed with fear. All of them told the same story, and the lieutenant realized with a shock that he had just been promoted commander of the Flatters mission.

Dianous stood the forty men remaining in the camp to arms. Fearing an immediate attack, he ordered the tents struck and the baggage piled up into a defensive redoubt. Ammunition boxes were unsealed and rounds issued. The men crouched behind their poor defences with hearts pounding and rifles cocked. The afternoon remained perfectly still; the heat was already draining out of the sky and cool shadows were lengthening among the thorn-scrub.

The wait felt like an eternity. As he crouched behind their feeble barricade, the full horror of the situation hit de Dianous like a thunderbolt. The mission's survival depended on the camels. Without them, they were stranded in hostile country, with the nearest

French outpost, Wargla, almost three months' march away. He knew he would have to try to get the animals back.

When it seemed that no attack was imminent, de Dianous ordered Pobeguin to detail twenty men for a fighting patrol. At four-thirty in the afternoon, the small band of soldiers set off towards the well.

They found the wadi deserted, except for the mutilated bodies of the dead and the carcases of camels shot during the battle. Scavenging birds were already homing in on their dead comrades and the slaughtered beasts. The mission's camels had vanished without trace.

There were no Tuareg in the wadi, but the *tirailleurs* could see them, perched like dark crows on the heights on the western side. De Dianous sent a small party under Pobeguin to reconnoitre the well, but within a few metres a dozen rifles cracked out from the western wall. The detonations echoed round the valley as the gunshots raised explosions of dust along the sandy bed. Though the shots went high, the range told Pobeguin that the enemy were using captured Fusils Gras. The Tuareg were not good shots, but they only needed to be lucky a few times, and here in the valley the *tirailleurs* were sitting ducks. The enemy numbered over three hundred men, the French party just twenty.

De Dianous recognized that the situation was hopeless: it was clear that there was nothing he could do, not even recover the bodies of his dead compatriots. If the lost camels had been in sight, he might have ordered a raid to seize some of them, but without knowing where they were, there was little his men could do except blunder round the wadi until they were picked off one by one or slaughtered en masse.

Squatting in the cover of the hillocks, the ex-sergeant from Provence made the first agonizing decision of his command. 'We'll go back,' he told Pobeguin. 'We can't do anything for the colonel now. It's best to withdraw, defend the camp, and try and save those who remain.'[55]

8

'They will tell the Christians how many you lost, and they will laugh at you'

After sunset, Atissi and the deaf-mute, Wangadi, the two Kel Ghela who had led the attack, joined the tribesmen in an exultant victory dance at the well. The place would be known ever after as Tajnut Tan-Kuffar, the Well of the Unbelievers. Fires had been lit, and now the Tuareg were roasting hunks of camel-meat from the butchered dead animals on red-hot stones. The news of the massacre had spread like wildfire through the valleys. Kel Ahaggar nobles who had not taken part in the ambush converged on the place to celebrate, gorge themselves and share in the loot.

The plan had worked perfectly, Atissi thought. Aitaghel had made fools of the Christians, leading them to believe he was sympathetic, enticing them, using the country to its best advantage. Flatters had been drawn in by the *amenukal*'s confusing behaviour, until escape was impossible. Aitaghel had planned the ambush in December at In Salah with the help of bin Bajuda, who had sent a contingent of his Awlad Ba Hammu Arabs, disguised as Tuareg, to assist. Most of the raiders were drawn from the Kel

Ghela and Tegehe Mellet drum-groups, with some of their best Kel Ulli. The third drum-group, the Taitoq, had taken no part in the attack – they had gone off to raid the Tuareg of the Ayr Mountains. The clans had gathered on Aitaghel's return from In Salah in January. It was Wangadi who had worked out the actual details.

Atissi suspected that, until December, Aitaghel had been in two minds about the French column. The first letter he had sent Flatters, refusing to open the route, had been agreed by the chiefs of all three drum-groups. The subsequent letters, more conciliatory in nature, had come from Aitaghel alone. In one of them he had stressed that he could not allow the Christians through his territory without payment of a very large sum of money. Atissi thought that the *amenukal* might at one stage have hoped to make a big profit from the protection fee, but had abandoned that idea when he had come up against the opposition of bin Bajuda and the Sanusi agent at In Salah.

On the other hand, Aitaghel might have realized after sending the first letter that the refusal was a bad move: it could only lead to a no-win situation for the Kel Ahaggar. If Flatters had been put off by it, there would have been no column to plunder, and inevitably, the Christians would have passed instead through the country of the Kel Ajjer, and the profits would have gone to Ikhenoukhen. The second and third letters the *amenukal* had sent Flatters could have been a deliberate ploy to ensure that he did not direct his caravan through Kel Ajjer territory. This would explain why Aitaghel had chided Ikhenoukhen for offering to help the Christians. Atissi did not know for certain whether the ambush had been a long-term or short-term strategy, but he did know that his uncle was a fox: he remembered well how he had deceived Ikhenoukhen at the storming of Ejmidhan during the war with the Kel Ajjer.

Among the celebrants, sitting a little apart, were the five Shamba guides who had betrayed their comrades. Sghir bin Sheikh had first realized that a large party was stalking the column when he had ridden north from Amgid with his Ifoghas in-laws. He had been working with Christians for years, but inwardly despised them. His eyes had been opened when he had arrived in Algiers with the Ifoghas guides sent by Ikhenoukhen to meet Flatters. He and his Tuareg relatives had been treated like dirt, left to fester without food or water in a flyblown hut until Captain Masson had arrived. Sghir had risked his life, and very nearly given it, to bring back Aitaghel's letter. He had even advised Flatters in Algiers not to try and pass through the Hoggar, or to trust the Kel Ahaggar, and the colonel had laughed at him. Then, after all his effort, Flatters had sent orders with Hamma from Amgid that he was dismissed, without any extra presents or bonus pay. That had been the last straw. Atissi had persuaded him to return to the caravan, bringing two guides, and play the part of the loyal servant, with the promise that he would receive a substantial share of the booty. His brother, 'Ala, had simply followed Sghir's lead.

Bu Jamaa had known about the planned ambush since December, when he had caught up with Aitaghel five days out of In Salah. The *amenukal* had already been acquainted with him, knowing him as Flatters' courier of the previous year. He had discovered that Bu Jamaa harboured a grudge against the Christians for having exiled his father after a revolt in the north. Aitaghel had brought him round by pointing out that the Christians had destroyed traditional society in Shamba country, and intended to do the same in the south. Bu Jamaa had returned to the column and used his influence with Flatters to introduce the treacherous guide Sidi Mohammad.

The other Shamba guides had not been informed about the plot until after Atissi had visited Flatters at Agendis. Like Sghir, they had been motivated by the prospect of loot. 'Ali bin Mahdallah was an outcast who had spent his life robbing caravans. Mohammad Bul-Ghiz had been a *goumier* for the French, but, whatever his true feelings, he had been unable to stand against the others; the prospect of loot was enticing, no matter how he felt.

Wangadi, Atissi and their men had been shadowing the

Christian column for weeks, even before it had left Amgid, waiting for the right opportunity to strike. They might have attacked on the *serir* of Amadghor, but the two leaders had decided to wait. Amadghor was open desert without cover, where the Christians' rifles would give them the advantage. Better to draw them into the labyrinth of the Hoggar, where the Kel Ahaggar could use their skills of deception and trickery to the full. Another chance had come at Agendis, but Aitaghel had forbidden it – the place was too near the *amenukal*'s camp, and a mass killing there would upset the womenfolk.

The ambush had not been without loss – the Kel Ahaggar had twenty-seven dead and many wounded – so Wangadi and Atissi had resolved not to follow up the ambush with an immediate attack on the Christians' camp. The Kel Ahaggar outnumbered them ten to one, and had no doubt they would kill them all, but the soldiers and cameleers would certainly take some of the Imuhaq with them, perhaps many, for this time, they would not be caught by surprise. That was a game that could be played only once.

Sitting painfully in the shadows, their arms and legs tightly bound, was a small group of captured *tirailleurs*. Among them were Privates First Class Mas'ud bin Sa'id and 'Ali bin al-Massai. Mas'ud had watched the bloody encounter from his vantage point on the hill, and there was one incident in particular he would never forget. A soldier of the 3rd RTA, bin Saad, had broken away from the fighting and had made a beeline for the camels. It was an incredibly brave act. He had actually succeeded in getting hold of a *mehari* when the traitorous guide Sheikh Bu Jamaa had blasted him in the stomach.

As he watched the scene, Mas'ud had become aware that another man was climbing up the hill towards his position, his comrade 'Ali bin al-Massai. They crouched together for a while, composing themselves and preparing to mount a rescue of bin Saad, but as they clambered down, they found the faux guide Sidi

Mohammad lying in wait for them. At spear-point he forced them towards the Tuareg milling about at the well. On the way they passed the wounded bin Saad and, realizing he was still alive, Mas'ud had insisted on carrying him. Five hundred metres further on he put the injured man down for a rest when a *mehari* wheeled in front of him, the camel normally ridden by Henri de Dianous, now claimed by 'Ali bin Mahdallah, who was dressed as a Targui. The traitor jumped down, drew a sword and promptly delivered two or three vicious cuts to the wounded bin Saad's head. He turned on the two *tirailleurs* and was about to kill them when Sidi Mohammad intervened, saying, 'These are my prisoners. Don't worry about them.'

Close to the well Mas'ud saw the rest of the Shamba traitors mixed up with the Tuareg. He and 'Ali were forced to kneel while the Kel Ahaggar decided their fate. After endless wrangling it was agreed that they should live, as slaves, and in the meantime, they would be tied up and left with another *tirailleur* of 1st RTA, 'Amar bin Hawa, who had lost a lot of blood from a ten-centimetre gash in his leg. He had been lying among the rocks when he was discovered by a Targui named Hamad and brought back. He, with two more *tirailleurs*, 'Abd al-Wahab and 'Abd Allah, had been subjected to a banana court. 'These men are *tirailleurs* and therefore French,' Sghir bin Sheikh had argued. 'If you let them live they will tell the Christians how many men you lost, and they will laugh at you.' The Tuareg needed little persuading, and the three *tirailleurs* were dragged off to be butchered.

Fortunately for 'Amar, his captor, Hamad, intervened, saying, 'He's had it anyway. Let him die quietly – give him to me.' Moments later 'Amar heard the screams of his less fortunate comrades as they were mercilessly hewn to death by Tuareg swords. 'Amar swore to himself that, if he survived, he would never forget the perfidy of the Shamba. For him, their dishonour was greater than that of the Tuareg. The Kel Ahaggar could no more help their treachery than a scorpion could help stinging, but for the Arabs, it was different. They lived by a code of honour, and that included loyalty to one's travelling companions. To harm a companion after eating 'bread and salt' with him was a heinous crime against the code – one that could result in ostracism from the tribe. In Arab eyes, these Shamba traitors had lost their honour for ever.

During the night ʿAmar was disturbed by the groans of a *tirailleur* even more badly injured than he himself. Leshleg bin ʿArfa had a bullet in the left leg, a spear-wound in the right side, and sword-cuts across the nose and the top of his head. Leshleg would have been killed, had the deaf-mute Wangadi not intervened and taken him under his protection. With him were two other *tirailleurs* Wangadi had earmarked as his slaves, a negro originally from Sokoto named Mohammad bin Lefaa, and an Awlad Naʾili of the 3rd RTA named Khenis bin Salah.

That night, the Tuareg buried their dead. In the morning the first thing ʿAmar saw was a charred and blackened corpse lying in the burned-out fire: the body of Colonel Paul Flatters. He had been stripped naked and roasted by the father of the Targui warrior he had shot. Atissi walked over to ʿAmar and demanded to know if the Christians would attack. 'Certainly,' the *tirailleur* said, 'because they have no water.' Atissi at once posted lookouts around the wadi, and took his brother Anaba, Sghir bin Sheikh, and ʿAli bin Mahdallah, to find out what the Christians were doing. They returned two hours later to report to Wangadi that the enemy had left everything and moved out. The camp was empty. The birds had flown.

9

'Some of us are bound to make it'

Henri de Dianous and his party had arrived back at the camp by sunset. After dark, the lieutenant called the roll. Of the original ninety-two men who had set out from Wargla, only fifty-six were left. Nineteen *tirailleurs* and eleven camel-men were dead or missing. All five Shamba guides had vanished, and de Dianous believed they were all dead apart from Bu Jamaa, whom the *muqaddam* thought had escaped on his camel. Since he hadn't returned, de Dianous assumed that he was heading north alone to get help. None of the Frenchmen yet had any idea that it was the Shamba who had betrayed them.

The *tirailleurs* and camel-men were stood to in all-round defence. The night was cold and silent, the sky filled with stars, and the men skinned their eyes for anything that moved. In the shelter of piled-up boxes and bags the five Frenchmen and the *muqaddam* held a council of war by candlelight. De Dianous said they could stay and fight, and perhaps recover some of the camels. The bellicose Breton Pobeguin supported him, and most of the other Frenchmen agreed; the *muqaddam* argued that they should return to Wargla.

For a moment the lieutenant's mind teetered at the prospect. Wargla lay fifteen hundred kilometres away, across the world's greatest desert, and they had no camels. They would have to cover this vast distance on foot, in truly horrendous conditions of heat and cold, with no food, and no water other than the little they could carry on their backs. Every step of the way would be dogged by the Tuareg, vastly superior in number, mounted on camels, well fed and watered, armed with captured Fusils Gras rifles, and operating in country they knew like the backs of their hands. De Dianous did not believe that any band of soldiers in history had ever achieved such a feat.

There was silence while he turned the proposal over in his head. He realized suddenly that the *muqaddam* was right. The *tirailleurs* were demoralized, the *sokhrar* were on the brink of desertion. An operation against the Kel Ahaggar would be suicidal. He knew that there was almost no chance of surviving a march back to Wargla, either, but it had to be tried, and it had to be done now, while the Tuareg were still celebrating their victory. 'We all must die,' he told them finally; 'whether it is by bullets or by thirst makes no difference. We will go back to Wargla: some of us are bound to make it.'[56]

The preparations were made in silence, under strict discipline. De Dianous ordered the crates of ammunition, food and silver francs broken open. He distributed the weight equally among the *sokhrar* and *tirailleurs*, together with the thirty full water-skins. Everything else was left behind. Pobeguin worried over the fate of the four salukis – he could not stand the thought of the Tuareg getting them – so de Dianous told him to take them. One by one the men were loaded up with their bulging packs, water-skins across their shoulders. In the absence of a guide, de Dianous detailed Pobeguin to lead the way with a compass. Their bearing was north-east, towards Wargla, fifteen hundred kilometres away. At eleven p.m. on 16 February, the fifty-six survivors of the Flatters mission set off on one of the most incredible and macabre journeys ever undertaken in the annals of the Sahara.

10

'Not one of them must escape us'

On 18 February, two days after the massacre, the Tuareg arrived en masse at the abandoned camp. Moving like jackals through the baggage, they smashed boxes and tore open sacks, collecting weapons, ammunition, clothing, cash, documents and provisions. They did not eat the dates, flour, couscous and biscuits, fearing they might have been poisoned by the Christians, but took the food with them anyway, as it might come in useful later. The documents – precious notes compiled by Flatters, maps, charts and tables of data put together painstakingly by Beringer, Roche and Santin – were scattered to the winds.

The Shamba traitors, all of them now dressed as Tuareg, joined in the looting eagerly. They knew where Flatters had kept the money but were disappointed to find that only four thousand francs remained, not much when divided between the three hundred and fifty warriors who had taken part in the attack. The Shamba helped themselves liberally to the loot, but they remained concerned that the survivors might get away. They did not dream they had not yet been suspected. The wounded *tirailleur* 'Amar bin Hawa overheard Flatters' former assistant Bu Jamaa saying, 'We will follow the tracks of the French. Not one of them must escape us.'[57]

After spending the night at the camp, the Tuareg dispersed to their tents with the booty, and the Awlad Ba Hammu headed for In Salah. The obese deaf-mute Wangadi packed his booty on to his stolen camels, saddled up his three *tirailleur* prisoners and played no further part in the pursuit. The hounding of the column was to be left to his cousin, Atissi, who was in no rush to get started. It would take the Christians weeks to get out of Kel Ahaggar territory on foot, he reasoned, and every day would be a deadly ache of fatigue, hunger and thirst. Once the desert had taken its toll, Atissi and his vultures would be waiting.

11

Saved Their Lives by Hiding among the Rocks

The first night the remnants of the Flatters Mission had covered thirty kilometres, marching at a fast pace, hardly stopping. They were desperate to put as much distance as they could between themselves and the enemy. As light came flooding into the wadi next morning, the Arabs discovered the tracks of hundreds of camels, not more than a few days old. The tracks were those of the Tuareg war-party that had stalked them. By mid-morning they had come to a well – one that had been deliberately bypassed by the Tuareg guides on the morning of 16 February. This was proof to de Dianous that the ambush had been carefully planned in advance.

Later the same day an alarm went up in the survivors' camp as the eagle-eyed Arabs spotted Tuareg riders in the distance. The men threw themselves prone and cocked their rifles. The enemy were distant black dots, just visible against the slate-grey landscape. They passed without turning aside, and Pobeguin speculated that they were returning home from the site of the massacre, laden with booty. Shortly afterwards there was another alarm: a tribesman was approaching from behind. Sheikh bin Ahmad, one of the camel-men who had been cleaning out the well with Flatters when the Tuareg had struck, had left the French officers and his rifle and run for it. He had hidden among the rocks on the western side of the wadi and, slipping away unseen in the night, had spotted his comrades' tracks and raced after them. He had caught them only just in time; after a four-hour rest at the well, they were about to get moving again.

They started out again at five p.m. and once again they tramped all night, covering another twenty-five kilometres. In the afternoon they came to a wadi where water was still running after the recent rains. They halted to fill their water-skins and rest, breaking camp by the wadi while it was still dark. Over the next two days, six more cameleers joined them, bursting into tears when they recognized their friends.

They all had harrowing tales to tell. Like bin Ahmad, they had survived by hiding among the rocks and, when they managed to make their way back to camp, had found it abandoned. Already racked by thirst, they had set off at a desperate pace to catch up with their comrades. Some, too badly wounded or exhausted, had been left behind. One pair of *sokhrar* reported having found the *tirailleur* bin Saad, dying in agony from the stomach wound inflicted by Bu Jamaa, and the sword-cuts doled out by ʿAli bin Mahdallah. There had been nothing they could do for him but leave him some water and flour.

12

The Enemy Had Caught up with Them

Once the plunder had been distributed, Atissi collected a force of about a hundred and fifty warriors and divided them into two parties. The smaller group would ride into the territory of the Kel Ajjer and raid the tents of the Ifoghas Tuareg, the tribe of marabouts who had provided several guides for the Flatters Mission. Atissi gave the raiding-party instructions to hit Ifoghas camps and run off their camels: they would learn not to bring Christians into Kel Ahaggar territory a second time. The larger group, consisting of a hundred riders, would follow the Christian column under his direction. They would harass them and wipe them out.

Or 22 February, six days after the massacre, de Dianous and Pobeguin led the men, dog-tired, thirsty and starving, to the *gelta* at In Sekan, lying under the shadow of the two-thousand-metre-high peak of Telertheba. They had already performed a remarkable feat of endurance, reaching the *gelta* on foot in a shorter time than it had taken the column to traverse the same distance by camel on the way out. It was a salutary tribute to the resilience and determination of the *tirailleurs* and *sokhrar*, to the toughness of the French and their skill in keeping up morale.

A price had been paid, however: three exhausted men had been left behind to die. The rest were so worn-out and racked with hunger that they felt they could not go on. Pobeguin examined the men's feet and found them a mass of blisters and bruises; in some cases their boots had fallen to pieces, obliging them to stump on almost barefoot. The engineer Joseph Santin was feverish, probably from malaria, and scarcely able to limp another step. De Dianous wondered if they would have to leave him here. The rations were almost finished. The lieutenant watched the four salukis lying in the shade with their tongues lolling. Others were also eyeing the animals hungrily. Dog-meat was not *hilal* to the Arabs, and ordinarily they would have shunned it. Now they could see the salukis only as food. 'We'll have to slaughter them,' de Dianous said.

Pobeguin stared at him incredulously. 'Not the dogs,' he said.

De Dianous turned away and ordered the Arabs to butcher the animals and divide the meat up. Curiously, no one was willing to carry out the execution – the salukis had been friends for so long. Finally a mulatto *tirailleur* named Bul-Qassim bin Zebla offered to do it, bringing out a sword that de Dianous recognized as having belonged to Flatters. He asked the mulatto where he had got it and bin Zebla replied irreverently that the colonel didn't need it any more. De Dianous said nothing. A dead man's sword was of little consequence at that moment. He told Bul-Qassim to kill the dogs. Pobeguin stalked off on his own, flinching as the dogs squealed and howled under the blade, though de Dianous noted wryly that the sergeant returned quickly enough when the smell of roasting dog-meat reached his nostrils, and he did not refuse his share. The meat was tough and stringy, and little enough split fifty ways, but after eating it the world began to look a different place.

De Dianous remained preoccupied: In Sekan was the last watering-place before the waterless *serir* of Amadghor, and there was not a man here who had forgotten how they had almost died of thirst crossing it from the north – and that with a full complement of camels. The weather was now much hotter than it had been in January, perhaps fifteen or twenty degrees up the scale. At thirty-five degrees Celsius the body's minimum water requirement rocketed from five litres to ten litres a day. The rate of water-loss for men on foot in the full heat of the sun, carrying heavy burdens, was tremendous; losing just five per cent of body moisture was enough to make a man pass out. The Shamba, masters of the desert, knew better than most that thirst was the great enemy here. Their folklore was rich in tales of men who had set off on foot in pursuit of lost camels and had succumbed to dehydration. Once it set in, a man had no more than six hours. The Arabs had seen men so desiccated that they had passed the point of no return, when, even had they found water, it would not help: at that stage a single mouthful of water would kill them.

Threatened with death by thirst, the Arabs would slit open the bellies of camels and drink the liquid from their stomachs. They would hunt oryx or addax and consume their gastric juices, or push their sticks down a camel's throat to make it vomit, and drink the nauseating mess. But de Dianous and his men had no camels, and there was no sign of desert antelope, so not even these options were open to them.

One of the cameleers told de Dianous that he had seen the tracks of onagers in the area. These wild asses were abundant in the Hoggar region. The lieutenant sent a party of eight men under Private First Class al-Madani to hunt for them. Al-Madani returned two hours later with a surprise – they had found no onagers but instead had discovered four Tuareg camels, left out to graze. Some of the men were for eating them at once, but de Dianous pointed out that they would carry the heavy water-skins across the Amadghor Plain. Hunger was manageable for a while, but dehydration would kill them in hours. De Dianous reckoned that the camels could carry enough water for them to make the five-day trek to the Tisemt saline.

The following day they struggled out into the arid wilderness of the *serir*. The night had been cool, but at sunrise they could feel the latent heat in the air. The eerie moonscape of the Hoggar fell slowly behind them. The far horizons were a shimmer of sand-mist, and beyond it the tantalizing dark needles of the hills seemed to mock them. If the march south had been a penance, the return was a walk through hell. By midday, when their shadows had shrunk to grey patches between their feet, the sun was a merciless red dragon spitting fire. The men limped and staggered along. Engineer Santin was still feverish and rode a camel festooned with water-skins. The slop of liquid was maddening to his ears. The men went silent, their mouths clogged with white mucus. Some picked up small pebbles and began to suck them, but even this Shamba trick provided little relief. Many tied *sheshes* tightly round their stomachs, to counter the thirst-induced tendency to bend at the waist.

De Dianous sent Sheikh bin Ahmad and two other *sokhrar* forward to find water. The cameleers lurched off and merged with the heat-haze, never to return. From now on the lieutenant took to rationing the water personally. Anyone who tried to open a skin without permission would find himself looking down the barrel of a revolver. They halted occasionally for a few moments' respite. During these intervals the Arabs would hunt for edible grasses, *tullult* and *afezu*.[58] The ears of *tullult* could be rubbed for seeds and used to make bread or porridge. *Afezu* seeds were no good for bread, but could be pounded and made into porridge or eaten raw. The Arabs dug out ants' nests to raid their stores of seeds, and looked for *tirfas*, a white fungus that grew on the stems of other plants. Beetles were collected avidly – grasshoppers were a special prize. Lizards could be eaten raw or cooked. If they were lucky they would find a *kibjan*, or monitor lizard, a half-metre-long reptile with meat that tasted like chicken. If they were luckier still, it would be a female, with a store of eggs the size of table-tennis balls. At night, the Arabs laid gazelle-traps, small wheels of straw and sticks with spokes centring on a hole. When it was buried under the sand, the gazelle would put its leg through the hole and be unable to withdraw it. Gazelle were wary animals and difficult to catch. The *sokhrar* dug long-eared fennecs and Ruppell's sand-foxes out of their burrows and clubbed hares with their sticks.

In spite of all these efforts, hunger and thirst took their toll. By 26 February two men had already dropped dead by the wayside and Tisemt was still some distance off. At about midday the lead scouts saw that the shimmer on the edge of the landscape was forming into human shapes. The scouts halted and shaded their eyes. Six riders had materialized out of the starkness and were moving towards them with the slow deliberation of panthers. De Dianous and Pobeguin peered at them, straining their bloodshot eyes. There was no doubt about it: they were Tuareg. After eight days of torture, the enemy had at last caught up with them.

13

Reduced to a Company of Wraiths

A frisson of fear ran through the ranks. The *tirailleurs* laid down their burdens, pressed rounds into the breeches of their weapons and prepared to fight. The *sokhrar* couched the four camels and drew their own rifles. All eyes were riveted on the approaching riders. It was Louis Brame, the infantry private, who first noticed that they were carrying a white flag. 'Keep them in your sights,' Pobeguin croaked. 'Damn the flag, we'll kill them and take the camels.' The Tuareg were wary and remained out of range of their Fusils Gras, dismounting at the base of a nearby hill. De Dianous watched them for a while, then detailed two *sokhrar* to go and talk to them.

The *sokhrar* returned with the news that the Tuareg were the owners of the four camels the mission had found near Telertheba. They wanted compensation, or the beasts returned. The *sokhrar* added that the Tuareg had also brought a message from chief Aitaghel, claiming that the Kel Ahaggar had not been involved in the murder of Flatters and his men. It had been the work of their enemies from the south, the Awlimmiden Tuareg, they said. They asked de Dianous to accompany them to Aitaghel's camp to confirm this.

The lieutenant was perplexed. He had not seen the perpetrators of the massacre at close hand and had no idea who had been responsible. After considering the proposition, he handed over two thousand francs to his couriers and told them to give it to the Tuareg. The cash might at least buy them some time.

As he had feared, the Tuareg did not leave after receiving the money, but hovered just out of range as the survivors lurched onwards, following on their heels like hyenas. When Rabah bin Hamedi, one of the cameleers, lay down on the ground to rest, saying he could go no further, the Tuareg picked him up and loaded him on the back of a camel, but after carrying him a short way, they snatched his rifle and hurled him down. Two of the Targui lifted him while a third drew his sword and plunged it up to the hilt in the helpless man's belly. Another Targui finished him off with a dagger-thrust in the neck.

The Tuareg remounted their camels and stalked after the column silently. Presently they caught up with two *tirailleurs* who had fallen behind and pounced on them, stabbing and slashing them with their swords until they collapsed, covered with their own blood, on the salty earth. The scavengers couched their animals and stripped the dying soldiers of everything but their trousers.

The next day was a passage through the inferno. A sledge-hammer sun beat down and a hot wind chafed them. There was no water to wet their cracked lips and bloated tongues or ease the torture in their kidneys. Every step on their blistered feet was a misery. Most had passed far beyond the limits of their endurance and were marching on pure survival instinct. To fall behind was to fall into the hands of the predator Tuareg, who dared not come near yet whose shadows were always lurking like evil spirits on the periphery of their vision. Some filled their water-bottles with their own urine and drank it. The Arabs drank mouthfuls of camels' urine, wincing at its bitterness. Pobeguin announced that they would find a water-point that day, and the men began to march faster, driven by their craving for liquid. Hunger retreated into the background. Thirst was a raging fire in their heads.

When they arrived at the *gelta* that evening, it was the answer to a prayer. As the men scrabbled to catch the liquid in their water-bottles and little bowls, de Dianous shouted at them to take it only in tiny sips. The Shamba showed the *tirailleurs* how to soak their *sheshes* and suck the moisture out of them little by little.

De Dianous declared that they would rest here for two days, and ordered the Arabs to kill one of their four camels. It was a sacrifice, but the worst of the Amadghor Plain was behind them now and they needed food. The cameleers hobbled the condemned animal and slaughtered it in the customary way, stabbing it in the jugular and slicing it across the neck. Blood cascaded out of the severed artery and they rushed to catch it in their bowls. Nothing was wasted – skin, tail, neck, thighs, hump, lights and even bones were cut or chopped up; the animal's great head was smashed open with stones for the brains, the tongue, the eyes and the nasal membranes. They divided the meat carefully into portions and cut the rest into strips, laying it out for the sun to dry the next day; the dried flesh would be a reserve for the journey ahead.

While the camel-men were engaged in cutting and drying next morning, de Dianous, Pobeguin and the other Frenchmen discussed the possibility of turning due east into the country of the Kel Ajjer, but after talking it over it with the *sokhrar* and *tirailleurs*, they discovered that no one knew the way, or where the crucial watering-places lay. De Dianous decided to stick with the northern route.

As they were talking, a survivor reeled into the camp, the *tirailleur* Sa'id bin Nayib, one of the two laggards attacked by the Tuareg the previous day. He was almost naked, laced in blood, and only just mobile. As his comrades administered water from a *shesh*, he described how he had been left to die, and how, stumbling around after the main party, he had come across the mutilated corpse of the cameleer Rabah bin Hamedi.

That day they spotted gazelle in the area, but the animals were too far away to shoot, and none stepped into any of their traps.

They set off at nine o'clock the next morning, heading for ₡ stump of Inzelman-Tikhsin, hanging, just visible, over the shimmer on the horizon. Santin and the wounded *tirailleur*, Sa'id bin Nayib, were mounted together on one of the three remaining camels. Pobeguin, still navigating on a compass bearing, was relieved when one of the Arabs located the tracks the caravan had left on the way out, wind-riffled but still recognizable. The tracker pointed out the unmistakable imprints of the mission's three horses, clearly defined. The sergeant wondered where those horses were now.

There was no water for the next two days, but the stages were relatively short. As they reached the *gelta* at Inzelman-Tikhsin, de Dianous remembered that this was the place from where they had sent the last dispatches home. The colonel had reckoned they would make In Azawa within twenty-five days from here. That had been on 29 January. It was now 2 March, thirty-two days later, and the mission was back again, reduced to a company of wraiths.

The food was once again exhausted, and, after drinking their fill, the men set about collecting *tullult* and *afezu* to grind into flour. Suddenly one of the *tirailleurs* laid a warning hand on Pobeguin's arm. Four onagers had come down to the *gelta* to drink. Pobeguin watched the small, muscular-looking little donkeys with their greenish coats and black flashes, and raised his hunting rifle carefully. He squeezed the trigger. The wild asses whirled and clattered off in a cloud of dust. When it cleared the men saw that one of the animals lay in the sand, its limbs quivering. The sergeant had put a slug clean through its skull. The men cheered. This was unexpected bounty indeed, and the carcase was hastily butchered for dinner. In the morning a *tirailleur* shot another onager, and they stayed at the *gelta* to butcher and eat it, which delayed their departure by three hours. Even then they marched only till sunset.

The following two days were waterless, and again the rations

...e heat grew more intense. On the afternoon of 5 ...arch, de Dianous sent two *tirailleurs* and two camel-men to look for water. They had been gone half an hour when a shout went up. The lieutenant looked up to see the men he had sent off sprinting in terror back towards the camp. Behind them loped a dozen Tuareg camel-riders.

'Stand to!' de Dianous ordered. The *sokhrar* and *tirailleurs* scrambled into firing positions and prepared to repel the attackers, but once again the riders stayed just out of range. After the runners had made the camp safely, de Dianous saw that the Tuareg had dismounted and scaled a ridge. They had skewered a piece of white cloth on a spear and were waving it. The lieutenant sent the *muqaddam* and two cameleers to find out what they wanted.

The Tuareg told the *muqaddam* they were a different group from the ones who had shadowed them – they claimed to be Kel Ulli living in the area. They wanted presents and clothes, and offered to sell two worn-out camels for seven hundred and fifty francs. The *muqaddam* told them he would have to go back to camp to get the money. The Kel Ulli agreed on the condition that one of the *sokhrar*, Sassi bin Shayb, stayed with them as a hostage. Once again de Dianous had no way of knowing whether or not these men had been involved in the massacre. The Tuareg, nobles or vassals, all looked the same to him. He doled out the money, knowing it was a gamble, and added a three-hundred-franc bonus – and to his surprise the beasts were duly delivered. That night several of his party sneaked over to the Kel Ulli camp to buy dates. The dates turned out to be the very ones the mission had lugged all the way from Wargla, pillaged from their abandoned camp three weeks before.

14

'They have given their word'

It was a three-day trek from Inzelman-Tikhsin to Amgid, and hour by excruciating hour the familiar landmarks came into focus: the long wall of the Tassili-n-Ajjer across the skyline, vanishing into the sand-mist towards the east; the massif of Tefedest to the west, terminating in the Hill of Demons, its double buttress peaks clearly picked out in the light. Beyond that, de Dianous knew, lay the gorge of Amgid, with its little running stream and yellow-eyed fish. Amgid was the gate of the Hoggar: once past it, they would be out of Tuareg country proper and on the way to the lands of the Shamba.

Those three days were fraught with tension. The Kel Ulli who had sold them the camels continually dogged their heels. The *tirailleurs* in the rear took pot-shots at them to remind them to keep their distance. On one occasion a mounted Targui fired at the column, to be answered a second later by a shot from Sergeant Joseph Pobeguin, whose rifle was always at the ready. Tuareg camel-riders were sighted on the horizon, travelling parallel with the column, appearing and disappearing like phantasms. One night five Kel Ulli walked out of the darkness, demanding to see the *muqaddam* and promising to supply dates and camels' milk. They quickly vanished to whatever dark region they had come from, never to be seen again.

On 6 March, the column located a camp they had used on the way out. They found the bones and skin of heat-mummified camels the column had left there and collected them as a great prize. The next day they arrived at a *ghedir*, or water-pool left by the rain, and de Dianous decided to halt. He gave orders to slaughter one of the camels they had bought from the Kel Ulli.

As soon as they started off, at three o'clock, the dark riders appeared. They had brought dates and biscuits to sell, again pillaged from the column's own abandoned stores. De Dianous bought back the mission's own provisions for an exorbitant sum, and the column marched deep into the night, hoping to throw off their unwelcome shadows. The lieutenant tried to focus his mind on Amgid, but could not resist the unconscious sense that a confrontation was building up. It was like the feeling Flatters had experienced prior to the ambush: nothing that he could put his finger on, but a series of small incidents and sightings, all giving the impression that wheels were turning behind the scenes.

When he mentioned this to Pobeguin, the sergeant nodded sagely. 'It will come at Amgid,' he said. 'That's where they will attack. Once past there, we are out of their country.'

On 8 March they started at ten o'clock in he morning. The end-wall of the Tassili-n-Ajjer was before them, rising up like a great reef out of the *serir*, dominated by a chiselled peak seventeen hundred metres high. The day grew hotter, the sun compressed in a tight fireball and the light so clear that they could see the honeycomb dunes of the Erg Guidi lying under the rock wall to the east. To the west, more low dunes of almost pure gold lay like a deep-pile rug on the stony plain. Soon, they were abreast of the great cliffs, and de Dianous knew they only had to follow that line to ʿAin Kerma and then the *geltas* of Amgid. He could almost hear the babbling of the little stream as it cascaded down the rocks, the plop of the fish as they flitted in its clear water.

He was jerked out of his daydream by a cry from Pobeguin. Seven dark riders had drawn up along their line of advance. They were waving a white flag. De Dianous shouted for the *muqaddam* to take two *sokhrar* and parley with them. The rest of the column threw off their packs and water-skins, and brought their rifles into firing positions. They watched as the *muqaddam*, a small figure in a ragged *gandourah* with two filthy, skeletal Arabs in tow, shuffled out to greet the Tuareg.

As the discussion went on and on, the men of the column fidgeted nervously. At last the holy man and his escort came shuffling back, and asked to see de Dianous and Pobeguin. The five of them squatted down together behind a wall of riflemen. 'These men say they know what happened to us, but claim they took no part in the massacre,' the *muqaddam* said. 'They have come to sell us camels, sheep and provisions, and suggest that we halt for some time here so that they can go and fetch them for us. They will help us get back to Wargla. They ask to speak to you personally.'

'It's a trick,' Pobeguin warned. 'They want to split us up, just like they did with the colonel. They want us to stay here so that they can build up a force big enough to attack us.'

'They say they are not Kel Ahaggar,' the *muqaddam* went on.

'They're lying,' growled one of the *sokhrar*. 'I recognized one of them – it was Atissi ag Shikkadh, the leader of the party that visited us at Agendis.'

De Dianous asked if he was certain, knowing even as he did so that the Arabs did not get such things wrong. He sent the *muqaddam* back to the delegation to tell Atissi that he refused to talk to him. Within minutes the holy man returned to say that Atissi had insisted his only wish was to help the column get back to Wargla. 'He is ready to swear on the Holy Quran,' the *muqaddam* said, 'that he has the best of intentions towards us.'

De Dianous sat up. As an Arab Bureau officer he had used the Quranic oath for years in native courts and knew how revered it was. Among the Arabs a man *was* his word, and to break such an oath meant the shattering of his reputation for life, not to mention the risk of losing his family and fortune and dreadful repercussions in the afterlife. He told the *muqaddam* that if Atissi was truly ready to swear an oath on the Quran, then he was prepared to talk to him.

Half an hour later, de Dianous came face to face with one of the men who had planned and executed the murder of his former commander, his comrades and fellow expedition members, and the theft of all the mission's camels – the main author of the nightmare the lieutenant and his party had endured for the past three weeks. De Dianous was backed up by five burly *tirailleurs* with loaded revolvers in their hands, but he was hampered by his lack of knowledge. He knew that Atissi was the nephew of Aitaghel and had visited the mission with a delegation at Agendis on 11 February. He had no way of knowing that the man before him had led the ambush, or that he had followed the party with the sole aim of finishing them off.

Atissi was accompanied by a Targui called Khatkhat of the Kel Ahem Mellen – the father of the two warriors who had ridden hard from Laghouat to bring the news of the column's departure. He and his band had dismounted from their camels and hobbled them by the forelegs. The animals wandered around, cropping desert sedges some distance away.

Atissi spoke with charm and persuasive rhetoric, insisting once more that he was concerned only with the safety of the column. When the *muqaddam* brought out a well-thumbed copy of the Quran from its cloth cover, Atissi placed his hand on it and swore solemnly by God that he would bring the mission thirty camels, twenty sheep and eight loads of dates within three days. After the ceremony he asked de Dianous to send twenty men to help fetch the animals and dates. Back in camp Pobeguin came over and pointed out the seven untended Tuareg camels. 'We could take them easily,' the sergeant said.

'No,' de Dianous replied. 'They have sworn on the Quran. They have given their word.'[59]

He asked for twenty volunteers. The men scoffed at him,

declaring that no one could trust the word of a Targui. De Dianous reminded them that the Kel Ulli who had sold them camels and dates a few days earlier had kept their word. Why should these Tuareg be any different, especially after taking such an oath? Again he asked for volunteers. There was an awkward silence. Finally, a grizzled camel-man named bin Lakhdar said he would go. A *tirailleur*, bin Buruba, and three other *sokhrar* agreed to go with him.

Soon after the five men had departed, hanging on the rumps of the Tuareg camels, a load of pulverized dates was brought to the camp. Taking this as a sign of Atissi's goodwill, de Dianous distributed them among the men. That afternoon, shortly after they had set off again, Pobeguin called him and pointed out a daunting sight. Riding parallel with the column, out of gunshot-range, was a mass of Tuareg camel-riders, heavily armed, perhaps sixty strong. De Dianous was reluctant to admit to himself that this looked like enemy action. He trusted the word of Atissi.

In fact, his experience had failed him. For Atissi, swearing on the Quran was no more than a strategem; he laughed at the incredulity of the Christians and their pet 'holy man'. The camels and sheep he had promised did not even exist and four of the five men de Dianous had sent to collect them had already been cut to pieces.

They had initially been transported towards Amgid on the backs of the camels, then deposited amidst a horde of Tuareg, who had immediately seized them. The *sokhrar* tried to make a run for it, but the veiled men caught them and sank swords and daggers into their flesh, slashed their throats, ripped out their stomachs and cut off their heads, arms and legs. The *tirailleur* bin Buruba was grabbed from behind by three men, who stabbed him in the back and lacerated his throat. As he staggered forward, choking on his own blood, other warriors stepped up and gleefully ran him through with their spears. Only the veteran bin Lakhdar was spared, tied up, and told that from now on he was a slave.

15

'Have you seen the red flag?'

All morning the column hugged the line of cliffs that marked the edge of the Tassili-n-Ajjer Plateau, and at ten o'clock they came to the watering-place at Tin-Tahert, known to the Shamba as ʿAin Kerma. To de Dianous's dismay, the Tuareg had got there first and were occupying it. Their camels were dotted across the bed of the gorge, snaffling grass. De Dianous ordered the tribesmen away at gunpoint and they submitted meekly, climbing a knoll nearby, leaving their camels unattended.

'Now is the time to grab the camels,' Pobeguin told him. The *tirailleurs* were ready to do it, but once again the lieutenant demurred. The column was almost through the gate of Tuareg country. He hoped desperately that they could escape without a face-to-face encounter.

The party stayed at the watering-place filling water-skins and bottles until late afternoon. Atissi turned up yet again with his white flag and, through a courier, invited de Dianous to come for a discussion. This time the lieutenant declined. He sent the messenger to ask what had happened to the five men he had sent off the previous morning. Atissi replied convincingly that they had been taken to get the promised sheep and camels and would be back the following day.

At four o'clock de Dianous ordered the column to move off. They tramped a few kilometres north along the gorge till they found a defensible place tucked under the cliffs. The Tuareg slunk after them silently. When the mission had settled down, Atissi sent a messenger to offer them pulverized dates, reaffirming that the sheep would arrive next morning. De Dianous bought six litres of the dates and distributed them among the men. The Frenchmen boiled them into a paste and many of the column rammed them down by the handful, but some of the *sokhrar* baulked. An hour later the world went mad.

The first thing de Dianous noticed was that his skin felt hot, as if he had a fever. His clothes were intolerably irritating and there was a rush of heat in his head. He began to scratch his arms and legs violently, and a moment later he was screaming and tearing at his clothes, trying to rip them off, rolling on the ground, babbling and crying. Seized with an uncontrollable and unfocused terror, he drew his revolver and blasted shots left and right. The *tirailleurs* had leapt to their feet the instant the lieutenant began yelling, but now they too had become unhinged, dancing like marionettes, grunting, howling and screeching like wild animals. Some belted off rounds from their rifles, laughing like imbeciles; others dropped to their knees and began to eat sand. Some tore their clothes off and rampaged around completely nude. 'The horses! The horses!' someone called. 'Don't let them escape!' Several men vanished into the night, ranting deliriously. Someone began to bark like a dog.

Louis Brame stared round at the orgy of madness dumbfounded, rooted to the spot, a cold sweat breaking out on his brow: this was one of the most terrifying things he had ever seen. Men he had marched with, worked with and sweated with, natives and Frenchmen alike, had suddenly been transformed into wild-eyed demons, roaring like beasts, cavorting naked, raving in voices he did not recognize.

Men vomited and fell over, retching, tearing out their hair by the roots, flailing their arms and legs like swimmers. He watched in astonishment as Joseph Pobeguin, the no-nonsense sergeant from Brittany, crawled in front of him on his knees, demanding in an alien basso-profundo voice, 'Do you want the red flag? Have you seen the red flag?' Brame looked on in disbelief as the sergeant vomited, then jumped to his bare feet, drew his pistol and started zigzagging about the camp, first in one direction, then another, shouting at the top of his voice, tearing off his clothes, leaping over the baggage until he struck his foot violently on a sharp rock. He hit the earth with blood pouring from the wound.

Brame was distracted by the crash of gunshots and saw two of the *sokhrar* jump on de Dianous, wrench him to the ground and wrestle the pistol out of his hand. The lieutenant let loose a string of invective in a voice that sounded like someone else's. Brame looked round desperately for Santin and Marjolet, and found them sitting in the lee of the rock wall staring into mid-space. He shivered: this was even worse than the bacchanalia around him. His countrymen didn't even appear to be aware of what was going on; they were lost in fugues of their own, oblivious to the world outside, stranded in some nightmare of their own making. Brame realized that some of the *tirailleurs* had not moved at all. They, like Marjolet and Santin, were frozen, gaping with blank eyes at something he could not see.

Suddenly Brame himself felt a flare of heat in his throat; his lips felt as if they had been branded with a hot iron. He clutched at his neck as fire seemed to flood through his veins. His skin felt as if it had been doused with hot pepper and he began to rake his arms, legs and neck with his own filthy fingernails. Brame's legs turn to jelly and he sat down on the ground, already blind and deaf to the insanity about him, passing into a dimension far beyond the Amgid Gorge, beyond the Sahara, beyond the petty dreams of railway engineers, beyond the bounds of space and time.

The madness lasted four hours, but it took the rest of the night to recover any semblance of normality. De Dianous was one of the last to come round, and the first thing he noticed was that he no longer had his pistol. He got up and staggered about, hunting for it, his legs unsteady, his head feeling as if it were clasped in a vice. Pobeguin was sitting propped up by a boulder, nursing a jagged gash in his foot. Brame and Marjolet still had crazed, otherworldly expressions on their faces. Several of the Arabs were lighting a fire from brushwood. The lieutenant found his weapon under a bush and went to ask them what they were doing.

One of the men explained that they were boiling water to make a concoction of sugar, butter and pepper. It would open the pores and purge the body of the poison they had taken. The Arab said he had been told about this remedy by Mohammad bin Raja, the mission's former guide, who had once seen some relatives seized with madness after eating a potful of locusts. The insects had undoubtedly been eating *bettina*, known in English as henbane, a plant that grew in certain places around the Hoggar Mountains. Henbane was a relative of the potato; the Tuareg called it *efeleh-leh*, and used its leaves as a poultice for pain, but if ingested, it caused excitement and hallucinations, followed by trance. For some it caused only trance – that was why some of the victims had sat staring into space. 'It was the dates,' the Arab told him. 'The Tuareg mixed it into the dates. They poisoned us.'

When de Dianous asked why the *sokhrar* had not eaten the dates, the Arab replied grimly, 'Because the men who brought them did not wait for the money. When the Tuareg give away something free, that is the time to worry.'

De Dianous still felt ill and unsteady, but he summoned all his willpower and self-discipline to focus on their situation. He was astonished that the Tuareg had not attacked while they were incapacitated; his guess was that Atissi had hoped the drug alone would do the trick, driving them off into the desert in ones and twos, where they could be picked off. It looked like he had partially succeeded – six *tirailleurs* of the 3rd RTA were missing; although de Dianous did not know it, they were lying under the rocks scattered through the gorge, unconscious from the effects of the drug, and only one of them, Ahmad bin Mas'ud, would survive. When he awoke twenty-four hours later, the column had gone without him, and as he struggled after it he came across the bloody remains of his comrades, murdered and mutilated by the Tuareg.[60]

Daylight came pouring into the gorge like liquid gold, creating lakes of shade beneath the cliffs. In the stark light of morning, the place, with its twisted columns, fluted rods, blocks and plinths of rock, looked unreal, like the melted-down turbines of some gigantic steamship in a Jules Verne novel. To the west, the slopes of the Amgid Erg were on fire, the sand-mist drifting incessantly up the windward slopes, boiling over the blade-like edges of the dunes.

Not long after sunrise de Dianous heard the Tuareg shouting that the sheep had arrived. The lieutenant thought first of the five men he had sent to get the animals. At least he had to find out what had happened to them. He dispatched a cameleer, Qaddur bin Genda, to confer with Atissi, and deliver an uncompromising message: 'Send back your warriors. If you want peace, do not keep more than ten men with you.' He instructed Qaddur to offer three hundred francs and a burnoose for the sheep. Atissi chuckled at the French predicament. They had had ample evidence of his duplicity, but still they were ready to believe him, such was the imperative of hunger. He pretended to accept Qaddur's offer in principal, but asked for a delegation of 'more trustworthy' men to debate the price. He particularly wanted the *muqaddam*.

The lingering effects of the *bettina* must have been responsible for the fact that de Dianous continued with this farce, even after having indisputable proof that Atissi was a liar, for instead of rejecting the proposal out of hand the lieutenant ordered another six good men to Atissi's camp, including the *muqaddam*, the camel-men Mohammad bin 'Isa, Sassi bin Shayb, and Qaddur bin Genda, and two *tirailleurs* of the 1st RTA. The group trudged over to the camp of the Targui chief, who rejected the *tirailleurs*, sending them back to de Dianous.

Minutes later a shout went up from the mission's sentries. Pobeguin limped forward on his injured foot and saw the two *tirailleurs* rushing towards them with a pack of 'masks' in pursuit on their *meharis*. 'We wanted to help them,' said *tirailleur* Mohammad bin Bul-Qassim, 'and Sergeant Pobeguin, with his sword in one hand and his revolver in the other, placed himself at our head and shouted, "Forward against the Tuareg!" But the officer [de Dianous] shouted, "No! No!" We had to obey the last order in spite of our wish to ignore it, and despite what the sergeant said.'[61]

As the men watched, the Tuareg rode down the *tirailleurs* and butchered them from the saddle, with spear-thrusts and powerful slashes of their swords. As the soldiers collapsed, the Tuareg left them in bloody heaps on the sand. They made a circling movement around the column, working their way ahead of them. One *tirailleur*, al-Mabruk bin Mohammad, incensed by what he had just seen, took careful aim with his Fusil Gras and shot one of the camels down at six hundred metres, pitching its rider into the rocks. The other Tuareg stopped and swarmed over the fallen animal like ants, hastily carving up the camel and taking the injured tribesman away.

Not long afterwards, the sentries drew de Dianous's attention to a knot of figures that had suddenly appeared on the cliffs above them, out of gunshot-range. He recognized them as what was left of the delegation he had sent to negotiate for the sheep that morning: the *muqaddam* and three cameleers. Behind them stood a host of Tuareg warriors, including Atissi.

As the column looked on helplessly, one of the *sokhrar*, Sassi bin Shayb, was dragged forward. A Targui placed himself in front of the man and drew his sword. For a second the masked warrior held it aloft and the sun flashed on the clean blade. Then he brought it down with such force on Sassi's shoulder that the sharp edge cut through the clavicle and bit deep into the chest, giving the onlookers the impression that his torso had been cut in half. As the Arab lolled forward with blood gushing from a cut artery, the Targui smashed the blade down again and again on his head and neck.

Sassi's broken body tumbled off the edge of the cliff and hit the rocks below with a wet thump. The Tuareg turned to the Tijani holy man, who had never in his life carried a weapon. 'Seeing the fate that awaited him,' said one man, 'the *muqaddam* tried to evoke the pity of his murderers, by making an appeal to their religious feelings, crying with all his strength, "O Tijani! O Tijani!"'[62]

It made no difference. As the holy man held up his rosary, the Targui executioner cut off his arm at the shoulder. The *muqaddam* shrieked and lurched backwards. Blood spattered the swordsman, who paused, as if to consider his handiwork. While two of his comrades held the holy man's maimed body, he brought the sword over in a cross-hatched cut that neatly severed 'Abd al-Qadir's head. The head rolled until it came to a stop against a rock. The headless body was flung off the cliff.

The executioner cast around for the other two *sokhrar*, and found them on their knees, sobbing and kissing the hem of Atissi's *gandourah*, begging for their lives. The swordsman looked at the chief. It was customary among both the Tuareg and the Arabs for a warrior to grant clemency to those who touched his garments and asked his protection. To everyone's astonishment, Atissi spared them.

The murder of the Arab and the *muqaddam* was the most brutal thing de Dianous had seen on this voyage. He knew at last that there were no sheep or camels waiting for them. Atissi's oath, and everything he had ever said had been a lie. The lieutenant no longer held out any hope for the five volunteers he had sent off two days earlier.

Wearily, de Dianous gave the order to move on to Amgid, the gateway to Tuareg territory, where he sensed the last drama would be acted out.

16

An Army of the Dead

It was a march of only ten or twelve kilometres, but they were the most hellish kilometres they had yet endured. De Dianous himself was too ill to walk and had to ride a camel. Pobeguin limped along behind him. Brame and Marjolet had to make a conscious effort to force their feet forward, while Santin staggered along like a dead man. The Arabs, too, were so dazed and sapped of energy after the night's experiences that they could march only a kilometre or so before they had to sit down again, and the leaders had to halt frequently to let them catch up. Even so, five men were lost, including Joseph Santin, who fell further and further behind until eventually he vanished. No one saw him go, and no trace of his body was ever found. He was undoubtedly caught, stripped and dismembered by the Tuareg.

By noon, the sky was a white-hot screen, blinding bright, draining every spot of colour from the landscape. De Dianous's tiny army came to the fissure in the ramparts of the Tassili-n-Ajjer that marked the entrance to the gorge. Away to the west the lieutenant's bleary eyes could make out the familiar jelly-wobble dune of the Amgid Erg. As he had expected, the Tuareg were already scattered among the rocks and the nests of boulders around the gap in the cliff. There were perhaps a hundred of them, these black-robed *junun*, peering threateningly out of the shadows. The column now numbered no more than thirty-nine men, half-starved, sick, thirsty, and beyond exhaustion.

When de Dianous couched his camel, he found he could no longer stand up. He had to be supported by two *tirailleurs*. Pobeguin was in no better shape to lead their troops into battle, so instead de Dianous called forward two of his most experienced soldiers, Privates First Class al-Madani and bin ʿAbd al-Qadir, and told them to attack. This was an almost impossible order. This little army had been marching continuously for almost a month, on starvation rations. They were weak, dehydrated and malnourished, their bodies were racked with pain, their feet were lacerated and blistered. Their bodies still contained the traces of the poison they had ingested less than twenty-four hours earlier – and they were up against an enemy that outnumbered them almost three to one, who had arrived on camels, were well rested, well fed and well watered, and who were holed up in good defensive positions. Yet none of the *tirailleurs* shied from the battle. They stood up as straight as they could and formed their ranks with slow deliberation. In their tattered, ragged, sun-bleached, emaciated state, they looked like an army of the dead. They knew, though, that they had one thing the Tuareg did not have: discipline. They were desperate and resolute, and they fully intended to sell their lives dearly. The *sokhrar*, most of them ex-*tirailleurs* or irregulars, took up position next to them.

The *tirailleurs* cocked their weapons. A rattle passed through the ranks as their callused hands worked the levers, shoving rounds into chambers. Al-Madani gave the order to advance. The *tirailleurs* and camel-men, some bare-footed, moved forward steadily. Shrouded heads popped up from behind boulders and at once a blaze of fire whipped out from the ranks, 11 mm rounds scorching air, whizzing and whining across the rocks. The heads vanished. Dark figures plopped out of the shadows. Spurts of white smoke appeared along the line of the rocks from the Tuareg positions. Bullets raised sputters of dust and gravel around the *tirailleurs'* feet. Stiff fingers ratcheted cocking handles; spent cartridge cases flew out and clinked on the stones.

The soldiers squeezed their triggers again and again, ignoring the defensive fire. Some of the Tuareg were using Fusils Gras, but they were untrained, and committed the classic amateurs' mistake of shooting high. Their volleys made no impression on the advancing men, who took aim carefully and made every bullet count. The Tuareg, astounded by the volume of fire splashing and ricocheting among the stones, saw their fellow tribesmen go down with half their heads sheared off, limbs mangled by 11 mm rounds, *gandourahs* splattered with gouts of blood. This was not their kind of war. They itched to be out there, face to face with the enemy, with a sword and a shield in their hands.

Atissi, crouching among the boulders, waited until the 'Christian' column was within about a hundred metres, then snapped out an order to attack. The warriors launched themselves from their hiding places, leaping towards the enemy, robes tucked up, shrieking, waving their swords and spears, shields held out in front of them. Other tribes might have quailed in front of them, but the *tirailleurs* did not turn a hair. They stood their ground and fired more rapidly, feeding in rounds and working levers with cool precision.

The *tirailleurs'* training paid off. The Tuareg were good fighters when they could let fear work for them, or when they had the element of surprise on their side, but they were no use against soldiers who stood shoulder to shoulder and refused to be cowed. As the elliptical Gras bullets belted through Tuareg shields and whopped into flesh, warrior after warrior collapsed, dead, dying or wounded in the sand. A few hurled javelins that fell aimlessly at the riflemen's feet. The attack lost momentum until, suddenly, the Tuareg found themselves running away from the very half-starved men they had stalked across the desert.

They took refuge among the rocks, leaving their dead warriors littering the ground, their bloodied robes smoking from the effects of close-quarter shot. Among the wounded the warriors dragged off the field with them was their leader, Atissi, his robes crimson with blood. He had taken a bullet in the side.

Three times the Tuareg tried to assault, and three times the attack broke up in the face of the deadly wall of fire and fell back. The third time, the *tirailleurs* went after them, firing as they ran. The Tuareg split into small groups and scrambled into the rocks. Those who had rifles or muskets fired back, and one *tirailleur* was hit in the chest by a rifle shot and vomited blood. Some of the Tuareg threw away their rifles and shied stones at the enemy instead.

Al-Madani and bin ʿAbd al-Qadir handled the soldiers splendidly, directing the fire left and right. Wherever a veiled head showed itself, a *tirailleur* would snap a round through it. It became a dangerous war of shadows, working round rocks, trying to outflank and encircle each other. Louis Brame, still intoxicated from the *bettina*, ran forward brandishing a revolver, firing it in the air. As he passed a crevice in the rock, a lithe Targui sprang out and skewered him in the neck with a spear. Brame froze and dropped his pistol. In the split second before he fell, he recognized Sidi Mohammad, the guide who had betrayed Flatters. The Targui withdrew his spear and stabbed Brame two or three times in the chest as he went down. A moment later Private First Class bin ʿAbd al-Qadir shot the treacherous guide in the head at point-blank range with his own revolver. A red circle appeared in the traitor's dark *shesh* as he slumped on top of Brame's body. The *tirailleur* knelt down to examine the Frenchman and found he was already dead; as he hauled himself to his feet again, he saw another, Paul Marjolet, running alone towards the gaping maw of the ravine, firing his revolver and shouting to the *tirailleurs* to follow. A bullet slapped into his chest and out of his back, spraying ripped flesh and a jet of blood. Marjolet crumpled into the sand.

The wall of the Tassili-n-Ajjer had turned flame-coloured in the dying sun. The light was behind the spectral army and in the eyes of the Tuareg. Night would be upon them in thirty minutes. At last Henri de Dianous shook off his lethargy, drew his own sword and pistol, and stumbled his way to where the fighting was thickest. A few of the enemy were in impregnable positions on the heights, still shooting. Al-Madani, simultaneously blasting off round after round and barking out orders, saw the officer staggering up to the line and shouted to him to go back. A bullet whammed into de Dianous's shoulder, spinning him round. He ignored the wound and the shouts of al-Madani and carried on towards the enemy. A second round crumped into his chest and bowled him over. Lieutenant Joseph Henri de Dianous de la Perrotine, who had worked his way up from private soldier to commissioned officer, lay on his back in his own blood, his dead eyes staring at the desert sky. He had predicted that some of the party were bound to make it back to Wargla. It was not his destiny to be one of them.

The light was fast fading, the sun behind them smearing streaks of blood-orange across the horizon. Al-Medani and bin ʿAbd al-Qadir bawled at the troops to withdraw. There was now no chance of entering the gorge, and if they stayed where they were, the Tuareg would encircle them. Pobeguin, the only Frenchman left alive, had taken no part in the fighting, but he knew they had won a victory of sorts. He estimated they had killed thirty-three Tuareg and wounded many more, including the chief, Atissi. The price they had paid was the deaths of Henri de Dianous, Louis Brame, Paul Marjolet and one *tirailleur*. Engineer Joseph Santin and five others were missing.

As darkness fell over the battlefield at Amgid, the last commander of the Flatters Mission ordered the column to pull out.

17

A Death Sentence from Their Own Comrades

The next watering-place, Jama'at Mirghem, was a smaller version of Amgid – the *gelta* was hidden behind a great stone in a narrow ravine cut into the side of the Tassili-n-Ajjer. The column marched non-stop for fourteen hours to get there. Only one man was left behind, the *tirailleur* Sa'id bin Nayib, who had been so brutally chopped up by the Tuareg a week earlier on the Amadghor Plain.

There were thirty-four survivors of the expedition now, and they had been moving almost continuously for two dozen days, on foot, across some of the worst desert on earth, carrying food, ammunition and water. They had suffered crippling cold and blinding heat; they had gone thirsty and starved; they had kept themselves alive with dog-meat and donkey-meat, roots, fungi, insects, lizards, wild grass, the skins of dead camels and their own urine. They had been betrayed, harassed, tantalized, cheated, tortured, poisoned and sold their own provisions by men whose only object was to annihilate them from the face of the earth. They had seen their comrades poleaxed in cold blood before their very eyes, and had fought a battle against overwhelming odds. Through all this, they had maintained discipline and cohesion; they had fought courageously, and though they had not gained the water-point at Amgid, they had delivered a blow that the Tuareg would not forget.

Yet the poisoning, the battle and the subsequent forced march had taken them beyond the limits of the tolerable. Their arrival at Jama'at Mirghem marked the end of the spirit that had kept them going so long. De Dianous was dead, and Pobeguin, who had ridden a camel all night, was still feeble from the *bettina* and unable to walk because of the wound in his foot. Although he was now coherent, Pobeguin's lack of mobility undermined his authority.

When they arrived in the gorge at about ten o'clock that morning, the sergeant posted sentries at the entrance, in case there were Tuareg lurkers. He filled his water-bottle from the *gelta* and drank in sips. At once he felt the liquid coursing through his body like a drug, revitalizing the cells and stimulating his brain. There were no provisions, and his only option was to order a camel slaughtered. Bul-Qassim bin Zebla, the mulatto *tirailleur* of the 1st RTA, who by now appeared to have appointed himself master-butcher, did the job with Flatters' sword.

As bin Zebla and the others went to work on the carcase, there was a cry from the sentries. The Tuareg had tracked them down: dark riders were hovering in the sand-mist beyond the gorge. There was an almost palpable groan of despair as the men picked up their weapons, loaded them, and tried to prepare themselves mentally for a fight they did not believe they could win. The sentries kept the Tuareg in their sights all day, but they made no attempt to come nearer. They had learned to fear the sting of Fusils Gras in the hands of trained riflemen, and this time they were taking no chances.

The men divided up the camel's meat. Some cooked it; others ate it raw. After dark, Pobeguin called for Private First Class bin 'Abd al-Qadir, who had helped lead the fighting at Amgid. The sergeant told the *tirailleur* that he had been hoping that Bu Jamaa would have brought help, but he had now given up and believed all their Shamba guides must have been killed or taken prisoner on 16 February. Pobeguin reminded al-Qadir that the mission's former guide, Mohammad bin Raja, had pitched his *douar* near Hassi Messeggem, which was about a week's journey to the north. Pobeguin's idea was that bin ʿAbd al-Qadir would make a run for Mohammad bin Raja's camp, where he could hire or borrow camels to get him to Wargla. There he would tell Sergeant Mohammad bin Bul Qassim, the Agha's military deputy, of the fate of the expedition, and bring back a rescue mission. Pobeguin warned al-Qadir that when he reached Hassi Messeggem, he was not to tell bin Raja or his Shamba neighbours that anyone else was alive, in case the local bandits and cut-throats got wind of it and came looking for easy pickings. Until he found the deputy, he was to pretend that the entire column had been slaughtered, and everyone else was dead.

Bin ʿAbd al-Qadir said he was ready to take on the challenge, but he could not manage it alone; he proposed taking three camel-men with him. Pobeguin refused: the departure of four of their fittest men would start a free-for-all and every man who thought himself strong enough would abandon the group, leaving the rest to their fate. Their only chance of survival lay in sticking together. To disperse into small bands would be to play right into the hands of the Tuareg.

Bin ʿAbd al-Qadir weighed it up, and decided to ignore the sergeant's orders. Around midnight, he and three *sokhrar* silently collected water-skins and small packets of camel-meat and climbed up the escarpment to avoid alerting the sentries at the entrance to the gorge.

Pobeguin woke next morning to find his party reduced to thirty men.

By the time the column started out, later that morning, the Tuareg had melted back into the desert. All day the stragglers checked behind them, but the 'masks' were nowhere in sight. They did not appear at sunset, nor at sunrise the next morning, nor throughout the following day. The men dared to hope that the veiled warriors had at last given up harassing them, but the disappearance of the enemy had an unexpectedly negative effect. The constant threat of attack had bound the group together, and without that external focus tribal and personal differences came to the surface, exacerbated by exhaustion, hunger and thirst.

Three days later, the survivors were climbing up the old trails into the Tinighert Plateau. The weather was hotter than when they had been here last, in January, and the men were on their last legs, moving sluggishly, resting more frequently and for longer. Their energy was almost visibly winding down. Their only asset was the two camels, now grotesquely thin and cadaverous. Little by little the men had thrown away everything not of immediate use, except the silver francs, carried in packs or loaded in bags on the camels' backs. One *tirailleur* refused to dump the money in his pack, and on 15 March he fell further and further behind. At camp that night, Pobeguin waited for him in vain. Two volunteers went back to look for him, and returned several hours later saying that the man was dead; there had been nothing they could do for him. Pobeguin noticed that both men were concealing bags of money in their burnooses.

By 17 March they had reached the well at Tilmas al-Mra, where they had last camped on 12 January. To everyone's enormous delight, they found a mummified camel there, and the starving men scrambled to cut up the rock-hard skin and crush the bones to make a stew.

Over the next two days the march became increasingly desperate. On 19 March, for the first time, the column split up, the leaders forging ahead to reach the next well before last light, leaving the slower ones far behind. It had always been their custom to pause so that the less able men could catch up, but now such considerations were thrown to the wind.

Things came to a head at camp that night, when the decision was made to slaughter one of the two remaining camels. The group instantly split into two, the northerners of the 1st RTA against the *sokhrar* and the four remaining Awlad Na'il soldiers of the 3rd RTA. Each side defended its 'own' camel, and insisted the other should be killed. Tempers flared, voices were raised, revolvers came out and rifles were cocked. It was only with a supreme effort of diplomacy that Pobeguin was able to calm things down.

No sooner had the chosen camel been slaughtered than the men began to fight again, this time over who would get the bigger scraps of meat. They screamed, pushed, wrestled and squabbled. The soldiers and camel-men, who had struggled so valiantly across the Sahara, on foot, for a month, had sunk to the level of animals. Pobeguin took charge of the meat set aside for the journey ahead and had a *tirailleur* stand over it, with orders to shoot anyone who tried to help himself. To make matters worse, the tail-enders staggered in after the meat had been divided and had to be content with the entrails. Some of the men did not make it to the camp at all that night.

They came in the following morning, and the group set off as usual. Hassi al-Hajaj, the well with an evil reputation, known as the haunt of bandits, lay only a few kilometres away, but in their current state it felt like the other end of the earth. They slogged on through the *hammada*, every pace a conscious effort of will. Almost at once, the column became strung out. As usual, the sun flayed them; within two hours the surface temperature was so high that those without shoes had to wrap bandages around their feet. The heat radiated back in their faces from the burning stones. By mid-morning they were suffering the effects of dehydration, fat tongues lolling against emery-paper lips, bending at the waist from kidney colic. They were well and truly at the end. At noon they sat down in the sun, unable to go any further.

Pobeguin tried to shift them in vain. He was riding the only camel left, his foot now badly infected from the injury sustained during the mad *bettina* orgy. He realized that they would all die of thirst if they just sat here, so he proposed taking the three fittest *tirailleurs* to Hassi al-Hajaj, and from there sending one man back with the camel, carrying water for the others, who would continue to plod on slowly until the camel arrived.

It took no more than two hours to reach the *hassi*, and once there, Pobeguin and the three *tirailleurs* drank and filled several skins. Pobeguin ordered the strongest of the three, Mukhtar bin Ghazal of the 1st RTA, to take the camel back as promised. Bin Ghazal set off south along the stony path and soon spotted a figure trudging along in the distance, his comrade, bin Ghoraib, also of the 1st RTA. He was the first of the column. The two men met up, and bin Ghazal gave bin Ghoraib a drink. They were out of sight of Hassi al-Hajaj, and there was no one else around. They had a camel, and they had water, and Hassi Messeggem lay only three days' trek away. They could make it – if they didn't have to wait for everyone else. In a heartbeat the two *tirailleurs* were mounted on the expedition's last camel and making for freedom.

Pobeguin and the other two *tirailleurs* waited at the well for hours in the shade of some thorn-trees, but it was almost sunset before they saw movement and found the first of the rear-party hobbling in. The men looked like ravenous, red-eyed corpses. At first they were too thirsty and exhausted to speak, but once the water had revived them a little, they recovered enough to tell Pobeguin that they had found the camel's tracks a little way out of Hassi al-Hajaj. The tracks had turned towards Hassi Messeggem. The two *tirailleurs* had absconded with the last camel.

At first Pobeguin could not believe it. The two men had virtually condemned the rest of the party to death. That camel had been their very last hope. Pobeguin had intended to slaughter it, to give the survivors the energy to reach Hassi Messeggem. Now they would never have the strength to get there.

The group arrived in dribs and drabs, each man in turn horrified by this latest act of treachery. These men who had survived daily harassment from the Tuareg had now been handed out a death sentence by their own comrades. For many this was the final straw. They cast around madly for insects, lizards, rats and edible plants – even sand-vipers – but Hassi al-Hajaj was a barren place, and there was little to find there. Some resorted to eating their own excrement.

18

They No Longer
Looked Human

For three days, the twenty-five survivors of the Flatters mission sat starving at the wells of Hassi al-Hajaj. Hunger had become a physical torment, a constant sour ache in the body. They tried everything they knew to alleviate it: rolling on their stomachs, tying their belts and *sheshes* as tightly as they could around their bellies, filling themselves with water to bursting point, sucking on stones. Nothing worked. Looking at each other, they saw only other animals with succulent, edible flesh. Finally, one of the *tirailleurs*, ʿAbd as-Salaam bin al-Haj, forced himself out of his torpor and suggested to Pobeguin that he should try to reach Hassi Messeggem alone. It was forty-five kilometres away, but ʿAbd as-Salaam was ready to try. If he did not get help, they would all die. Reluctantly, Pobeguin agreed.

ʿAbd as-Salaam took his rifle and some water and started off on the path towards the Messeggem Valley. Pobeguin had forbidden anyone else to go with him, but several men who had for three days sat as motionless as lizards suddenly found the energy to slink away. When Pobeguin asked where they were going, they replied, 'Hunting.' No more than a kilometre from the camp ʿAbd as-Salaam heard the scuff of footsteps behind him and he turned to find three or four of his comrades bearing down on him. They no longer looked like his comrades; they no longer even looked human. Their eyes were red-rimmed and sunken, massively out-sized in their skeletal faces; their thin, blackened lips were drawn back over vulpine teeth. Their faces held an expression so savage that for a second 'Abd as-Salaam shivered. Then they were on him, jerking him down, rifles to his head. Two crisp shots rang out, killing him instantly.

The men stripped the clothes off the body and drew the sharp little knives they used so efficiently for skinning and butchering camels. One of them was Bul-Qassim bin Zebla, the 'master-butcher'. He used Flatters' old sword to sever the dead man's arms, legs and head and within minutes 'Abd as-Salaam's body had been dismembered into unidentifiable hunks of bloody flesh. The men were so famished that they began to chew the raw meat while they brought out wood and dry grass and lit a fire, heating stones and laying the flesh on them. The intoxicating smell of the cooking meat almost made them faint.

At sunrise the following day, the mulatto Bul-Qassim and the others returned to the well. One of them was carrying charred meat in his pack. He offered it to Pobeguin, telling him it was the flesh of a moufflon they had shot the previous night. The sergeant stared at the burned flesh in horror. He recognized it as human, and understood at once what had happened. He saw how low they had now sunk – yet he also knew he was powerless to do anything about it. While the other starving men fell on the food, Pobeguin turned away in disgust.

It might have been the unexpected food that gave the survivors the fillip they needed, or the fear that more of them would end up in the cooking-pot. That morning, Pobeguin persuaded fourteen of them to attempt the march to Hassi Messeggem. Al-Mabruk bin Mohammad, the *tirailleur* who had shot down the Targui camel-man near 'Ain Kerma, and a comrade of his from the 1st RTA, Ahmad bin Tahir, were dying of malnutrition; seven others were either unable to walk, or had lost the will to try. It was only with an act of superhuman will that Pobeguin managed to get himself up. He had eaten lizards and grasshoppers for three days and his foot was now so bloated from the infection that he had to drag it along.

It was a dismal little bunch that tottered away from the well-field that morning: a procession from a vision of purgatory. They were walking skeletons, the bones pressing through their skin, the flesh taut on their faces, their eyes huge and lifeless, their hooded cloaks in rags and tatters. The sun came out and grilled them as they hobbled along, panting. The going was so painful that they had to stop every few minutes, and over the whole day they made no more than three kilometres. At their best, these men had marched thirty kilometres or more in the same time, but their strength had deserted them. Hassi Messeggem, the promised land, was as distant as the moon.

The two *tirailleurs* Pobeguin had left dying at Hassi al-Hajaj hung on to life, surrounded by men too weak to help them. Darkness fell over the desert, bringing with it the end of all hope. The dying men lingered on until the early hours of the morning, when camel-man Jadid bin Mohammad, who had been watching them with clinical detachment, pronounced them dead. He whispered to his friend bin Zanun, who drew his knife and prepared to carve them up.

Instantly, the other men were awake. Jadid told them that al-Mabruk and bin Tahir had died quietly in their sleep, and argued that it was no crime to eat their corpses. Two *tirailleurs* of the 1st RTA, bin ʿAuda and bin Ahmad, objected, swearing that no one would touch the corpses of their comrades. The men had been brave soldiers of their regiment and deserved proper burial.

For a moment there was a stand-off as all seven of the men weighed survival against death with honour. For bin Zanun, survival triumphed. He ignored the others and bent over the dead al-Mabruk with his knife. Bin ʿAuda and bin Ahmad cocked their rifles. Jadid drew his revolver, put it to bin ʿAuda's head and shot him at point-blank range. Blood and brains sprayed bin Ahmad, who squeezed the trigger of his own weapon. A bullet whoffed past Jadid's ear, missing him by a fraction. The camp, so lethargic until that moment, exploded into violent action. More shots rang out and flashes split the darkness. When the smoke cleared, bin Ahmad was lying dead with a slug of lead in his chest, and Jadid had vanished.

There were now four men left in the camp. None of them was able to walk to Hassi Messeggem, and all were aware that help would not arrive before they succumbed to starvation. They sat down and held a requiem for the dead that turned into a barbaric feast. They had been prepared to fight over the corpses: now all four set to work to lop hunks off them. By dawn most of the flesh had been gobbled up.

Three kilometres away the Pobeguin party had heard the barrage of gunfire. Their first thought was that the Tuareg had returned, and at dawn the sergeant sent two men back to the well to investigate. They came trudging back at noon with a harrowing tale of cannibalism and madness. At once four *tirailleurs*, including Private First Class al-Madani, Private bin Bahariyya and the self-appointed 'master-butcher' Private Bul-Qassim, all of the 1st RTA, declared they were going back to the *hassi* to avenge the deaths of their comrades, bin ʿAuda and bin Ahmad. Though Pobeguin suspected that revenge was not their only motive, he was too frail to argue.

When the four avengers arrived at the well, they hunted for Jadid. Unable to track him down, they cornered bin Zanun instead, and while two men held him, another put a bullet through his heart. They carved up his body and barbecued his arms, legs, hands and feet. Next morning they reeled back into Pobeguin's camp carrying skins of water and Zanun's flesh. Pobeguin was once more faced with a terrible dilemma: eat or die. He had not eaten properly for seven days, and the sight and smell of the meat literally held out to him by his *tirailleurs* proved too powerful to resist. Knowing that there was no other way of gaining the strength to make Hassi Messeggem, he finally gave in. He took the meat and crammed it into his mouth.

The capitulation of the last French NCO was a signal that any remaining moral standards had collapsed. The bonds that had held the group together had evaporated step by step. Now they were no longer a social unit, but a mob of primitive individuals, each concerned only with his own survival – and those still alive back at Hassi al-Hajaj were their prey. In the afternoon, six men, amongst them al-Madani and Bul-Qassim, went back to the well, shot dead the three who remained, sliced the meat into strips and roasted it on red-hot stones. They stayed there the night – but no one slept. Trust and loyalty were ideals of the past: every man knew that the moment he relaxed his guard he would become the next dish on the menu. They lay on the sand all night with their loaded rifles in their hands, starting at every noise and every flicker of shadow.

The next day they returned to Pobeguin's camp carrying water and more human flesh. On the way they found Jadid, the *sokhrari* who had murdered two *tirailleurs* four days earlier. He was lying under a tamarisk tree in foetal position, dying from hunger and thirst. Bul-Qassim lost no time in slitting his throat with Flatters' sword and the rest of the band closed in like wolves, stripping the body, dismembering it with their knives and bayonets. They ate the meat raw, marching along gnawing at a hand or a foot, a thigh-bone, a bicep or a pectoral.

For the rest of the day and all the next, they did nothing. On the night of 29 March, in Pobeguin's camp, al-Madani noticed that the stars were occluded. His heart sank. This could mean only one thing: the sirocco was on its way. In the morning the sky was leaden, and there was a brooding silence that made the skin crawl. Far away to the south, beyond the Tinighert Plateau, the men could make out a band of darkness creeping across the far horizon like a brushfire.

That day they started out for Hassi Messeggem again, but within an hour the smoke-coloured strip across the southern skyline had become an inferno of dust hundreds of metres high, its edges fraying into cat-o'-nine-tails lashes. For Sergeant Joseph Pobeguin it was the Sahara's final dirty trick. Human flesh, eaten against his instincts, had given him a last chance to trek the forty kilometres to Hassi Messeggem, where he would find help. The storm had taken that chance away from him. The wind hit them with a crack like a thunderclap and they were enveloped in a surge of dust and grit in a billion whirling vortices. The drone of the storm was terrifying. The sleeping desert had come alive and was now trying desperately to hurl them off the edge of the escarpment. Pobeguin had seen sandstorms before, but nothing like this. The force of the wind was so great that it was impossible to walk. Visibility was down to about three metres and there was no shelter from it anywhere. The men lay down on their faces, letting the sand whip over them, praying that it would stop.

The storm sucked away the little moisture their bodies had retained, and soon the water in the skins was finished. Pobeguin said they should stay where they were till it blew over, but al-Madani knew that they would soon die of thirst. They could not make it to Messeggem; their only option was to return once more to Hassi al-Hajaj. Abandoning the Frenchman, they turned into the eye of the storm. All afternoon they battled the sirocco's massive power, their *sheshes* across their faces, their eyes so full of dust that they stumbled on almost blind. There was no sunset that evening, only an imperceptible yielding of one degree of darkness to another. Yet the night held out some hope – sandstorms usually abated at sunset, only to begin again in the morning. Somehow they found the well, drew water and swigged it down.

When they had slaked their thirst, they remembered their hunger. That night they lay awake with the craving for food churning in their bellies, drowsing on a hair-trigger, every man hoping secretly that one of their number would pass away and provide sustenance, but each desperate that it should not be himself. No one died, and there were no human sacrifices that night.

In the morning Bul-Qassim, al-Madani and another *tirailleur* set out to look for Pobeguin. They found him not far from the well under a tamarisk tree, where he had dragged himself in a last effort to reach water. He was wearing one of the *gandourahs* he had been so proud of, now reduced to a ripped and tattered rag, with a leather belt notched impossibly tight around his middle in a futile attempt to ward off the thirst-pangs. He was clutching his precious hunting rifle to his chest, and rambling dementedly that he was going to die. Al-Madani proposed giving him water but Bul-Qassim shook his head. He pulled out his revolver and loaded it.

Al-Madani ordered him to stop, but the mulatto laughed at him. Bul-Qassim stood over the helpless Frenchman and pumped five rounds into his body. The man who had written so confidently a few days out of Wargla that he had 'good, big eyes' did not even see his murderer coming.

19

Bones He Did Not Recognize

Mohammad bin Raja had pitched his *douar* under the eaves of Tademait, not far from the well of Hassi Messeggem. The camp was a ring of tents with openings facing inwards to a corral where the flocks of goats and sheep and herds of camels were hobbled at night. His tent was decorated with rugs, water-skins hanging from uprights, heavy wooden couscous bowls, ornate saddle-bags, earthenware pots, and a rotary quern for grinding grain into flour. It was divided by a curtain into men's and women's quarters. On the afternoon of 2 April 1881, bin Raja led his best *mehari* to the gap of his tent, couched it and saddled up, with the help of his small sons. He slung his rifle over his shoulder, cocked his knee over the saddle-horn and let the camel take his weight as it rose. He tugged the halter gently, setting the beast's head towards the well.

Bin Raja had last seen Paul Flatters in the company of Shikkadh at Jebel Khanfussa on 25 January. He had been glad to leave the column. The Shamba called the desert 'The Land of Fear', and with good reason – the threat of raiders was never far away. Bin Raja's life had taught him to be on his guard, especially with the Kel Ahaggar. He had been a notorious raider himself, in his youth, and he had seen his share of bloody fights, but he feared the

Tuareg capacity for deceit. He had warned Flatters about them. The absence of Aitaghel had struck him as suspicious, and he did not believe that the *amenukal* was prepared to allow Christians through his land so easily.

A few days after he had reached home in February, Flatters' last courier, Qaddur bin Muissat, had passed through, hot-foot for Wargla, carrying dispatches from the column. Qaddur had left the caravan at Inzelman-Tikhsin on 29 January. Squatting in the shade of bin Raja's tent, quaffing tea, Qaddur told his host that Shikkadh had ridden north from the caravan, rather than south to the Hoggar. Both Arabs pondered this for a moment. Qaddur said that Shikkadh claimed to have pitched his tent in the Igharghar, but both of them knew that few of the Kel Ahaggar lived so far north. Bin Raja suggested that Shikkadh had gone to report to a raiding-party that was shadowing the Flatters caravan.

After Qaddur had left, Bin Raja had travelled to ʿAin Saba. He returned near the end of March to receive a shock. In his absence, his herdsman said, four men had turned up on foot at the *douar*, men who had been with the Flatters Mission. They were in a terrible state – famished, dehydrated and physically exhausted. They had brought appalling news: the Flatters caravan had been wiped out by the Kel Ahaggar. Everyone else was dead.

They had refused to answer any further questions and, after resting at the *douar* for a few days, they had hired camels from bin Raja's brother-in-law, Brahim, who had taken them to Wargla. Now bin Raja was waiting for Brahim's return to find out if there were any more details. He had suspected the worst all along but could not believe that all but four men of the mission had been killed.

The day was clear, the sky unblemished. Bin Raja's camel cast a spider-like shadow before him on the erg. In the far distance he could see, clearly illuminated by the downing sun, the massed boulders and drunken rock colonnades of the Tinighert Escarpment, the same one that the caravan had climbed that cold morning in January. The weather had changed since then: freezing nights had been replaced by hot days. The sirocco season had begun six days earlier, with a caustic wind from the south bringing shrouds of dust. Bin Raja usually rode out towards Hassi Messeggem at this time of day to meet his camel-herd. His herdsman took the camels to graze in the wadis every day at first light, and brought them back in the late afternoon.

After a while, bin Raja's keen eyes picked out his camels. At first they were no more than a flaw on the surface, a line of humps distorted by the guttering light. It was some time before they came into full view and bin Raja could see the familiar figure of his herdsman walking behind them. Then he noticed that there were three more men with him, all on foot. He was curious.

Close up, the men were scarecrow figures, thin as cadavers, their skulls showing through the taut skin of their faces and their *gandourahs* in tatters. They watched him, hovering nervously. Their eyes seemed unnaturally bright and too large for their faces. As bin Raja couched his mount and slid out of the saddle, he realized that he knew them. These were soldiers of the 1st RTA who had accompanied the Flatters Mission: the veteran Private First Class al-Madani bin Mohammad, Private ʿAbd al-Qadir bin Bahariyya and Private Bul-Qassim bin Zebla. Bin Raja remembered bin Bahariyya, in particular, as the *tirailleur* had fallen into the well here at Messeggem and broken his arm. To bin Raja, who had heard only days ago that the entire mission had been massacred, it was as if they had risen from the dead.

Later, back at his tent, bin Raja slaughtered two sheep to feed the guests. While the meat was roasting on hot stones, the *tirailleurs* gobbled down camels' milk and couscous.

'Where are the others?' bin Raja asked.

Al-Madani waved a thin hand towards the wells. 'There,' he said. 'Some of them.'

'And where is Colonel Flatters?'

'Dead,' al-Madani replied. 'All of them dead.'

After they had eaten there was an ominous silence. Al-Madani inquired tentatively if bin Raja would lend them camels to go back and pick up the men they had left behind. They were at Hassi al-Hajaj, two or three days' journey across the Tinighert Plateau. The Shambi agreed, and said he ought to accompany them. There was another awkward silence as the men eyed him blankly. It was obvious that his suggestion was unwelcome, and bin Raja sensed that the *tirailleurs* were holding back. They were no longer the same men he had known. Two months earlier, even in their civilian clothes, they had looked like soldiers. Now their martial bearing had deserted them.

'I will come with you,' he repeated.

After dark that night, bin Bahariyya took bin Raja aside and asked if he could leave a small sum of money in his *douar* for safe keeping. The 'small sum' turned out to be two thousand one hundred and seventy-five francs of the mission's money, in silver. The *tirailleur* had carried it a thousand kilometres on his back across the desert, through heat, cold, thirst, starvation and atrocity.

They set off at first light the next day. At the well, bin Raja found five men, mostly cameleers, sitting quietly, staring into space. All of them were badly emaciated and had the same haunted look as the three *tirailleurs*. Bin Raja and his small party climbed the escarpment and crossed the plateau towards Hassi al-Hajaj. It took them two days to get there. Near that well they found two more survivors, barely alive, whom they loaded on to the camels. Not far away bin Raja came across what was left of a camp, and began to sift through the remains curiously. There were the burned-out ashes of a fire with bones scattered about it – bones bin Raja did not at first recognize. It was only when he knelt down to examine them that he realized they were human, hands and feet, charred from the fire. The flesh had been eaten.

Bin Raja stood up slowly, and took a long, accusing glance at the *tirailleurs*. They had not wanted him to know about this. The reason for their odd manner back at the *douar* became clear. Their abnormally large eyes glittered at him uncomfortably. Suddenly bin Raja's gaze lit on a burnoose, half-buried in the sand, and he strode over to look at it. Nearby was a pair of sunglasses, partly burned, a leather belt, a revolver with one shot in the chamber, and two rifles. One of the weapons was a hunting rifle. The last time bin Raja had seen it, it had been slung from the shoulder of Sergeant Joseph Pobeguin, the most alert soldier of the mission.

20

'Such treachery, such perfidy, such savagery'

Bin Raja arrived back at his tents on 7 April. The solemn procession of human wrecks following him was all that was left of the Flatters Mission. Ten had made the final march to Hassi Messeggem, carrying the remains that had once been Joseph Pobeguin, but only eight had arrived. Bin Raja had found the two missing men wandering deliriously on the way. With the two others he had brought back from Hassi al-Hajaj, that made a round dozen. He had also collected all the artefacts he could find: Pobeguin's burnoose, belt, sunglasses and weapons. He had been stunned by the men's story – not only the grisly tale of cannibalism, but the fact that anyone had managed to survive such a journey at all. Bin Raja had spent his entire life in the desert, but had never heard of anything like it.

At his camp, there was another surprise waiting for him. The place had been invaded by fourteen Shamba *goumiers*, who had ridden fast from Wargla on the orders of the military deputy, Sergeant Mohammad bin Bul-Qassim. They were the advance guard of a rescue-party three hundred strong, led by the sergeant himself, that was now on its way. The first news of the mission's fate had reached Wargla on 28 March, when the four men who had come from bin Raja's camp had been led into the oasis on camels: Private First Class bin ʿAbd al-Qadir and his three *sokhrar* companions, who had left Pobeguin's party on the night of 11 March and had been guided to Wargla by bin Raja's brother-in-law, Brahim. Shortly after their arrival the story was confirmed by Mukhtar bin Ghazal and bin Ghoraib, the two 1st RTA deserters, who had struggled into town with the camel they had stolen. They had also been carrying large amounts of cash, which they had been too tired to conceal from the deputy's men.

The fourteen-man advance party had pulled out all the stops on their ride from Wargla, covering the 624 kilometres in an incredible seven days. Speed had been of the essence, because the deputy had also been informed by spies that a raiding-party of Awlad Ba Hammu Arabs from In Salah was on its way to wipe out the survivors. ʿAbd al-Qadir bin Bajuda, the sheikh of the council, wanted no one telling tales. The raiding-party turned tail when it heard of the deputy's approach, and the twelve *tirailleurs* and camel-men were escorted to Wargla safely, arriving on 25 April. Here they were subjected to interrogation by the Arab Bureau. On their own testimony, the two deserters, bin Ghazal and bin Ghoraib, were arrested pending courts martial. The man who murdered Pobeguin, 'master-butcher' Bul-Qassim bin Zebla, was also thrown in jail.

A few days after their arrival, Sheikh Bu Jamaa and ʿAla bin Sheikh rode in, carrying silver francs and what appeared to be booty from the mission. They were promptly arrested by the deputy. Interrogated by Captain Spitalier of the Arab Bureau, Bu Jamaa protested his innocence. He had known nothing about the planned ambush, he claimed, but had warned Flatters that Sghir had been plotting with the Tuareg. On the day of the massacre, 16 February, he had been away hunting gazelle when the camels had been taken off to the *tajnut*, but had caught up with the colonel and told him he had been betrayed. He claimed Flatters had scoffed at him, replying rudely that he was fed up with Shamba tricks.

During the attack, Bu Jamaa went on, he had been standing near Sghir, and had fired at the Tuareg until Sghir had stopped him. Then he had leapt on his *mehari* and fled. He claimed to have left the area two days later and followed the tracks of the survivors for four days with Sghir and 'Ala bin Sheikh, and the two other Shamba guides. On 21 February they had turned east towards the Tassili-n-Ajjer, eventually arriving at the tents of Sghir's Ifoghas father-in-law 'Abd al-Hakim. It did not escape Captain Spitalier that this testimony was as full of holes as a pepperpot. If Bu Jamaa had truly known nothing of the plot, how was it possible for him to have warned Flatters? Why had he waited two days before leaving the area? Why had he stayed with the traitor Sghir instead of going to get help? If he did know that the colonel had been betrayed, why had he warned him only when it was too late? These questions, and the undeniable fact of his sudden acquisition of riches, led Spitalier to indict him before a court martial.

The last the outside world had heard of Flatters was from the dispatches brought by Qaddur bin Muissat dated 29 January, more than two weeks before the disaster. Ironically, on 24 March, eight days after Flatters had been killed, *La République Française* published a piece stating that, according to an unconfirmed report, the colonel's party had arrived at In Azawa on 14 February. 'One can consider the crossing of the Hoggar accomplished,' crowed another paper, *L'Exploration*. 'The principal aim of the expedition is attained.' This claim was probably based on a letter from Aitaghel that had arrived at Wargla at the end of February, and which it also published, that said, '[Flatters] arrived in our territory, the Hoggar, in good health, and departed in the same state. Beyond the Hoggar we are no longer responsible, because our authority ends there.'[63] Before Aitaghel's lying message had reached the French authorities, General Cerez, commandant at Oran, had passed on a disquieting rumour picked up from a Shambi who had come from the south, who told him Flatters 'has been stopped by the people of the Tidikelt from marching further, and some of his men have been massacred'.[64] A week before the first survivors turned up at Wargla, the Governor-General had replied to Cerez, saying this rumour could be 'categorically denied'.

By the time the rescue-party had reached bin Raja's camp on 7 April, news of the disaster had broken in the French press. The Maltese news agency Havas had picked up the story a week earlier and sent a brief dispatch to the papers. The following day the *Gazette de France* announced: 'Colonel Flatters and his escort, who had gone far into the Sahara to establish the route of the Trans-Saharan Railway, have been massacred by bands of Tuareg, of a rebellious tribe.'[65] Though *Le Figaro* and *Le Petit Journal* ran the story within days, the pieces were muted and wary. Neither the journalists nor the public wanted to admit that the unthinkable had happened: Duponchel's 'handful of tribesmen armed with mediaeval weapons' had actually defeated a major French initiative in the Sahara. Where was 'the might of France' now? Where was 'the national genius' that Duponchel had avowed so confidently would 'rule supreme'? What had happened to Henri Duveyrier's 'noble, kind and honest' Tuareg?

It was not until the true horrific details filtered through that outrage began to take the place of reticence. By mid-April, indignant articles had appeared in *Le Français, La France, Le Journal Débats, Le XIXème Century*, and *La République Française*. Edmond Magnier, director of *L'Evénement*, ran the headline 'Avenge Flatters!' at the top of a caustic piece:

> We march from insult to insult, from defeat to defeat, from humiliation to massacre. The honour of our name, our lawful influence, the security of our establishment in Algeria, the grandeur and the economy of our projects on the African continent, demand that we make a prompt and energetic response against such treachery, such perfidy, such savagery. We have the right to call for revenge without mercy on the savage hordes, pillagers and murderers, who have drenched the desert sands with the

blood of our unfortunate countrymen. These are not soldiers that the atrocious Tuareg have butchered and poisoned, they are the heroes of progress.[66]

Adolphe Duponchel, who had declared the previous year that failure was inevitable, felt compelled to rub it in. 'Reorganized into two phases,' he wrote, 'of very high cost, ordered to follow an eccentric route, straying far from the known trade routes and the flat land to risk itself in the mountainous region of the savage Tuareg, who had, besides, formally refused to give it passage through their territory, this expedition was bound to go wrong. Fleeced and pillaged on the first encounter, it was pitilessly massacred on the second.'[67]

The romantic image of the Tuareg that had so beguiled the High Commission in 1879 had finally begun to die. Colonel Belin, commandant at Laghouat, proposed sending a column of a thousand troops to wipe the Kel Ahaggar off the face of the earth. Captain Bernard, an artillery officer who had been with the first mission, was sent to make an official inquiry, and proposed an armed task force, 'to show these savages that we are powerful enough to cross their country without their permission'.[68]

21

'The Kel Ahaggar had no part in the affair'

The prospect of retaliation caused consternation in Aitaghel's camp near Tazruk. Atissi was dumbfounded to find out that some of the survivors had actually reached home safely. Wounded in the fight at Amgid, he had ordered his raiders to abandon the hunt and returned to the Hoggar, convinced that the desert had done his job for him. None of the Kel Ahaggar had believed that any man could possibly survive a journey on foot, without food or water, across such terrain. They had reckoned without the astonishing toughness of the French, the camel-men and the *tirailleurs*, many of whom were settled Arabs from the *tell*.

The Flatters massacre had turned into a Pyrrhic victory for the Kel Ahaggar, who themselves had some sixty warriors dead and many more wounded. They were few – the three drum-groups together probably numbered no more than a thousand men, women and children – and they had already been decimated in the war with the Kel Ajjer. They could not afford such casualties. They had seen the effectiveness of the French Fusils Gras at Amgid, and now they had proof of the courage and resilience of French-led and French-trained troops. Aitaghel's first thought was that a larger column of such men, sent with the determination to wreak vengeance, would cripple the Kel Ahaggar for good.

He was so unnerved by the prospect that he tried to put the blame on others. 'Those who killed the Christians are the [Kel Ulli] of Ayr and the people of Ajjer,' he claimed in a letter to Tahir al-Hassidi, the Ghadames merchant who had recommended Flatters before the expedition. 'They died in the region of Ayr. It is the undernamed [Kel Ulli] who massacred them; the Kel Ahaggar had no part in the affair . . . at the time these Christians were killed the Kel Ahaggar were on a raid against the Kel Ajjer and had not yet returned to their homes . . . I gave them a guide whose mission was to conduct them to the territory of the Ayr. I lost the best of my men in this affair, who were also killed [i.e. by the Ayr].'[69]

Aitaghel not only had the effrontery to name seven Tuareg chiefs of rival tribes as the authors of the killing, but also added several excuses – and it was these that inadvertently gave the game away: 'They did not pay me for the right of passage,' he complained; 'they are not among those who enjoy the protection of Islam.' He also argued that he had had no instructions from the Ottoman government to allow them to pass. This was the only truthful claim in the entire letter – and begged the question as to why, in that case, he had given them guides.

Tahir al-Hassidi was concerned enough to pass on a copy to Consul-General Féraud in Tripoli. Féraud promptly wrote to Belkhu, the *amenukal* of the Ayr Tuareg, who was highly indignant at the false accusation and in turn rushed off a letter to the Kel Ahaggar chief, warning him that when the French came to revenge the massacre of their column, the Hoggar Tuareg need not think of trying to take refuge in his country.

In fact, many of the Kel Ahaggar who had taken part in the killing were already heading for the Ayr Mountains.

While Aitaghel was desperate to evade responsibility in the eyes of the French, he was equally anxious to gain kudos from the Ottoman Turks. Ten days after the massacre, on 26 February, he wrote to the Ottoman governor of Ghadames, Abu Aysha:

You suggested that we should keep watch on the [caravan] routes and protect them against hostile elements; that is what we have done. We have applied ourselves to preserve the routes against invasion by the enemies of Islam . . . I inform you of what happened to the Christians, that is to Colonel Flatters, who came to our land with his men armed with fifteen hundred guns, with the intention of crossing the country of the Hoggar to go to the Sudan. They came to the Hoggar but the people of that country fought them for the [sake of] the holy war, in the most energetic manner, and massacred them – it is finished. Now, my dear friend, it is absolutely necessary that the news of our great action should arrive in Constantinople. Tell them there what happened, that is that the Tuareg have waged against the Christians the perfect holy war.[70]

Aitaghel's tendency to spin a web of lies, playing both sides against the middle, is a fascinating insight into the Machiavellian character of the Tuareg. The name of the game was survival, and any falsehood was worth it: this was the lesson the outcast *tawaraka* had learned over their thousand-year exile. The *amenukal* even tried to persuade the *tirailleur* prisoner, Leshleg bin ʿArfa, that he had been against the action. 'I was unable to stop what happened,' he said. 'If people had listened to me, the French wouldn't have died, but there was no one who was able to help me.'[71] Aitaghel went so far as to ask Wangadi, Leshleg's captor, to release him – and even Leshleg himself suspected this was a deliberate ploy to curry favour with the French. In any case, Wangadi refused to let the young *tirailleur* go, on the grounds that he was likely to lead the enemy straight to his camp.

The Ghadames merchants did not attempt to disguise their glee. In mid-April 1881, Féraud intercepted a message from one of them proclaiming the Flatters débâcle was 'no less than a great victory by the Hoggar Tuareg over the French Army in Algeria'.[72] Despite this, and Aitaghel's incriminating letter to Abu Aysha, no link was ever traced between the Flatters incident and the Divine Porte. Ottoman *vali* Rasim Pasha was able to point out smugly that the massacre had taken place in the Hoggar Mountains, far beyond his jurisdiction. The Ottomans left it to the Italians to voice their satisfaction. 'As far as Colonel Flatters goes,' wrote an Italian journalist, 'one can say on behalf of Tripoli: *mors tua, vita mea*' – your death is my life.[73] For the time being, at least, the moribund Ottoman Empire had out-manoeuvred the French in the Sahara, and the caravan trade continued to flourish on their side of the border. Though they were never able to prove it, the Arab Bureau remained convinced that the Sanusiyya had been behind the whole affair.

22

'It is better to throw a veil over the deplorable things that happened'

The Shamba Arabs did not emerge any more honourably from the Flatters débâcle than the Tuareg. In May and June, Sheikh bin Ahmad and two more camel-men turned up at Laghouat. They had been missing since de Dianous's party had crossed the Amadghor Serir in early March. After the lieutenant had sent them in search of water, they had lost their way, and had turned east across Amadghor towards the country of the Kel Ajjer. On 12 March they reached the tents of Sghir bin Sheikh's father-in-law, ʿAbd al-Hakim, where they had found the mission's five Shamba guides, including Bu Jamaa. Knowing nothing of their treachery, the *sokhrar* had greeted them delightedly. In return the Shamba had tried to kill them.

Their host, ʿAbd al-Hakim, had saved them, but Bu Jamaa then attempted an even darker stratagem. He and ʿAla bin Sheikh were about to set off on their journey back to Wargla, and they agreed to take the camel-men with them. After six days' journey, the two Shamba marooned them in the desert, saying, 'We don't want your blood on our hands, but we can't have you going to the French and telling them what happened. We're going to leave you here.'[74]

The three *sokhrar* retraced their own tracks, and after almost dying of thirst and starvation a second time, arrived at the camp of Ikhenoukhen, who took them under his wing. Sheikh bin Ahmad and one companion were dispatched with a caravan to Ghadames, where they were helped by Father Louis Richard of the White Fathers. He sent them back to Algiers via Tripoli. The third camel-man, Baraka bin 'Isa, joined a small caravan being guided by Sghir bin Sheikh, who also intended to return to Wargla with his loot. After many days' journey the caravan arrived at a Shamba *douar*, where Sghir was informed that Bu Jamaa and his brother 'Ala had been arrested by the Arab Bureau in Wargla. Seeing the way the wind was blowing, Sghir at once turned round and went back to the Ifoghas. Baraka meandered on alone from camp to camp until, finally, he reached Wargla safely.

Sghir bin Sheikh never returned to the north. He hid out with the Ifoghas until he was killed in a raid by the Kel Ahaggar some time later. That he played a major part in the betrayal of Flatters is confirmed by a letter sent in March to the Ghadames merchant Tahir al-Hassidi by a friend. 'We have been told that a man of the Shamba named Sghir and his companions made a great profit out of the affair [the massacre of the Flatters Mission]. The Shamba are installed with the Ifoghas and are wary of going to Wargla,' al-Hassidi read.

If the testimony of Sheikh bin Ahmad was not enough to prove the guilt of Bu Jamaa, it was confirmed by the depositions of two *tirailleurs* captured during the massacre. 'Amar bin Hawa, who had been spared at the intervention of his captor, Hamad, came in on 18 June. Hamad, who turned out to be an Ifoghas, took the *tirailleur* back to his tents in Kel Ajjer country, then released him. Like Sheikh bin Ahmad, 'Amar travelled with a caravan to Ghadames and was repatriated from there. He described to his interrogators how he had personally overheard Bu Jamaa tell the Tuareg, 'We will follow the tracks of the French. Not one of them

must escape us.'[75] Private First Class Mas'ud bin Sa'id of the 3rd
RTA turned up in January 1882, having escaped after eleven
months' captivity in Tuareg camps. He confirmed that he had
seen Bu Jamaa shoot the *tirailleur* bin Saad during the action at
the *tajnut*.

By this time, Bu Jamaa had already been court-martialled and
acquitted for lack of evidence. The furore was over. The French
government was engaged in the invasion of Tunisia and in putting
down a rebellion on the Moroccan border, and it had taken no
action against the Tuareg. They were aware that airing their dirty
washing in public would serve only to evoke embarrassing questions about the way the Flatters Mission had been conducted.
They thought it better to exercise a degree of damage limitation,
accentuating the positive and papering over the unpleasant cracks.
For the present, at least, the Tuareg had won.

Neither the deserters nor Bul-Qassim bin Zebla were ever court-
martialled. On 5 October 1881, the Commandant of the Algiers
Division, General Loysel, sent a dispatch to Governor-General
Louis Tirman, explaining the difficulties in prosecuting men who
had been subject to such extremes: 'Must they carry the moral
responsibilities for their acts?' he asked.

> It would be difficult to affirm, and even assuming that there is
> sufficient proof to establish that they have really done what they
> are accused of doing, the extenuating circumstances would be so
> strong that they are likely to be acquitted. In these circumstances
> it seems to me facetious to expose the horrible drama that
> unfolded in the solitude of the Sahara to public curiosity, and I
> think it is better to throw a veil over the deplorable things that
> happened near Hassi al-Hajaj.[76]

Instead, the army doled out the Military Medal to Private First
Class bin 'Abd al-Qadir of the 1st RTA, who, according to
Colonel Eugène Belin, was 'the only one who deserves to be

recompensed for the energy he showed in coming first to Wargla to bring news of the disaster'.[77]

Bin 'Abd al-Qadir and seven other *tirailleurs* returned to their regiments and soldiered on. Bu Jamaa went back to his job as a guide for the Arab Bureau in Wargla, and was still working there in 1896.

23

'The same Tuareg who shed the blood of our first martyrs'

The camel-man Sheikh bin Ahmad's arrival in Ghadames set in motion another tragedy that became a footnote to the Flatters massacre. While being cared for by the White Fathers, the Arab was questioned by Father Louis Richard, who was in the process of planning a trek to the oasis of Ghat. The plan had been thwarted by the news of the Flatters affair, which had reached the White Fathers' headquarters in April. Richard had managed to get himself accepted in Ghadames, despite being cited in the Italian press as a member of the secret French conspiracy in the Sahara. The courtyard of his Arab-style house was constantly packed with the sick and needy of the town, who came in search of his help and were never turned away.

Richard's sights were still set on Timbuctoo, but his superior in Algiers, Archbishop Charles Lavigerie, had forbidden any precipitate move in that direction, especially in the wake of the Flatters fiasco. Lavigerie had instructed Richard to expand phase by phase: first establish a base in Tripoli, then in Ghadames, then in Ghat. The final move on Timbuctoo could be made from there. Richard had been warned that both Ghadames and Ghat were heavily infiltrated by their arch-enemies, the Sanusiyya Brother-hood, who were still believed responsible for the murder of Fathers Alfred Paulmier, Philippe Menoret and Pierre Bouchand in 1876.

Father Richard had struggled hard against the Ottoman admin-istration, which had blocked him at every turn. Officially, it was forbidden for any foreigner to travel beyond Tripoli. The rule was not strictly enforced but allowed the *vali*, Rasim Pasha, a get-out clause if any 'accident' should befall foreign nationals travelling through the Sahara. Richard was prepared to risk the antagonism of the Turks, but he could not get round the opposition of his superior. In May 1881, when Sheikh bin Ahmad limped into Richard's mission in Ghadames and described what had happened to Paul Flatters and his caravan, Richard was strangely encour-aged. The cameleer told him that the attack had succeeded only because Flatters had allowed the party to be split up. The fault, he said, lay with the colonel. He had trusted the treacherous Tuareg and had not exercised the proper caution. Had he been more circumspect, the massacre would not have happened.

Father Richard took this as a lesson learned and vowed not to make the same mistake himself. In any case, the Tuareg would have little reason to pillage a group of poor priests. When bin Ahmad was well enough to travel, Richard penned a letter to Archbishop Lavigerie and asked the Arab to deliver it to the Archbishop's residence on his way through Algiers. The letter repeated what the *sokhrari* had told him, and begged for permis-sion to travel to Ghat. Charles Lavigerie was convinced enough to grant the request.

Richard asked the authorities in Wargla to send a Shambi guide he knew named Sayah bin Bu Sa'id, and in the meantime he recruited some local Tuareg to buy camels and help organize the trek. These included a man called al-Khajam, his son Bettina, his brother-in-law, 'Isa, and a slave called Jaddur. When the Shambi Sayah arrived in Ghadames, he was immediately suspicious of al-Khajam and his crew. He walked around the market listening to gossip and discovered something that horrified him. Al-Khajam had been in touch with another Targui named ʿIda ag Qemum, one of the men responsible for the murders of Norbert Dournaux-Dupere and Eugène Joubert in 1874, and of the three White Fathers in 1876. Sayah later got someone to identify ʿIda and followed him to a house in Ghadames, and, by asking around, found out that the house belonged to Mohammad Bu Etteni, a prominent slave merchant who was violently anti-French, and a member of the Sanusiyya.

Sayah reported this to Louis Richard, but the priest shrugged it off, saying that he was not employing ʿIda; his guide was al-Khajam, who didn't even belong to the same tribe. Sayah accepted this, but asked for a notarized waiver stating that if anything untoward befell the White Fathers, he would not be held responsible. When he discovered later that al-Khajam had agreed to payment in full after the journey rather than the customary half in advance, he was even more convinced the Targui was being paid to lead the White Fathers into a trap. Even the governor, Abu Aysha, advised Richard to head for Wargla rather than through the Sanusiyya-controlled region south of Ghadames.

A week before Christmas 1881, Father Louis Richard left the town riding a horse, with two others from his order, Fathers Alexis Pouplard and Gaspard Morat, on camels. Richard had decided to ignore Abu Aysha's caveat, and was making for Ghat by the shortest possible route. On the second day, al-Khajam's brother-in-law, ʿIsa, declared that he was going to ride ahead to a well a few kilometres away, to find out if it had water. Against the protests of the Shambi guide Sayah he went off alone, and did not return until sunset. When Sayah demanded to know why he had taken so long to ride such a short distance ʿIsa claimed to have spotted moufflon and gone to hunt them. When Sayah asked where the meat was, ʿIsa replied that he had given up the chase, afraid of losing his way. The Arab guffawed and said it was a new experience for him to meet a Targui afraid of losing his way in the desert.

That evening after dinner, as Father Morat knelt to pray, 'Isa crept up behind him and plunged a dagger into his back. Morat rolled forward with blood gushing down his spine. Alerted by the cry, Father Richard raced to help him. He found both 'Isa and al-Khajam barring his way with drawn swords. Richard was a head taller than either of them, and powerfully built, and, incredibly, he managed to ward off their sword-thrusts with his arms and deliver a salvo of deadly punches, knocking both men off their feet. While they picked themselves up he dashed for his horse, hoping to save Pouplard, who was out of sight, but as he stuck his foot in the stirrup, al-Khajam's nephew Bettina peppered him from close range with a naval blunderbuss, searing the flesh off his back.

One of the Shamba had run from the camp to warn Father Pouplard of the attack and, finding him in one piece, the Arab led him into the rocks on the bank of the wadi, hoping that they might be able to escape after dark. No sooner had they reached the lip of the watercourse, than 'Ida and two other Tuareg emerged out of the shadows and blocked their way. 'Ida raised his sword and smashed it down on Pouplard's skull so hard that the blade cut into the bridge of the nose. As the priest collapsed, the three warriors slashed his body. The second White Fathers mission to the south was at an end.

Cardinal Lavigerie was stunned by the news. 'It was the Tuareg,' he wrote in a circular letter to the White Fathers Missions, 'the same Tuareg who shed the blood of our first martyrs, who spilt that of these brothers. They brutally massacred them three days only after their departure from Ghadames.'[78] Though the *Vali* of Tripoli arrested three of the murderers, Lavigerie asked for them to be pardoned, adding more fuel to the Tuareg conviction that the French were not prepared to avenge the deaths of their compatriots. Shortly after the murders, the Sanusi agent

Thani slipped out of Ghadames at night, on a camel. He holed up at the Sanusiyya's sanctuary at Jaghbub Oasis, on the Egyptian border, and never returned to Tripolitania.

24

'A long and dishonourable captivity'

From the moment the story broke in the press, there were doubts that Flatters and his men were really dead. On 11 April, Governor-General Tirman received intelligence that a number of survivors of the massacre, including Paul Flatters himself, were being held by a Shambi renegade, who wanted to exchange them for members of his family under arrest in Algeria. A few days later, in Tripoli, Consul-General Féraud received a report from Ghadames that an Arabic-speaking French officer had survived the massacre and was currently under the protection of a Targui. While neither of these reports had any foundation, escapees who returned at intervals over the next two years kept the pot boiling. If the Tuareg were still holding prisoners from the massacre, why not Flatters himself?

For one thing, Flatters was not, at first, officially declared dead. Since he had not been serving with his regiment, the Civil Code concerning soldiers who died on military service could not be applied to him. An inquest was required, and no one had the authority to state definitively that the colonel was deceased. It was not until July 1881, when Bu Jamaa was interrogated at Laghouat and confirmed the death, that the question was solved legally – but Bu Jamaa was not an entirely credible witness, so many remained unconvinced.

Two years later, in February 1883, the former guide Moham-mad bin Raja was contacted by the French authorities. For a while he had been in their bad books: the Arab Bureau had learned about the stolen cash ʿAbd al-Qadir bin Bahariyya had left with him at Hassi Messeggem, but bin Raja had returned only half of it, claiming to have spent the rest. Now they needed his skills again, this time to rescue Leshleg bin ʿArfa of the 3rd RTA, who had been enslaved by Wangadi and was still living in his tents. Bin Raja tracked Leshleg down to the camp of Wangadi's son in the Wadi Amgel, where he was herding goats alongside the negro slaves. The Shambi waited until Leshleg's master had left the *douar*, then went to confer with him.

Leshleg had been a prisoner for two and a half years, and had an amazing story to tell. Carted off on camel-back from Tajnut Tan-Kuffar, just hanging on to life, he had been saved and nursed back to health by Wangadi's beautiful young daughter, Sallam. After recovering he had accompanied Wangadi on raids against rival tribes, fallen ill, recovered again, and taken part in more raids; in one of them his party had taken seven hundred camels. He also had news of the two other *tirailleurs* enslaved with him. Bu Lefaa, the Sokoto native, had proved so dishonest that Wangadi had sent him back to the Sudan. The other soldier, Khenis bin Salah, had been killed horribly by the Tuareg for stealing a goat. He had been stretched out and branded on his legs and arms with a red-hot iron, then had fifty hot stones placed one after the other on his bare chest.

Bin Raja arranged for Leshleg to abscond by night and meet two of his men in a nearby wadi. The operation was conducted suc-cessfully, and Leshleg reached Wargla on 4 June 1883. Bin Raja would certainly have been killed had he been discovered, and for his valour the French awarded the former raider two hundred francs and a superior firearm of his choice.

Leshleg was officially the last known survivor of the Flatters expedition, but for some the mystery lingered on. Twelve years later, a native of Tunisia named Jebari, a former military interpreter who had a small publishing business, issued a pamphlet entitled 'The Survivors of the Flatters Mission'. He claimed to have met Paul Flatters and the other Frenchmen at an assembly of Tuareg notables in the Sahara. They were not dead, he claimed, but had suffered a 'cruel and dishonourable captivity' for fourteen years. He had identified Jules Roche, whom he said now went by the name of Ghenushen, and who spent his days in melancholy dreaming. As for Paul Flatters, he had become a Targui in speech and dress, and now lived at the oasis of Tagaiss with his adopted Targui son, Ismau, whom he adored.

That Jebari was believed, despite the obvious discrepancies and inaccuracies in his report, demonstrates the power of myth – the same power that had led Flatters himself to accept Henri Duveyrier's romantic idylls about the Tuareg in the first place. In fact, Jebari was fêted in France, introduced to Sarah Flatters, and his offer to ransom the captives for thirty thousand francs taken seriously. The one important lesson the Flatters débâcle had had to deliver had still not been learned.

Once again, its effects were to prove harmful. In May 1896 a Franco-Spanish nobleman named Antoine de Vallombrosa, marquis of the obscure province of Mores, in Sardinia, set off from Tunis by camel to reach Timbuctoo. He was a firm believer in Jebari's stories and was determined to make contact with Flatters on the way. The marquis had not even reached Ghadames when he was attacked by his Tuareg and Shamba guides. He shot three of them with his revolver before bleeding to death from a spear-wound in the neck.

25

'The colonel was most inferior to his task'

To those who accepted that he actually was dead, Paul Flatters became in death what he had dreamed of becoming in life, a national hero. 'It became the death of Siegfried or Achilles,' wrote Sahara expert Professor E. F. Gautier, thirty years later. 'Everything was there to strike one's imagination. The massacre had taken place in the desert, land of mirages, and the importance of the disaster was great because so very few returned.'[79] It was Gautier, a professor at the University of Algiers, who did most to discredit the Flatters legend. 'The colonel was most inferior to his task,' he wrote. 'He carried with him, one might say, a dead soul, heavy with personal sorrows; what took him into adventure was less the attraction of danger than that of death; his end had something of the suicide about it, with the aggravating circumstance that it was collective. Perhaps one could sum it all up in one word: depression.'[80]

Gautier's verdict set the tone for posterity, so much so that many historians have dismissed Flatters as a tragi-comic 'Colonel Blimp', an incompetent, blundering Victorian eccentric whose main motive in embarking on the expedition was to seek 'an honourable death'. According to historian René Lecler, writing in 1954, Flatters was 'as strange a leader as [it was possible to find] anywhere in the

Sahara'.[81] In 1968 author Brian Gardner echoed Gautier, dismissing Flatters as 'tired, depressed and fatalistic'.[82] More recently Douglas Porch described him as 'a man used up by middle-age', who was 'more at home in a bureau than a bivouac'.[83]

The last of these accusations is easily dispensed with. Shortly before his return to Paris in 1877, aged forty-nine, Flatters rode a thousand kilometres to Wargla and back by horse to escort an American journalist. He was senior commandant at Laghouat and could easily have sent a junior, but he preferred to go himself. This is not the action of a man 'more accustomed to the bureau than the bivouac', but that of a man with an unbridled passion for the desert. The fact that Flatters wrote books and articles does not prove that he preferred a cloistered life, nor – even in the 1880s – was a man 'used up' at the age of forty-nine. As for being 'a strange leader', Flatters was eminently qualified for the job – he knew the Sahara and its people, and spoke fluent Arabic. It is hard to imagine that there existed anyone better qualified.

Neither is there any evidence that Flatters was clinically depressed. On the contrary, many of those who knew him as commandant at Laghouat spoke of his lively intelligence and *joie de vivre*. He planned, organized and led a major expedition into an area then totally unknown to Europeans, and he did this without the benefit of modern technology, communications, medicines or geographical data. This was the enterprise not of a buffoon, an incompetent or a 'dead soul', but of a man of organizational ability, tenacity, courage and determination. He betrayed a certain natural testiness at times, but in general his letters display a lively and cheerful disposition. Far from being 'on the brink of suicide', Flatters was a man driven by a dream, a man prepared to surmount any obstacle to follow it. Had the mission been organized as he had originally proposed back in 1877, with three hundred riflemen, and instructions to assume the kind of pugnacious mien the Tuareg understood, it would almost certainly have succeeded.[84]

Flatters did make tactical mistakes, but most of them followed from the assumption that the expedition was 'peace-loving', and that the Tuareg were actually the honourable and chivalrous men Henri Duveyrier believed them to be. Flatters' main fault was that he abandoned his inner convictions to embrace an ideal imposed on him by men who knew less than he did. This, as it turned out, was his ultimate sacrifice.

It is easy to forget that the late Victorian era was a time when inner convictions counted for far less than they do today. Society and its conventions were everything, the individual nothing. To rebel against social convention was the height of vulgarity; Godliness was synonymous with social virtue. Flatters' glowing personnel reports clearly indicate that he was a man who conformed to prevailing ideology. If society believed that the Tuareg were 'noble savages', then it would have been unthinkable for a man like Flatters to gainsay it. What society believed was the truth, no matter how contradictory his personal experience might be. In any case, he must have been perfectly aware that had he argued, the job would simply have been given to someone else.

It took the destruction of the Flatters Mission to change society's ideas about the Tuareg. Henri Duveyrier, their principal author, was sent to Tunisia in 1881 to assess the best way of revenging Flatters, and actually offered to lead a punitive mission against the Kel Ahaggar, turning scourge of the people he had idolized. The punitive mission was not sent, and Duveyrier never gained an opportunity to expiate himself. Subjected to excoriating censure for his misleading views, he came in time to believe that his entire life had been a lie. On 27 April 1892, eleven years after Paul Flatters had disappeared in the Sahara, Henri Duveyrier walked quietly into the woods near his home and shot himself in the head.

PART THREE

THREE

'AVENGE FLATTERS!'

1

'Two sultans with the same title'

In October 1900, hundreds of Tuareg camel-riders converged on a camp of fifteen or twenty moufflon-hide tents near Tazruk, on the eastern side of the Hoggar Mountains. The riders were tricked out in their best dark robes, *sheshes* and veils, and carried swords, spears, shields and rifles. There, on the undulating stony ground among peaks shaved and shattered into cones, trapezoids and natural arches, the Kel Ahaggar paid their last respects to Aitaghel, the *amenukal* who had died after leading them for more than thirty years. Aitaghel had been a crude statesman, but he had held the confederation together despite the devastating war with the Kel Ajjer, the threat from the Christians, the dissent of the Taitoq and the influence of his rival, Khyar ag Hegir. The task that now faced the three drum-groups and their Kel Ulli was to choose a new chief. Presiding over the election was an outsider, Sheikh Abdin, a marabout of the Kunta Arabs of the Sudan, who claimed direct descent from the Prophet Mohammad. Abdin was fanatically anti-French. He was married to a Kel Ahaggar woman and was renowned both as a fighter and as a holy man. For many days the veiled warriors sat round campfires drinking tea, stuffing themselves with couscous, mutton and goats' meat, tweaking their veils from one arrangement to another, posturing, blustering, swaggering, debating and launching into streams of rhetoric.

They were faced with a difficult decision. By tradition, Aitaghel's rightful heir should be Mohammad ag Wurzig, the son of his elder sister, but the Kel Ulli disapproved of him. In the past, these despised vassals, descendants of the Isebeten, the aboriginal people of the Hoggar, had never been asked their opinion, but the Kel Ulli had acquired camels and weapons of their own. Now they were independently powerful, and more numerous than the Imuhaq, and their views had to be taken into account. The Kel Ulli regarded Mohammad ag Wurzig as effete, too old and too feeble to be a warrior. They preferred Aitaghel's nephew through his younger sister, Atissi ag Shikkadh.

Atissi, like Aitaghel, had at first been afraid that the French would hunt him down. Once he had recovered from the bullet-wound he had taken at Amgid, he had led a party back to Tajnut Tan-Kuffar to burn all evidence of the massacre. As the years had passed and no retribution had fallen on him, his swagger and self-assurance had returned. He had been confirmed in his belief in Tuareg invincibility and superiority. For the Imuhaq, the blood-feud was a sacred duty. The fact that the Christians had not even attempted to avenge the deaths of their brothers was, in Tuareg eyes, an open admission of cowardice. Atissi's adoption of the sobriquet 'Son of the Leopard' was indicative of his arrogance and boastfulness. Back in 1881, he was reputed to have personally strangled several helpless survivors of Flatters' Mission and poisoned the dates with his own hands. His treatment of Henri de Dianous and his party, going so far as taking an oath on the Quran, demonstrated his relish for the sadistic that went far beyond the necessities of strategy.[85] Even in a culture where brutality, double-dealing and egotism were a way of life, Atissi was extreme. Now the Son of the Leopard had been chosen as *amenukal* of the Hoggar.

Mohammad ag Wurzig was not happy about this. He objected,

rightly, that his cousin was his junior, and not even in direct line for the chieftainship. Although all the Kel Ulli and a few of the nobles supported Atissi, some of the traditionalists backed Mohammad's claim. When the convocation looked like breaking up in disarray, the marabout Sheikh Abdin proposed a compromise. Placing both hands on his rosary, he declared, 'You will be two sultans with the same title!' He then tore his own *shesh* into two and put half each on the head of both Atissi and Mohammad.

2

The Spectre of the Trans-Saharan Railway Revived

Six years earlier, Major Joseph Joffre had defeated the Awlimmi-den Tuareg outside Timbuctoo. He had marched a column of *tirailleurs* and spahis more than eight hundred kilometres along the Niger River in six and a half weeks. Employing the classic infantry tactics of the day, Joffre, later to become a notable field marshal in the First World War, formed his men up into neat ranks and pumped fire into the hordes of veiled men. A hundred and forty Tuareg were killed. The following day the local chiefs came to sue for peace. The mysterious 'golden city' that Alexander Gordon Laing and so many after him had died trying to reach was mysterious no longer.

The French now controlled both ends of the ancient trade route, but the Kel Ahaggar still owned the middle ground, and anyone crossing the desert had no choice but to pass through their territory. In the Sudan, the French were hemmed in everywhere by the British. Casting around for a chink in the British armour, they settled on Nigeria as the most exposed of their rival's colonies, but to bring pressure to bear in time of war they would need to be able to move a modern army across the Sahara in a matter of days

– and that would require a railway. Suddenly, fifteen years after it had been put to sleep, the spectre of the Trans-Saharan Railway was revived.

Adolphe Duponchel's original idea, derailed by the High Commission, had been to route the railway through In Salah. The town where Aitaghel and bin Bajuda had planned the Flatters massacre was the key to the Sahara, but it had always been an obstacle to the French. While the allegiance of its inhabitants to the Sultan of Morocco was nominal, the British giant stood behind the sultan with a big stick. It was not for nothing that Paul Flatters had feared his letters falling into the hands of a British consul. That situation changed in 1890, when a new Anglo-French agreement gave the French a free hand in the Sahara.

In Salah was the capital of the Tidikelt, the eastern extension of the great Tuat Oasis, the Street of Palms. The Hoggar Tuareg got their supplies of dates and grain from the Tuat-Tidikelt. Back in 1881, having repented of his demand for their annihilation, Eugène Belin had pointed out that a French occupation of the Tuat Oasis would paralyse Kel Ahaggar supplies, so by moving into the Tuat the French could kill two birds with one stone. Not only would they secure a major stepping-stone on the route of the new Trans-Saharan Railway, but they would also get a stranglehold on the Kel Ahaggar's market.

First, though, the job that Flatters had set out to do must be completed: a line through the Hoggar Mountains must be surveyed. On 23 October 1898, a new expedition set out from Wargla for the Sudan via the Hoggar Mountains: the first official French expedition dispatched into the Sahara since Flatters' death. Led by Fernand Foreau and Major François Lamy, it adopted precisely the stance that Paul Flatters had recommended in 1877. There was no more talk about the undesirability of 'frightening the natives' or disguising *tirailleurs* as camel-men. This was a mission of colonial conquest, consisting of a thousand camels and a military escort of three hundred soldiers – exactly the number that Flatters had specified. It had taken twenty-two years and the deaths of more than a hundred men for Flatters' plan to be taken seriously.

On 20 January 1899, Foreau and Lamy left their main column in the Anahef Massif, where de Dianous's party had slaughtered their salukis on their desperate march back to civilization. With thirty Shamba irregulars they rode a hundred and forty kilometres by camel in two days, arriving at Tajnut-Tan-Kuffar on 22 January. Guided by a Kel Ajjer boy named Thaleb, who had not even been born when Flatters was trying to cross the Sahara, they found the well long since filled in by floods and marked by a single tamarisk tree.

They remained only an hour in the wadi and spent most of that time hunting around for relics of the massacre. 'No vestige of that painful occurrence remains,' Foreau wrote, 'and we have found no more than a few little fragments of calcinated bone, a left humerus, quite a long way from the well . . . and a little bit of the sole of a shoe of incontestably European make.'[86] Before leaping back on to their camels, they stood in silence for a moment, in honour of those ill-fated pioneers.

Atissi's riders had trailed the Foreau–Lamy column, but dared not attack. There was no way Atissi could mistake the overtly martial nature of this new expedition. The Foreau–Lamy escort wore their blue Armée d'Afrique tunics and tarbooshes; the officers and NCOs sported their dress uniforms and kepis. They marched in strict military formation, and wherever they halted for a few days, they built a strong defensive position. They even carried two 42 mm Hotchkiss mountain guns. On the night of 9 December, near Amgid, where Henri de Dianous had fought his last bloody battle, three Tuareg approached their camp. The mission's sentries grabbed them, divested them of their spears and swords and confiscated their camels. The Tuareg claimed to have been looking for pasture and begged to be released, especially when, the next day, they realized how large the caravan was.

Foreau and Lamy agreed to let them go, on the understanding that they delivered a letter to Atissi, stating that the French were not here for revenge, but just wanted to pass through in peace.

Atissi received the letter, but he was convinced that the long-awaited retribution had arrived. As Foreau and Lamy traversed the Amadghor Serir over the next few weeks, they found signs of quickly abandoned Tuareg *douars*, and hundreds of camel-tracks leading south: Atissi had ordered the Kel Ghela to evacuate the whole area. The expedition had been hoping to replace their exhausted camels in the Hoggar, but found every camp deserted; the entire Tuareg population had pulled out.

On, 2 February 1898, the column arrived at In Azawa, the wells that had glittered so brightly in Paul Flatters' imagination. Foreau and Lamy and their band had become the first Europeans to traverse the Hoggar Mountains from end to end.

It took their *tirailleurs* three days to build a redoubt overlooking the wells, and when it was completed, Lamy manned it with a detachment of twenty-five soldiers under a French officer and two French NCOs. Six years later, the redoubt was christened Fort Flatters.

The peaceful character of the Foreau–Lamy mission was not to last, however. On 7 March, as they pressed on south across the country of the Kel Awi and Awlimmiden Tuareg, they were attacked by a raiding-party four hundred strong. This time the French were ready for them, dug in behind a well-constructed barricade, and the dark riders were repelled on their first charge by volleys from the *tirailleurs* and a barrage of shells from the mountain guns. The battle lasted only twenty minutes, leaving the Tuareg with nine dead, sixteen wounded and thirty captured. They withdrew at once, and did not trouble the expedition again. Five months later, on 28 July 1899, Fernand Foreau and François Lamy led their men into the town of Agadez, having blazed a trail along which French influence would soon extend from Algeria to the Sudan.

In December the same year, a hundred and forty-five *tirailleurs* and irregulars, commanded by Lieutenant Théodore Pein, and a geologist, Professor A. G. Flamand, crossed the Tademait Plateau and approached In Salah. At the village of Igosten, about twenty kilometres to the east, a thousand *ksurians* and Awlad Ba Hammu Arabs came out to squash them. The Arabs were sent packing in less than two hours, leaving fifty-six dead. The following June the Tuat-Tidikelt Oasis became a French *territoire*, with its headquarters at the *annexe* of In Salah.

3

'This outrage demands to be avenged'

In March 1902, a woman called Fatma wult M'sis was travelling with a caravan she owned through the rocky Muydir Plateau. Her camels were carrying dates and grain for sale in the Hoggar. Though Fatma's father was an Arab of the Shamba, she was Kel Ghela through her mother and therefore, by Tuareg tradition, of noble descent. As an inhabitant of the small oasis of In Ghar in the Tidikelt, about fifty kilometres west of In Salah, Fatma was officially a subject of the new French Territory of the Oases, created the previous year.

Not long after the caravan entered the Wadi Talzaghet, Fatma's guide called her attention to a band of camel-riders who had appeared suddenly from the cover of an adjacent gully. The party was not large, and Fatma saw at once from the riders' purple robes, rifles, swords, spears and saddlery that they were noble Tuareg warriors of the Kel Ghela, relatives through her mother. They were followed by a small contingent of negro slaves.

To the lady's astonishment, the men did not greet her, but rode up to her camel-men, levelled rifles and spears at them and ordered them to hand over the camels, the goods and all their belongings. Incensed, Fatma urged her camel towards them, shouting in Tamahaq that she was a noblewoman of their tribe, but the bandits took no notice. At close quarters, Fatma received an even bigger shock – despite the warriors' tightly drawn veils, she recognized one of them: her maternal uncle, Baba ag Tamaklast.

To Fatma, this was an utter disgrace. She couched her camel and berated Baba in no uncertain terms: did he think that he could deceive her by hiding behind his veil? He had dishonoured the family and shown himself up to be nothing more than a common thief. Her uncle dismounted and called his slaves and while two of them held Fatma, another thrashed her savagely with a club. 'It is God who has put me in your path,' Baba yelled, his words punctuated by thuds of the stick and Fatma's screams. 'You have betrayed your kinsmen and prostituted yourself to the French. I will punish you as you deserve.'

Baba and his men left her lying in the desert with her camel-men, badly bruised and shaken but not seriously hurt, and made off with her camels and goods. Baba had told her that God had put him in her way, but Fatma thought otherwise. Only eight days earlier her brother, Mohammad bin M'sis, had been attacked by the same gang of Kel Ghela in Muydir, and he too had been relieved of his merchandise, *mehari*, baggage-camels, sword and rifle. Mohammad, known throughout the Tidikelt as a warrior and a poet, had worked as a guide and interpreter for the French at In Salah. It could be no coincidence that both brother and sister had been robbed.

It was not God who had put Baba ag Tamaklast in the path of his nephew and niece, but the co-*amenukal* of the Hoggar, Mohammad ag Wurzig. He had prompted Baba to harass travellers living under French authority as a deliberate ruse to provoke a backlash against Atissi. The 'two chiefs' solution proposed by the holy man Abdin two years earlier was not working: it had, predictably, plunged the Hoggar into chaos. The Kel Ulli especially regretted this compromise because they now had to pay tribute to two masters instead of one, and many were forsaking both *amenukals* for a third party, Musa ag Amastane, nephew of

Aitaghel's old rival, Khyar ag Hegir. Like his uncle, Musa was a moderate who believed in conciliation with the French.

Mohammad ag Wurzig was crafty enough to understand that the Christians would hold Atissi responsible for any subversive acts against their 'subjects'. The French had never forgotten Atissi's role in the Flatters massacre, nor his inhuman treatment of the survivors. To make matters worse for himself, the Son of the Leopard had opened his chieftainship by sending a threatening letter to the commandant at In Salah, Captain Gaston Cauvet. 'If you come to the Hoggar,' he had written, 'I will destroy you by force or by ruse; if you prevent my caravans from revictualling in the markets of the Tidikelt, I will come and cut down the palm trees of the oasis.'[87] In Cauvet's eyes, this amounted to a declaration of war.

When Fatma got back to the Tidikelt, she lost no time in riding to In Salah. She swept into Cauvet's office and told him, 'You know, Captain, that I am a noblewoman and this outrage demands to be avenged. I have come to ask your aid to obtain just reparation and to make them return the goods they have stolen.'[88] Cauvet, an alert, passionate extrovert with brilliant-blue eyes, close-cropped hair and an explosive extrusion of whisker, was immediately engaged. He saw in Fatma's complaint just the kind of pretext he and his superior, Chief Commandant Colonel Henri Laperrine, had been looking for. Since Aitaghel's death the desert south of In Salah had become more disturbed than it had been in years. Camels belonging to the Shamba of the Tidikelt, pastured in the wadis in In Sokki and around Hassi Inifel, had been rustled at regular intervals by Tuareg raiders. A damsel in distress under French protection, harassed by the Tuareg while going about her lawful business, was the ideal excuse to send off a punitive raid – one that would sort out the Kel Ahaggar once and for all.

Cauvet and Laperrine had both been subalterns in the Armée d'Afrique at the time of the Flatters disaster, and neither had ever forgotten the insult to France. Cauvet sensed that the time was ripe for revenge, but he had only a handful of regular troops under his command. He did have one important resource, however: his deputy, Gaston Cottonest, a tall, stringy, thickly bearded lieutenant from Dunkirk. Cottonest was a remarkable officer, cool-headed, energetic, and capable of inspirational leadership. He was a fluent Arabic-speaker, a superb camel-rider, and a hard-as-nails desert veteran with a deep affection for the Arabs. He was one of the new men of the French Empire, a modernist: flexible, bold, and prepared to flout convention and cock a snook at the rules. In short, Gaston Cottonest was the ideal soldier for a guerrilla war.

Cottonest was called into the office, and the commandant told him that he was to lead a counter-raid against the bandits who had robbed Fatma and Mohammad bin M'sis. 'You can take forty reservists of the *makhazni* from Wargla,' Cauvet said, 'and recruit ninety men from every local Shamba clan that has a grudge against the Kel Ahaggar.'

The lieutenant considered it for a moment. 'The bandits' trail will long ago have gone cold,' he said. 'There will be very little chance of finding them.'

Cauvet nodded agreement and said the important thing was to demonstrate to the Kel Ahaggar that their mountains were no longer the refuge they had been – that the French could – and would – reach them there. Cottonest was to embark on what was officially to be called an 'administrative tour'. He would reconnoitre the Muydir Plateau and push as far as possible into the heart of the Hoggar Mountains, the central plateau of Atakor, as yet unexplored by Europeans. Cauvet did not believe that the Kel Ahaggar would confront the column; he thought they would probably melt away, as they had done before the Foreau–Lamy expedition. 'I think your mission will yield some happy results,' he said, 'even if only from a geographical point of view . . . but it will be a good result if we can promenade in the heart of their country.'

He instructed the lieutenant not to engage the Tuareg in combat, except in self-defence.

Finally, he handed Cottonest an 1890-model Lebel carbine. This was a great prize. The world's first magazine-fed rifle, the Lebel had an accurate range of more than a thousand metres, and fired a copper-jacketed 8 mm bullet at a muzzle-velocity of a thousand metres a second. The increased velocity meant that the smaller, hard-nosed rounds had a more powerful impact: at close range they could knock a man's arm clean off. The Lebel's cylindrical magazine held only five rounds, but could be reloaded quickly with a clip. Cottonest examined the weapon with deference.

As he stood up to take his leave, he inquired, impertinently, if these orders had come from Colonel Laperrine.

'No,' Cauvet said. 'Colonel Laperrine does not need to be informed at this time.'

4

Many Old Scores
to Be Settled

The evening of 22 March, Gaston Cottonest met the 126 Arabs who were to accompany him. They were dressed in sand-coloured *gandourahs*, hooded burnooses and *sheshes* looped around their faces, kept in place by wide black bands. Each man had brought his own *mehari* and carried a French-issue 1874-model Fusil Gras and a hundred and twenty cartridges.

They were local Shamba from the Tidikelt, drawn from nine or ten Shamba clans and divided into three sections, each section led by a sheikh: ʿAbd al-Qadir, Duro, and the formidable Tuareg-fighter Qaʾid Baba, who two years earlier had inflicted crushing counter-raids on Taitoq and Ifoghas marauders. Cottonest was aware that these Arabs owed only superficial allegiance to the French – most of Duro's section had actually been in action against the Pein–Flamand mission at Igosten. The lieutenant hoped that their grudge against the Tuareg was stronger than any they felt against their colonial masters.

The nucleus of the patrol was the thirty-six *makhazni* reservists from Wargla, fit, dedicated, well-trained young men, who were crack shots with their Fusils Gras. As a guide, Cottonest had recruited Fatma's brother, Mohammad bin M'sis. He was not only fluent in both Arabic and Tamahaq but a seasoned rider and

guide who knew the Hoggar intimately – and he was driven by
a desire for personal revenge. The patrol was to be followed by a
small baggage-caravan of twenty-five camels, which would carry
reserve rations, ammunition and medical supplies.

Before dawn the next day the Arabs rounded up their camels
and brought them in to be loaded in the open space between the
ksur. They led their mounts over to where their saddles and
equipment were piled and jerked on the headropes to barrack
them. The *meharis* slumped disdainfully to their front knees, sank
to their back knees and settled carefully on their hocks. The Arabs
brushed the dust off their withers, fitted saddle-pads, smoothed
out folds, then eased the saddles into place. They crouched down
on the animals' right side, slapped them lightly to make them raise
their bellies and fed the girths underneath, then knotted them to an
iron ring fixed on the saddle with a thong of leather. All these
operations were performed with meticulous care. Every Shambi
knew that one small mistake could result in a slipped saddle, a
gall, or even a fall from the camel's back.

When they had tested the tightness of the saddle, they hung on a
pair of water-skins, each holding about twenty litres, and saddle-
bags containing enough flour, couscous, rice, tea, coffee, sugar and
dried meat for thirty days. Finally, they slung their rifles across
their backs, picked up their head-ropes and waited for the signal to
mount. Gaston Cottonest cocked his lanky leg over the saddle and
the Arabs followed suit. The *meharis* rose, grunting, to their feet.
The Arabs formed into loose groups and stalked out of the oasis,
through the thickets of palms and across the sand-sheet, their
burnooses flying. Despite the fact that one of the camels trailed
behind it a wheeled device for measuring distance, no one could
have mistaken this for a scientific expedition. The men had the
grim, determined look of warriors about to go into battle. Many
old scores were to be settled on this 'administrative tour'.

For the first few days the column travelled slowly, descending
the escarpment of Tigentuin and moving across a *serir* punctured

by knolls, cliffs and inselbergs like fairy castles. The stones that clinked and grated beneath their camels' feet were black with age, honed and sharpened by sun, wind, rain and sand for aeons. Soon they dropped into the Wadi Botha, where the flood-waters draining off Tademait raised lush pastures. They drifted along at a snail's pace. If they found rich grazing early on, they remained on it for the entire day, unloading their animals quickly and hobbling them by the forelegs, turning them loose on the swathes of grass. If the grazing was poor, they pushed on until sunset. After dark they would let the camels graze again, bringing them into camp and knee-hobbling them only when it was time to sleep.

After dark a small galaxy of cooking-fires would flicker up. The Arabs ate together in groups, devouring couscous, rice or fresh-baked bread, crouching round communal dishes, each man feeding himself with his right hand. There were no tents or beds on this expedition; the Arabs laid their rugs around the fire and slept close together, their rifles in their hands, wrapped in their burnooses under the watchful eyes of their lookouts. Progress was deliberately slow. Cottonest could not afford to lose any camels on this trip, nor did he want Kel Ahaggar scouts to work out that he intended to breach the Atakor.

Moving like this, the patrol worked its way slowly to the south-east towards the Muydir Plateau, roughly in the direction of the Amgid Gorge. After the Wadi Botha, the going was hard, but Cottonest basked in the knowledge that he was breaking ground that not even the Foreau–Lamy mission had covered. On 4 April the patrol crossed the defile of Khangat al-Hadid into the heights overlooking the Igharghar, where Flatters' party had passed on their way to Jebel Khanfussa. Up on the *hammada* a hot wind assailed them, emptying the water-skins and dehydrating the men. Cottonest led them down from the plateau into the Igharghar, heading for the wells of Gharis.

It was here that they encountered the first sign of enemy activity. When the Arabs examined the wells, they found they had been deliberately filled with sand. This was a shock. Knowing they must find water at once, Cottonest ordered the patrol to turn south along the Igharghar, and later that day they came across a shallow pool in the wadi. The Arabs dismounted and scraped up the liquid in their bowls, managing to fill a few skins. It was enough to slake their thirst, but not enough to water the camels. The trackers saw no sign of the Tuareg, but they knew they were being trailed. That night, to elude the enemy, they climbed up on to the plateau after dark and made a forced march across terrain so rough that they had to dismount and lead the *meharis* on foot. It was pitch-black. The scouts stumbled over stones, lost their footing and plunged down escarpments. Cottonest himself fell headlong into a ravine, crashing into sharp rocks, dislocating his right shoulder, breaking a finger and spraining his left ankle. At daybreak they descended through a pass to In-Tabariq, where they found a well in the shadow of the rock wall. To the north-east they could see the thirteen-hundred-metre-tall peak of Khan-fussa, where Flatters had met his first Tuareg guide, Shikkadh. It was about a day's march away. Far across the *serir*, beyond the miasma of dust on the skyline, lay the great buttress of the Tefedest, with its bow-shaped tail, Wudan, capped with the peak of the Hill of Demons.

The well yielded enough water for the camels, but Cottonest felt the position was too exposed, and didn't linger. The animals were watered quickly and the skins filled, then the patrol followed the fractured line of mesas due south to the well of Asseksem, where the plateau creased away to the west, its sheer walls panning out in minor key through a wasteland of ruts and canyons. Cottonest decided that Asseksem would make a suitable base-camp for surveillance of the Muydir. He ordered the patrol to dismount and construct a defensive sangar of stones, in case of attack. That done, he called his three sheikhs, Qa'id Baba, 'Abd al-Qadir and Duro, and instructed them to take small parties and scour the plateau for news of Baba ag Tamaklast and his bandits. If possible,

the scouts were to retrieve the stolen camels, and if not, they were
to bring back other livestock instead.

The scouting parties were all back by 18 April, with no camels
but five hundred and ten head of sheep, fifty-three donkeys and a
bevy of Tuareg women and children. The men had run away as
soon as they had seen the patrols coming. Cottonest treated the
prisoners well, and sent them home with their donkeys and enough
food to live on. He claimed the sheep in compensation for the
stolen goods and had Mohammad bin M'sis take them back to In
Salah.

The sheikhs had also acquired some interesting intelligence.
Baba ag Tamaklast had retreated to Ideles, the tiny hamlet of
palms and gardens on the western edge of the Hoggar's Atakor
Plateau, first put on the map by Duveyrier in the 1860s. Qa'id
Baba had captured some Kel Ulli,[89] and had sent them off with a
message for Atissi, informing him that they were calling his bluff.
Far from attempting to destroy them 'by force or ruse', the Son of
the Leopard had fled at their approach and was hiding out in the
Tassili-n-Ajjer.

Cottonest was delighted to hear that Baba was at Ideles. The
lieutenant's injuries were much improved after the week's rest, and
he ordered the patrol to strike camp next morning. The Arabs
were now on the scent and they moved fast, covering long distances in a day. Soon the ramparts of Wudan were in clear focus.
The patrol headed due east, passing under the skirts of the mountain, then turned south into the plain of Amadghor, following the
walls of Tefedest. They climbed up on its shoulder, forging a path
directly across the wind-blasted valleys into the heart of the
Atakor. Valley gave way to valley. The troop passed through
ranks of fluted peaks, knapped and hammered by time, the
bleached skeleton of a world from which all flesh had long ago
been flayed. Day by day the great central fortress of the Hoggar
reared out of the sand-mist.

Cottonest had scouts outriding the main body, who soon came

into contact with the Tuareg. They were mostly Kel Ulli. On the first day they ran into seven riders and opened fire, but only one of them tumbled out of the saddle; the rest made off as fast as their mounts would go. When the Arabs examined the dead man, they found he was a tribesman of the Issekermaren, a vassal clan of the Kel Ghela. The same thing happened the next day, but this time the Tuareg abandoned their camels and scuttled off into the rocks. The beasts were rounded up and added to the mission's loot.

The same day they rode into a Tuareg camp, skin tents pitched under an overhanging cliff. The men had all run away, so Cottonest interrogated the women, children and slaves. The women maintained that their menfolk had the best intentions to the 'visitors', but the young boys and slaves let slip that the warriors were gathering to hit Cottonest with a massive ambush, which was being organized by Mohammad ag Othman, Atissi's second cousin and the chief of the Tazruk Valley.

Cottonest realized that speed was now crucial, and on 24 April he had his raiders ride all night again. As the dawn came up in a rage of flame and smoke over the apron of Atakor, they were in sight of Ideles. It was a disappointing prospect: seven or eight mud-brick houses, some shacks of palmetto fibre, a few patches of garden, and about thirty palms. The lieutenant had his riders couch their camels in the nearest wadi and went in on foot with a small advance party. Once again the Tuareg showed no stomach for a fight. They leapt on to their *meharis* and lit out into the hills with Gras rounds frying the air, ricocheting around them. Not to be outdone, Cottonest's *makhazni* mounted and peeled off in hot pursuit, whooping and cheering, firing from camel-back, bowling four or five of the enemy out of the saddle.

The rest of Cottonest's party ransacked the village. In a house they were told had belonged to Aitaghel, the lieutenant was surprised to find Fusils Gras, cartridges, a mobile oven from Flatters' mess equipment and various French-issue cooking pots and vessels – all collected after the massacre or taken from de Dianous's abandoned camp in the Wadi Tidaqqaten twenty-one years earlier. Cottonest ordered his men to demolish the house. He had the largest palm tree in the grove cut down and stripped, and mounted the trunk in a two-metre oblong of bricks constructed from the rubble. On the trunk he erected a Tuareg oryx-hide shield, inscribed in French and Arabic with the legend: *Flatters Mission: 16 February 1881–25 April 1902.* When it was done, he stood back and saluted solemnly, while the Arabs fired a volley in the air. Twenty-one years had passed since Paul Flatters had fallen at Tajnut Tan-Kuffar, but the long-awaited retribution had begun.

5

The Tuareg Had
Outrun Them

That night, one of the Arabs deserted to the Tuareg with his rifle, camel and equipment. Cottonest was worried, both about the effect on morale and about the information the deserter might give the enemy. He was also disquieted by the fact that none of the Tuareg he had met had given battle – this appeared to him to confirm the slaves' gossip, that they were melting away in order to gather a sizable force.

He discovered from the local Haratin share-croppers who worked the gardens and palm groves that his quarry, Baba ag Tamaklast and his men, had moved to Tazruk, a slightly larger village than Ideles, that stood more than eighteen hundred metres high on the eastern slopes of the Atakor. Cottonest wasted no time in giving chase, even though it meant stepping right into the dragon's lair. He hoped to be able to catch up with them and deal with them piecemeal before they could join up with local chief Mohammad ag Othman.

It took them only three days to make Tazruk, and once again his troop met with no resistance. It was clear that here, too, the Tuareg had moved on. Questioning the local Haratin carefully, Cottonest learned that Mohammad ag Othman had just scooted into the hills with Baba ag Tamaklast and a band of Kel Ulli; they were planning to ambush his party as it passed through the steep defiles of the central Hoggar and massacre him and all his men. Cottonest ordered a search of the settlement, and his men came up with two French military water-bottles, one still bearing the name and address of the shop where it had been purchased: *Bazar du Voyages, place de l'Opéra, Paris*. They also found more Gras cartridges, French-issue boxes, and a pair of stirrups that had belonged to Flatters himself. On the strength of this evidence, Cottonest ordered Tazruk demolished and burned. When the moon came up at midnight, the raiding-party set off on the trail of the fugitives.

Cottonest and his troop were now on the very rim of the plateau, at an altitude of almost two thousand metres. This was a land of fluted peaks and plunging mountainsides, not the kind of desert the Shamba were used to. Narrow tracks rose at steep inclines through twisting passes, falling away into sandy valleys forested with tamarisk trees. In places there were ribbons of green sedge growing along tiny streams, and vast dun-coloured wadis coiling around the foot of hills that appeared to be no more than heaps of loose boulders. Tazruk itself stood on a rocky panhandle, and Cottonest was obliged to follow the contours of the hills rather than cutting across the valleys, where the going was impossible for the camels.

They slogged on along the precipitous tracks for the rest of the night and all the next day. For most of the time they were obliged to walk, manhandling the *meharis* through the stony gullies. They tramped on almost without a break into the next sunset, and on and on into the night. At about three o'clock the next morning they dropped down through the Col of Azru into the sandy plain of Tahifet, where they halted for a brief rest among tamarisk groves. They had been trekking non-stop for twenty-seven hours, and had covered no more than forty kilometres. Many of the camels had cuts and bruises on their feet. Cottonest examined them and selected forty of the best, with their riders, to form a flying column.

The riders mounted up almost at once and set off across the undulating plain at a fast trot. They ground was covered in fresh tracks, and soon Cottonest came across the carcase of an exhausted camel. This was the first indication that they were gaining on the enemy, and it spurred them forward. Further on, there were more abandoned camels, and camel-calves, then a slave, and baggage that had been dumped on the track. Halting to examine it, Cottonest found a conical tent of European manufacture, embroidered with the maker's name: *Benjamin Eddington, London*. It had once belonged to the ill-fated Marquis of Mores. After that, he came across two female slaves, and finally, not long before sunset, a lame, worn-out mare belonging to Mohammad ag Othman himself.

Night fell like a dark curtain, shrouding the hills from view, and Cottonest called a halt. His men were dropping with fatigue. They had covered sixty-seven kilometres from Tazruk over execrable country in the past thirty-six hours, much of it on foot. The guides told Cottonest that they were unlikely to catch up with the fugitives at night. Most probably Mohammad ag Othman and his band had turned south out of the Atakor, along the Wadi Zirzir into the wild country towards the Sudan. Reluctantly, the lieutenant had to admit that the Tuareg had outrun them.

6

He Had Violated
Hallowed Ground

On 4 May, they regrouped and made camp at Taghawhawat, not far from Tamaghasset. While the Arabs lit fires and began to cook couscous and bake bread, Cottonest dispatched scouts to quarter the area, looking for enemy movement.

An hour later two Arabs raced back to the camp and reported breathlessly that the patrols had run into one large and two smaller bands of Tuareg warriors. They estimated the enemy to be two hundred and sixty strong. The veiled men had opened fire on them and two of their troop were missing, presumed dead. The rest of the scouting party had stayed in the field to observe the enemy build-up. Cottonest snapped out an order to strike camp. The men doused their fires, slung their kit over the backs of their *meharis* and mounted up with their rifles in their hands. They rode hell for leather until they made contact with the scouts, determined to retrieve the bodies of their dead comrades, but by the time they reached the forward position the Tuareg had vanished into the mountains and the missing Arabs had returned.

For the next two days Cottonest's raiders moved slowly round the edge of the Atakor, intending to loop back north in the direction of In Salah. The lieutenant had hoped to catch Baba, but was not looking for a showdown with the Tuareg. His orders were to avoid an engagement unless in self-defence, and he had already carried out Cauvet's instructions to show the flag: he had made it clear that a French patrol was capable of pursuing bandits into the very core of their 'sacred fastness'. Yet he had the feeling that the Tuareg had no intention of letting him get away with it. He had desecrated their hallowed ground, and they could not permit him to escape. His soldier's sixth sense told him that the predators were circling and a trap was carefully being laid.

On 6 May, Cottonest became the first European to see the village of Tamanghasset, today the capital of the Hoggar region, then no more than a huddle of hovels inhabited by Haratin cultivators on the banks of a wadi. One of his scouts engaged a Haratani in conversation and found out that a few days earlier the place had been full of Dag Ghali – a Kel Ulli tribe – mounted, and tooled up for battle. There had been at least three hundred of them, and they had gathered to strike the French patrol at Taghawhawat. Having lost their chance, they had slipped away into the hills to await a better opportunity. Cottonest realized that these were the parties his scouts had encountered three days earlier and concluded that his pursuit of ag Othman had not been wasted – it had prevented the enemy from combining in time for a concerted attack.

An hour before first light next morning the Arabs mounted their camels and Cottonest turned the patrol north towards the village of Tit, some forty kilometres away; the lieutenant intended to cover the distance in a single push. They would water their animals at the spring there the following day. The sun came up as they rode out of Tamanghasset, setting afire the massed clouds, floss caught on the needles of the Atakor above them. To the south, the raddled labyrinth of blocks and ridges sparked into an ocean of flame.

That morning a party of outriders Cottonest had sent to cover his rear ran to catch up with him, to report that they were being tracked by a large Tuareg war-party. He knew how to deal with this. He ordered his fighters to halt, dismount and scatter into the rocks in ambush positions. His ploy failed when the enemy spotted them and once again faded away into the labyrinth.

7

All the Roads of All the Centuries

The day was hot and very still. The Shamba camels trooped on steadily in three bunches, pressing close together. The Arabs drew in their *sheshes* against the heat, adjusted their burnooses and worried their heels against their camels' coarse withers. At midday the stocks of their Fusils Gras were almost too hot to touch. By early afternoon their canteens and skins were empty and they were looking forward to the prospect of water.

At three-thirty that afternoon the lead scouts sighted the outlying palmetto huts and enclosures of the settlement. Cottonest called Duro and instructed him to take his troop, clear the village and select a lying-up place beyond Tit on high ground. The Arabs set off at a trot. Shortly after them came Qa'id Baba's troop, splintering into two squads and boxing around the settlement's perimeter on both sides, about two kilometres away. Qa'id and his men were to rendezvous with Duro on the far side of the village and return to the main force to report.

Cottonest, at the head of his forty *makhazni*, watched the scouts' camels shovelling up dust as they disappeared towards the village. He ordered his men to push on steadily at walking pace. About a hundred metres behind the *makhazni* came the

251

baggage-caravan of twenty-five beasts, escorted by 'Abd al-Qadir's Arabs. A five-man group brought up the rear.

Tit lay on a flat *serir* of gravel, scattered with beds of sand and nests of boulders, low dunes and broad ridges of shattered granite. A dull greyness had taken the polish off the western sky, and the stillness was ruptured suddenly by a wind that dragged a pall across the horizon. Shrouds of sand-smoke whipped along the periphery of Cottonest's vision. After the main party had been riding for about twenty minutes, the lieutenant thought he spotted movement far to his right. He ordered half a dozen *makhazni* to investigate. The camel-riders sped off, vanishing quickly beyond a curtain of blown sand.

At about four o'clock he saw them hurtling back, waving their rifles frantically, and pulled up his camel to meet them. The men gasped out that they had crossed the lip of the Wadi Tit and had seen a host of Tuareg hiding inside, a little way from their kneeling camels. They had been spotted. The enemy had sprinted for their animals and were riding after them. As Cottonest looked up, he saw a sight he would never forget. Three hundred black riders had suddenly sprung out of the bowels of the earth and were bearing down on his column through roils of dust. They were no more than eight hundred metres away.

It was a shock: Cottonest had been expecting an attack, but the enemy had waited until precisely the right moment to launch their assault. Despite all his caution, he had been caught with his force divided, and now his seventy men were outnumbered more than four to one. He paused for a fraction of a second. Scanning the ground, he estimated that he had about five minutes before the Tuareg hit them. It wasn't much, but he was determined to make use of every second.

The ground was flat and open *serir*, but to the lieutenant's left the carpet of gravel was broken by the debris of lava pillows, blocks and slabs. Beyond that was a fractured terrace that had once been the ground level, eroded into gravel plinths about fifteen metres high, walls of soft sand piled like a skin over rubblestone screes. The nearest plinth was capped with a granite bulge in its centre, standing about sixty metres tall. Cottonest decided that this high ground would be his last resort. For now there was no time to deploy his men there, and in any case it would mean abandoning the mounts. He snapped out a crisp order to ground camels and stand to. The Arabs jerked their *meharis* down, rolled out of the saddle and arrayed themselves behind the beasts. Fusils Gras breeches clacked as the men cocked their weapons. Cottonest ordered them to hold their fire and placed himself coolly in front of them to make sure the order was obeyed.

For an eerie moment the only sound was the shoosh of the wind. The black riders moved slowly into range, all three hundred of them close together in a single mass. They came on defiantly at a walking pace, their camels' heads twisted back under control over the clawed cross-spikes of their saddles. The *meharis* undulated forward across the flat earth, a flowing stream of movement. The warriors were poised, straight and proud on their camels' withers, bare feet clasped on their necks, veils tightened to post-box slits, their black, blue and purple *gandourahs* flowing behind them like banners. The camels' feet wove soundlessly across the stones, leather girths clicking, the sound of the riders' flapping robes like riffled paper. Suddenly a roar went up from the massed ranks, low at first, but growing steadily louder: '*Ghafia Dag Ghali! Tala Marabitin!*' – Peace of the Dag Ghali! Grace will be given to the Marabitin![90]

Cottonest could barely understand, but he grasped the word 'peace' and for a split second wondered if the Tuareg might be friendly. That thought was disposed of abruptly when a single shot punched out from the flank, punctuated with a puff of smoke. The Tuareg broke into a trot, their fastest camels now pulling forward into the lead. Ignoring his order, the Arabs started shooting, yelling curses at the enemy as they fired. The Fusils Gras spat. Rounds fizzed and walloped into the massed riders. Some of the Arabs were good shots and many of their bullets smacked home into flesh, sending the masked men skittering off their mounts.

The warriors came on without turning a hair. Twenty metres from the Arab position, they hurled their javelins. The spears whispered through the air and slumped into the *serir*. Most fell short of their targets, but the Tuareg used the momentary hiatus to couch their camels and step gracefully out of the saddle. They carried spears and shields in their left hands and rifles in their right. 'To our great surprise, almost all of them had rifles,' Cottonest said later. 'They were big men with an imposing walk who came straight towards us with a real disdain of danger.'[91]

Although they did not know it, these Tuareg were the last defenders of their hills, the final guardians of the place that had been their refuge for a thousand years. Ironically, few of them were Imuhaq, and therefore, by Tuareg tradition, not warriors at all. Many of the noble Kel Ghela had melted away in the face of danger, leaving the tribes that had been their vassals to make a stand. The bulk of the force that advanced on Cottonest's party were Dag Ghali, direct descendants of the ancient Isebeten from whom the Imuhaq had once taken this land by force. With the Dag Ghali were numbers of Issekermaren, vassals of mixed Arab ancestry, and Iklan, black slaves whose ancestors the Imuhaq had stolen from the Sudan. Nor were they led by the belligerent Atissi who had threatened to destroy the French. Among their leaders was Musa ag Amastane, the noble Kel Ghela who had favoured negotiation.

Seconds later the Tuareg flung themselves on the nest of Arabs, shrieking their war cries, their swords slicking, their spears glittering. The Shamba began to fall back, still firing, their shots drumming a staccato tattoo across a foreground thick with smoke. They retreated into the rocks and boulders behind them. For a nasty moment Cottonest thought the Tuareg would outflank them and cut them to pieces. His only chance was to disengage and move to a distance at which the Fusils Gras would be effective.

The lieutenant ordered his men to withdraw to the terrace he had marked out earlier and the Shamba broke off the engagement. They pulled out skirmishing, scrambled up the rise, threw themselves down on the summit and began punching off rounds like madmen. Bullets skeetered across the rocks, snapping off fragments in deadly shrapnel bursts, gouging furrows in the *serir* around the advancing men. 'We were immediately in position and started to fire again,' Cottonest said, 'arranged in a semi-circle on the top of the hill. The Tuareg understood our tactics; they threw themselves behind the rocks that we had just abandoned and a terrible fusillade roared out from both sides. On the right and the left the Tuareg continued a slow enveloping movement that was partly stopped by our fire.'[92]

Cottonest took up a post slightly away from the rest, on the right side of the elevation, where all his men could see him. He had with him his interpreter and two runners of the *makhazin*. He took careful aim with his Lebel, cracking shots into the midst of the encroaching masses, who were firing as they advanced. On his left and right his men were pumping out rounds so madly that Cottonest had to order them to slow down. The main body of Tuareg warriors was now sixty metres away, but their skirmishers had run and crawled up, halving the distance. The Arabs were still bashing off bullets with abandon, and Cottonest was concerned that they would exhaust their ammunition. The nearest of the enemy, many armed with Remington rifles, were lying among the stones, popping up like jack-in-the-boxes to shoot off rounds at close range.

Suddenly Cottonest's position was blitzed with intense fire and a neat red hole was stamped through his interpreter's forehead, the round emerging from the back in a cascade of blood. The Arab slumped down among the rocks without a sound. At almost the same time one of the lieutenant's runners screamed as a bullet slammed into his chest. The Arab coughed blood and crashed down quivering, blood drenching Cottonest.

The lieutenant paused to insert a clip into his magazine, unaware that a Targui had drawn a bead on him from twenty-five metres. One of his runners, Mohammad bin Merizig, on his left, spotted the danger and sprang in front of him, ready to fire, but before the Arab could squeeze his trigger, a round gouged a track across his left hand, shattered his right forearm, hit the blade of the sabre thrust through his bandolier and ricocheted into Cottonest's right shoulder. Bin Merizig gasped and dropped his rifle, the blood from his mauled right arm spattering over both of them. Cottonest reeled. His shoulder was numb, the blood soaking his uniform. He steadied himself and, ignoring his own wound, plastered a field dressing round the Arab's mutilated right arm. The dressing was immediately saturated with blood. Cottonest ignored his Lebel, picked up bin Merizig's Fusil Gras, and growled at the Arab to hand over his ammunition and leave the line. The young *makhazni* refused to leave, and continued feeding him cartridges with his left hand until, five minutes later, he passed out from blood-loss and shock.

At almost the same moment, Sheikh ʿAbd al-Qadir was hit by a slug that pierced his left side and lodged against his spine. The sheikh wilted in a heap, paralysed and speechless, and was propped up behind a rock by his men.

By now the Arabs' fury had subsided and their shots were more carefully aimed. They waited calmly for a veiled head to appear before drilling it through with a bullet. Black-clad figures thrashed down among the rocks, or wobbled back with blood spurting from chest wounds. A wedge of warriors, many of them drenched in blood from wounds in the upper body, made for the patrol's camels, hoping to retire from the fray. The Arabs got them in their sights and let rip with a savage broadside. Bloody rosettes blossomed on the back of the warriors' dark robes as they were bowled over into the gravel. The camels jerked up, roaring, as the rounds zipped into their big frames, and many collapsed, dead. Only three Tuareg managed to escape – Cottonest thought they were Kel Ghela. He noticed with dismay that one had jumped on his own *mehari* and was lurching off across the desert, taking all his geographical notes, photographic equipment and films. He got the retreating warrior in his sights but hung fire for a moment – it was a difficult shot, especially with an injured shoulder, and he didn't want to hit his *mehari* by mistake. By the time he had decided to shoot, the Targui was out of range.

The sandstorm had abated. The battle had been raging about forty-five minutes when Duro and Qa'id Baba suddenly emerged from the lingering sheen of dust in a solid wedge of camel-riders moving swiftly from the left flank. Cottonest realized that the storm must have prevented them from hearing the gunshots. The Tuareg had given no thought to the detached troops and had posted no pickets or rearguard. The two sections split. Duro led his men left of Cottonest's position in a shroud of dust and couched their camels between the Tuareg and the wadi, cutting off their line of retreat. Qa'id Baba and his men worked round to the right of the knoll, dismounted, spread out – and hit the enemy with enfilade fire so intense that the Tuareg almost stopped shooting.

Cottonest saw his chance. He stood up and yelled at his men to charge. The Arabs picked themselves up. A few drew sabres but most shoved rounds into the breeches of their rifles. They plummeted down off the ridge into the Tuareg ranks, screaming out their own war-cries, and the Tuareg were caught by surprise. Hand-to-hand fighting was their forte, but the Shamba fell on them with devastating force, smashing their skulls with rifle-butts, parrying spear-thrusts on their stocks and letting rip with round after round at a range so close that many of the enemy were sent sprawling with their robes on fire. Everywhere there were thrashing knots of bodies, swords clashing and ripping into flesh, barbed spears gouging, rounds crackling through the hide of Tuareg shields, splurges of blood splattering the sand, the screams of the wounded and dying.

It was too much for the Tuareg. They abandoned the Arab camels and ran, under covering fire from a group that had sagely withdrawn on the first sign of a charge and had posted themselves on a ridge a little less than a kilometre away. Those who managed to get on their camels found themselves running smack into Duro's Arabs, who picked them off one by one. Warrior after warrior slumped out of the saddle. The Shamba followed up their shooting, tracking down the injured men and slitting their throats or putting bullets through their skulls. Duro then ordered his men to mount up and pursue those who had got through the net.

Cottonest's squad advanced slowly and cautiously on foot, dealing with pockets of resistance piecemeal, delivering the *coup de grâce* to any warrior they found lying wounded. The sky was still glowering from the storm and the sun was already over the skyline, a pale egg-yolk glimmering wanly through swells of magenta dust. By six-thirty that evening the shooting had drifted away far into the distance as Duro's men chased the last of the fugitives. Gaston Cottonest walked back to the camels, his uniform and beard stiff with congealed blood. The numbness in his shoulder had worn off, giving way to biting pain. The Arabs were gliding across the battlefield like figures in a dream, collecting weapons, dragging bodies out of the rocks to be counted. The dead were thickest around the foot of the ridge. Many bodies were smouldering from the effects of close-contact gunshots. Suddenly the skies opened and it began to pelt down with rain.

Seventy-one Tuareg had been killed in the fighting at the knoll, and another twenty-two were accounted for by Duro's pursuing Arabs. Almost sixty more later died from their wounds: in total, about half the Kel Ahaggar force. The Arabs rounded up ninety-one camels and collected eighty-three rifles, including Remingtons, and a large number of swords, shields, spears and daggers.

Cottonest had two dead and ten wounded, and his men had fired fourteen thousand cartridges. As he surveyed the dreadful carnage through the surge of the rain, Gaston Cottonest knew that Paul Flatters had finally been avenged.

That day marked more than the death of a hundred and fifty Kel Ahaggar fighters. The Tuareg had kept the secrets of the Hoggar inviolate for a thousand years. Now their enemies had penetrated their refuge, and survived. The Tuareg, most of them Kel Ulli, had fought with a total disregard for danger, but the fourteen thousand cartridges fired by their enemies speaks for itself – that, and the courage of the Arab irregulars, led by a single Frenchman, who were fighting in an unknown region, outnumbered four to one. All the roads of all the centuries had led here to the tiny hamlet of Tit, where in little more than an hour, on 7 March 1902, the legend of Kel Ahaggar invincibility had been shattered. An age had ended. The myth was gone.

8

'I did not overstep
my orders'

At first light on 19 May, as Cottonest's patrol prepared to leave the well at Matlag Ma'amar in the warren of canyons south of In Salah, they spotted riders in the distance: a relief mission, led by Colonel Henri Laperrine himself. It was a timely morale-booster for the ten wounded, especially Sheikh 'Abd al-Qadir, who was at death's door. After two months of speaking Arabic, Gaston Cottonest was at last able to use his native tongue.

Laperrine, who is usually credited with having dispatched the Cottonest mission, had actually known nothing about it until after it had left. If Cauvet had informed him, he would have been obliged to ask Algiers for approval, and Cauvet knew perfectly well he would never get it. 'I had no orders,' he later said, 'therefore I did not overstep my orders. The distinction is perhaps a trifle subtle . . . but it exists none the less.'[93] Cauvet had deliberately bamboozled the authorities in Algiers by failing to report the mission until it could not be recalled.

It had taken two remarkable men, Gaston Cauvet and Gaston Cottonest, to exact vengeance for the Flatters massacre, and both possessed precisely the quality Paul Flatters had lacked: the ability to stick to their own convictions and to ignore conventional wisdom. Colonial empires had been built by men like these.

Cottonest's patrol rode back into In Salah four days after meeting Laperrine. They had been away sixty-two days and had covered almost seventeen hundred kilometres, much of it in country previously considered impenetrable. All but five of the patrol were irregulars, and only one third had any military training. Yet this little band of men changed the face of the Sahara for ever. The repercussions of the battle of Tit, wrote *méhariste* Captain Lehuraux, were unimaginable.

In one day, the prestige the mysterious veiled men, these notorious robbers of the desert, had accumulated over centuries, was dashed. Their best warriors had disappeared. The mountains themselves, that invincible citadel of which the Kel Ahaggar were so proud, which they thought impregnable, was penetrated by the French, who had crossed it without difficulty. So the Tuareg found themselves eclipsed, and from then on they could no longer terrorize the peaceful populations of the oases, nor indiscriminately fleece inoffensive caravaneers.[94]

Tuareg power had always been based on prestige, an abstract quality that existed only in the eye of the beholder. This prestige was itself derived from fear, and the fear was based on a deliberately calculated bluff. The Tuareg, though few in number, were masters of psychological warfare. Now their millennium of bluff had been shown up for the sabre-rattling it had always been, even though relatively few of the warrior caste had actually fought at Tit. Mohammad ag Othman, Atissi's second cousin, had been killed there, and Musa ag Amastane had fought and escaped. Atissi had long since vanished into the Tassili-n-Ajjer with many of his 'noble' Kel Ghela, and Sidi al-Keraji, of the Taitoq.

Gaston Cottonest's action did not, of itself, destroy the Kel Ahaggar. Ever since the Hawwara had first arrived in these hills, their society had been on the brink of tearing itself apart from within. The Isebeten had struck a balance with the environment, but the Imuhaq had overstrained its resources. Even the precious camels had mostly been pastured outside the mountains. It was the eternal competition for material assets that had given Kel Ahaggar society its cut-throat edge, creating a people who were endlessly at war, among whom almost anything was permitted in the name of survival.

By the late 1870s the supremacy of the Imuhaq had been threatened by the rise of a warrior Kel Ulli, armed with swords, spears and rifles, and camels of their own. The war with the Kel Ajjer had accelerated the process by claiming the lives of hundreds of 'nobles'. Aitaghel had managed to hold the federation together, but his letters and actions suggest that he was constantly under pressure from rival factions, and Sidi al-Keraji of the Taitoq, in particular, had never fully accepted his authority. The cracks had begun to show with the fatal division of authority between two *amenukals*, neither of them adequate to deal with the new world in which the Tuareg found themselves. Mohammad ag Wurzig proved ineffective, and Atissi was a bully who believed he could intimidate the enemy by threats he was unable to carry out.

Atissi returned to the Hoggar Mountains after Cottonest had gone and began organizing a new round of camel-rustling in the Tidikelt, but the Kel Ahaggar turned increasingly to Musa ag Amastane. Musa had fought at Tit, yet he had always remained in favour of dealing with the Christians. Gaston Cauvet, who knew of Musa's reputation, deliberately sought to enter into negotiations with him.

In October 1902, he sent a second mission into the Hoggar, led by Lieutenant René Guillo-Lohan, partly to suppress Atissi's camel-raids, and partly to search for Musa. Riding at the head of a hundred and sixty-six men, including *tirailleurs*, spahis and *goumiers*, Guillo-Lohan followed Cottonest's route through Ideles, where he found the monument to Flatters had been destroyed. He resurrected it. He also visited the battlefield at Tit and discovered that the Tuareg had not buried their dead, just attempted to cover their bodies with stones. He was told that, two days after the battle, Tuareg warriors had flocked to the site as if to confirm with their own eyes that their people really had been defeated. The lesson had obviously been well learned, for René Guillo-Lohan's patrol encountered no resistance. Laperrine was delighted. Guillo-Lohan had tested the waters in the wake of Tit, and found them cold. Kel Ahaggar power was broken.

On 11 January 1904, a little less than two years after the battle, a hundred Kel Ghela warriors swept into In Salah. At their head was Musa ag Amastane, veil drawn tight, clad in his best purple robes. Musa's career had out-spanned that of Gaston Cauvet, who had ultimately been given his marching orders for the unauthorized Cottonest patrol. Musa was greeted instead by Captain François Metois, the new commandant of the *annexe*, clad in full dress uniform and kepi, at the head of the entire garrison of *tirailleurs*, spahis, and Laperrine's recently trained regular camel corps, the Compagnies Sahariennes. Over days of feasting and discussion, Musa pledged to halt all hostilities by the Kel Ahaggar. He announced that he would open up the old trade route through Amadghor, and guaranteed its security in return for the protection of France.

Metois told him that, in French eyes, he, not Atissi, was the real *amenukal* of the Kel Ahaggar. For the first time in their long history, the Imuhaq had become the subjects of a foreign regime.

The Sahara had been conquered and the ancient trade route with the Sudan was open again. There was no longer any barrier to the building of the Trans-Saharan Railway. In 1912, a new mission was sent across the Sahara under Captain Nieger, to survey a route from In Salah to Lagos. Nieger made the crossing in eight months, and reported that the construction of a railway no longer posed any serious problem.

It was too late. Now it was in their grasp, neither the French government nor the public were interested. The Indian summer of steam-and-steel technology was over; the era of the motor-car and the aircraft had begun. Sixteen years after Musa's visit to In Salah, a regular air service was running between Algiers and Timbuctoo. Though plans for the Trans-Saharan were revived periodically, Duponchel's dream never got off the drawing-board. Many had died for it, an entire way of life had been destroyed for it, but there is not and never has been a railway across the Sahara.

Epilogue

In 1910, a French administrator, A. Bonnel de Mezières, arrived in Timbuctoo to conduct an official French inquiry into the death of Alexander Gordon Laing. He was introduced to the eighty-two-year-old nephew of Mohammad bin 'Abeid – the man who had murdered Laing and his Arab companion in their sleep in 1826. Bin 'Abeid's family still had in its possession a golden brooch in the shape of a cock that had been given to Laing by his wife, Emma Warrington, daughter of the British Consul-General in Tripoli, whom Laing had married shortly before he began his journey. De Mezières was taken to a tree on the caravan-route to Arawan, under which he unearthed two skeletons. French medical officers at Timbuctoo confirmed that one was an Arab boy, the other a European adult.

Like Paul Flatters, Alexander Gordon Laing had been avenged for the savage attack he had suffered south of In Salah, eighty-three years earlier. 'The Tuaricks are a strange people,' he had written, 'living mostly upon plunder, or the tribute which they collect: Whatever they demand, must be given them; a refusal would be the signal for plunder and murder.'[95] His remains were buried in Timbuctoo, the city he had given his life to reach.

Twenty years later, in 1930, the African Society of London erected a monument to his memory at the place where his remains had been found. By that time the old caravan trade had ended. Motor-lorries now left their tracks on the desert surface and aircraft spanned the emptiness from Algiers to Timbuctoo. The 'strange Tuaricks' had already become a tourist attraction. Laing would not have recognized this twentieth-century Sahara, and almost certainly he would not have liked it. The great desert he had known had been a wilder, more dangerous place, yet it had been vital and authentic. Tuareg society might not have been entirely pleasant, but it was unique. The age of Tuareg supremacy had lasted a thousand years, but Laing's incredible journey had sounded its death-knell. In 1826 he had found a society unchanged since the Arab traveller Ibn Battuta had passed this way in the fourteenth century. By 1930, it was gone.

Postscript

Adolphe Duponchel published a second book about his project, *L'Afrique Centrale et le Transsaharien*, in 1881. He blamed Charles de Freycinet for the failure of his earlier plans. The engineer believed that the former Minister of Public Works had wasted finance on exploration that could better have been spent on the actual construction of the line. Duponchel died in Paris in 1903, aged 83.

Gaston Cottonest received no reward, medal, or even thanks for his achievement. The battle of Tit went virtually unacknowledged in the press. On his return to In Salah, Cottonest was relieved of his post and transferred back to France. He never returned to Algeria. One of the most successful *méhariste* officers in French history, Cottonest's experience and talents were wasted – a salutary example of the power of late-Victorian political correctness.

Gaston Cauvet was held guilty of insubordination over the Cottonest patrol, sacked from his post as commandant of In Salah, and retired from the army.

Henri Laperrine went on to become a legendary name in the history of the French Sahara thanks to his brainchild, the Saharan Companies: regular Shamba *méharistes* commanded by French officers and NCOs. Contrary to popular belief, these soldiers did not pacify the Sahara, they only policed it. The real work had been done by old-style Arab irregulars, like those who had made up Cottonest's patrol. Laperrine rose to the rank of general. He died of thirst in the Sahara in 1920, after his aircraft crash-landed on the inaugural flight between Algiers and Timbuctoo.

Atissi ag Shikkadh spent the rest of his life in exile in the Tassili-n-Ajjer and across the border in Ottoman country. The date and circumstances of his death are unknown.

Musa ag Amastane did not adopt the title of *amenukal* until it had been independently confirmed by the Kel Ahaggar council. In 1905 he was officially invested as *amenukal* in the name of France by Captain Dinaux, at Tamaghasset, and presented with the red burnoose of office (a practice borrowed from the Ottoman Turks). Thereafter he ruled as a French ally, and with French military might behind him became the most powerful *amenukal* in Tuareg history. He died on 27 December 1920, and his descendants are still recognized as *amenukals* of the Kel Ahaggar.

Sidi al-Keraji, chief of the Taitoq, had never accepted the authority of Aitaghel and the Kel Ghela. He returned to the Hoggar after surrendering to Henri Laperrine, and in 1905 was invested officially as *amenukal* of the Taitoq drum-group. His clan joined the Senussi revolt in 1916 and, after its failure, most moved south into Niger. By 1994, only nine Taitoq families remained in the Hoggar.

The Ottoman Vilayet of Tripoli: Vali Rasim Pasha's success in the Sahara was short-lived. In 1884, the Kel Ajjer revolted against Ottoman rule and captured Ghat, killing forty Turkish soldiers. The *Vali* retook the oasis the following year, but by then the Saharan caravan trade was in decline. Its most valuable commodity, ostrich feathers, were being produced more cheaply in ostrich farms in South Africa. The vilayet ceased to exist in October 1912, when the Ottoman Sultan signed the Treaty of

Lausanne, ceding the area to Italy. In 1951 Tripolitania and Cyrenaica became the independent kingdom of Libya.

Ikhenoukhen of the Kel Ajjer offered, after the Flatters massacre, to join the French in a punitive campaign against the Kel Ahaggar, but the French government refused. The old *amenukal* died in 1884, shortly before his drum-group attacked Ghat, and was succeeded by his nephew. At the time of his death he was reputed to be over a hundred years old. If this was true, he would already have been in his thirties at the time of Laing's murder.

The Sanusiyya Brotherhood rose in revolt against the Italians in 1916 and invaded Algeria, capturing Janet. Many of the Kel Ahaggar joined the revolt. In the same year the Sanusi also launched an invasion of British-controlled Egypt, in support of the Ottoman Empire. They were routed by British armoured car patrols at Siwa. The Sanusi were persecuted by the Italians and consequently became allies of the British in the Second World War. In 1951, the head of the Sanusiyya, 'Idris, was brought out of exile and ruled the country as King 'Idris I until 1969, when he was deposed by Colonel Mu'ammar Gaddaffi. The complicity of the Sanusiyya in the Flatters massacre and the murder of the White Fathers has never been conclusively proved.

Sultan 'Abdul Hamid II was deposed by the Young Turks' revolt in 1909. The Ottoman Empire lasted only another nine years. The Turks became allies of the Germans in the First World War and were defeated in the Middle East by the Allies. In October 1918, the empire was divided between Britain and France.

The White Fathers: Charles Lavigerie was made a cardinal in 1892, but died in the same year without ever realizing his ambition to see his mission established in Timbuctoo. This was achieved two years later, after the capture of the town by the French. The

White Fathers Mission still exists today. It continues to be involved in missionary work in north Africa and elsewhere, and also runs the Pontifical Institute of Arabic Studies in the Vatican. In 1987, the Italian Mariantonietta Peru, one of its lay students, became the first woman ever to cross the Sahara from west to east by camel and on foot.

Notes

1. Gardner, Brian, *The Quest for Timbuctoo*, p. 87.
2. Grévoz, Daniel, *Sahara 1830–1881: Les Mirages Français et la Tragédie Flatters*, p. 79.
3. Physical surveys have proved conclusively that Tuareg males average 5 feet 7 inches, slightly smaller on average than European males. The tallest Targui ever found was 6 feet 3 inches. Virtually every description of the Tuareg, even today, insists on their tallness – either enduring proof of the power of myth over actual experience, or a victory for Tuareg psychological warfare. See Briggs, Lloyd Cabot, *Tribes of the Sahara*.
4. Leclerc, René *Sahara*, p. 129–30.
5. Henri Duveyrier was informed by a Targui that the word 'Tuareg' was of Arabic origin, and meant 'the Abandoned of God', because for a long time the Imuhaq had refused to accept Islam. This is not supported by any etymological evidence: the Arabic word for those who do not accept Islam is *kuffaar*, and the term for pagans is *wathaniyyin*. There is no Arabic term for 'the Abandoned of God', or even such a concept in Islam. I speculate here that the word may be based on an archaic form of the verb *taraka*, meaning to leave, but another possible base is the verb *Taraqa* (*T* being emphatic), meaning to strike. The literal meaning of the word *Tawariq* in this case would be 'misfortunes' or 'calamities'. The exact meaning and origin of the word Tuareg remains unknown.
6. See note 3 above.
7. Bovill, E. W., *The Niger Explored*, p. 58–9.
8. Grévoz, Daniel, *Sahara 1830–1881: Les Mirages Français et la Tragédie Flatters*, p. 79.
9. Ibid., p. 88.
10. Duveyrier's conception of Tuareg nobility was influenced by the work of Jean-Jacques Rousseau (1712–78), one of the philosophers of the French Revolution. Rousseau believed that people were essentially kind and good, but were corrupted by civilization. He idealized the 'noble savage' as an unspoiled individual, and felt that the nearer a person lived to the

earth, the 'better' he was likely to be. The nature of Tuareg society provides little evidence to support Rousseau's theory.

11. Leclerc, René, *Sahara*, p. 129–30.
12. Grévoz, Daniel, *Sahara 1830–1881: Les Mirages Français et la Tragédie Flatters, p. 72.*
13. Ibid., p. 177.
14. Ibid., p. 117.
15. Ibid., p. 121.
16. Ibid.
17. Brosselard, Henri, *Voyage de la Mission Flatters au Pays des Tourags*, p. 103.
18. Mélia, Jean, *La Drame de la Mission Flatters*, p. 97.
19. Ibid., p. 99.
20. Grévoz, Daniel, *Sahara 1830–1881: Les Mirages Français et la Tragédie Flatters*, p. 150.
21. Ibid., p. 159.
22. Cassou, Marcel, *Le Transsaharien – l'Échec Sanglant des Missions Flatters 1881*, p. 167.
23. Grévoz, Daniel, *Sahara 1830–1881: Les Mirages Français et la Tragédie Flatters*, p. 162.
24. Pettier, René, *Flatters*, p. 113.
25. Daumas, General Eugène, *The Ways of the Desert*.
26. Féraud believed that Aitaghel had actually visited Ikhenoukhen to deliver this tongue-lashing, but this seems unlikely, as it would have represented a journey of several weeks, and it is clear that Aitaghel rode to the Tuat in December. It is more likely that he simply sent a letter.
27. Cassou, Marcel, *Le Transsaharien – l'Échec Sanglant des Missions Flatters 1881*, p. 125.
28. Ibid., p. 97.
29. Ibid.
30. Grévoz, Daniel, *Sahara 1830–1881: Les Mirages Français et la Tragédie Flatters*, p. 171–2.
31. Cassou, Marcel, *Le Transsaharien – l'Échec Sanglant des Missions Flatters 1881*, p. 125.
32. See Bernard, Captain F., *Quatre Mois Dans le Sahara – Journal d'un Voyage Chez Les Tuareg, Suivi d'un Aperçu sur la Deuxième Mission de Colonel Flatters*, p. 130.
33. Ibid.
34. Pottier, René, *Flatters*, p. 119.
35. Ibid., p. 120.
36. Grévoz, Daniel, *Sahara 1830–1881: Les Mirages Français et la Tragédie Flatters*, p. 169.

NOTES 273

37. Peyre, Joseph, *Proie des Ombres*, p. 56.
38. Porch, Douglas, *The Conquest of the Sahara*, p. 116.
39. Mélia, Jean, *La Drame de la Mission Flatters*, p. 132.
40. Ibid.
41. Ibid., p. 133.
42. Pottier, René, *Flatters*, p. 127.
43. Derrécagaix, Lieutenant-Colonel V., *Exploration du Sahara, Les Deux Missions du Lieutenant-Colonel Flatters*, p. 119.
44. Mélia, Jean *La Drame de la Mission Flatters*, p. 135.
45. Barbier, J. V., *A Travers le Sahara, Les Missions de Colonel Flatters*, p. 141.
46. Mélia, Jean, *La Drame de la Mission Flatters*, p. 135.
47. It is possible the Tuareg were telling the truth. As the saline had probably not been used in their lifetime, it is unlikely that they had visited it previously. On the other hand, they may have been deliberately covering up for the raiding-party under Atissi and Wangadi that was already following the Flatters mission.
48. Almost certainly this was Atissi's raiding-party. It was an Arab axiom that when desert travellers found tracks crossing their own, it spelled trouble. I believe that at least some of Atissi's raiders had come directly from the place where Bu Jamaa had met Aitaghel, at Menyat, five days from In Salah. Without doubt bin Bajuda's Awlad Ba Hammu had come directly from the Tuat.
49. This may have been Baba ag Tamaklast, whose action twenty-one years later was to lead to the destruction of Kel Ahaggar power at Tit in 1902.
50. Grévoz, Daniel, *Sahara 1830–1881: Les Mirages Français et la Tragédie Flatters*, p. 89.
51. According to Bu Jamaa's own statement, he and the *muqaddam* Sidi 'Abd al-Qadir visited Flatters at this time and warned him that Sghir bin Sheikh was trying to foment a mutiny among the camel-men. 'You must not allow Sghir to leave the camp, Colonel,' Bu Jamaa claims to have told him. 'He is a friend of the Tuareg, and is capable of doing something against the mission.' Both Flatters and the *muqaddam* were dead by this time, and could not refute his testimony. Bu Jamaa also had good reason to whitewash his own part in the betrayal.
52. Bu Jamaa made this claim in an official deposition some time afterwards, when there were no other witnesses, and when he had every reason to try and paint himself in a favourable light.
53. Some reports put both Flatters and Masson with the horses on the western edge of the wadi when the attack reached them. Witnesses who may or may not have seen the events at close hand maintain that the colonel's first instinct on seeing the charging warriors was to walk

forward and greet them. This is not as improbable as it sounds, because Flatters certainly knew the Tuareg often welcomed guests by executing a ferocious mock charge: it had been described by Henri Duveyrier, among others. It may explain why he and Masson moved towards the advancing enemy. When the officers realized the Tuareg were genuinely hostile they made a dash for their horses. Flatters took the bridle from Sghir bin Sheikh and had one foot in the stirrup when Sghir brought his sword down on the colonel's skull. Still alive, Flatters drew his pistol and fired left and right before the Tuareg enveloped him. This version of Flatters' death, while not impossible, seems unlikely, depending on how far the two men were from their horses when the attack developed.

54. Cassou, Marcel, *Le Transsaharien – l'Échec Sanglant des Missions Flatters 1881*, p. 127.

55. Pottier, René, *Flatters*, p. 137. De Dianous has been criticized by historians for failing to take any action. However, it is important to stress the relative numbers involved – at least three hundred and fifty Tuareg against only twenty *tirailleurs*. At Amgid, later, a determined effort by the *tirailleurs* failed to dislodge the Tuareg from the watering-place despite inflicting heavy casualties. It is clear that, in this situation, and given the numbers at his disposal, there was little the lieutenant could have done.

56. Pottier, René, *Flatters*, p. 137.

57. Cassou, Marcel, *Le Transsaharien – l'Échec Sanglant des Missions Flatters 1881*, p. 131.

58. Tamahaq *tullult – Aristida pungens, afezu – Panicum turgidum*.

59. Cassou, Marcel, *Le Transsaharien – l'Échec Sanglant des Missions Flatters 1881*, p. 131.

60. Ahmad bin Mas'ud arrived back in Wargla in 1881 after being kept prisoner in a Tuareg camp.

61. Bernard, Captain F., *Quatre Mois Dans le Sahara – Journal d'un Voyage Chez Les Tuareg, Suivi d'un Aperçu sur la Deuxième Mission de Colonel Flatters*, p. 130.

62. Mélia, Jean, *La Drame de la Mission Flatters*, p. 154.

63. Grévoz, Daniel, *Sahara 1830–1881: Les Mirages Français et la Tragédie Flatters*, P. 176.

64. Ibid.

65. Grévoz, Daniel, *Sahara 1830–1881: Les Mirages Français et la Tragédie Flatters*, p. 176.

66. Pottier, René, *Flatters*, p. 148–9.

67. Mélia, Jean, *La Drame de la Mission Flatters*, p. 176.

68. Ibid.

69. Bernard, Captain F., *Quatre Mois Dans le Sahara – Journal d'un Voyage*

Chez Les Tuareg, Suivi d'un Aperçu sur la Deuxième Mission de Colonel Flatters, p. 140.

70. Ibid., p. 142.
71. Mélia, Jean, *La Drame de la Mission Flatters*, p. 172.
72. Martel, M. A., *La Politique Saharienne Ottomane*. Note Féraud 12/4/81.
73. Grévoz, Daniel, *Sahara 1830–1881: Les Mirages Français et la Tragédie Flatters*, p. 200.
74. Cassou, Marcel, *Le Transsaharien – l'Échec Sanglant des Missions Flatters*, p. 149.
75. Ibid.
76. Mélia, Jean, *La Drame de la Mission Flatters*, p. 168.
77. Ibid., p. 169.
78. Bodley, R. V. C., *The Soundless Sahara*, p. 181.
79. Leclerc, René, *Sahara*, p. 181.
80. Grévoz, Daniel, *Sahara 1830–1881: Les Mirages Français et la Tragédie Flatters*, p. 120.
81. Leclerc, René, *Sahara*, p. 153.
82. Gardner, Brian, *The Quest for Timbuctoo*, p. 186.
83. Porch, Douglas, *The Conquest of the Sahara*, p. 90.
84. It is worth noting here that Atissi shadowed but did not dare attack the Foreau–Lamy Mission in 1898–9, which adopted an aggressive attitude and was escorted by 300 armed regulars – exactly the number Flatters originally asked for.
85. Some scholars, including Tuareg expert Jeremy Keenan, have theorized that Atissi deliberately allowed the last survivors to go free as a dire warning to the French. In view of bin Bajuda's dispatch of a raiding-party to finish off the survivors, and Aitaghel's desperate attempt to convince the French authorities that his people were not involved, this seems unlikely.
86. Foreau thought that the humerus belonged to René Masson *because* it was a long way from the well, indicating that he believed the version of events outlined in note 53 above.
87. Porch, Douglas, *The Conquest of the Sahara*, p. 261.
88. Ibid.
89. The Kel Ulli were of the Dag Ghali group, the chief vassals of the Kel Ghela, and the principal inhabitants of the area through which Cottonest was passing.
90. The first chant was ironic. The second was intended to encourage the Marabitin clan among the Cottonest patrol to mutiny.
91. Brunon, M. R., *La Découverte du Hoggar & Le Combat de Tit – Mars–Avril–Mai 1902*, p. 240.

92. Ibid.

93. Porch, Douglas, *The Conquest of the Sahara*, p. 261.

94. Brunon, M. R., *La Découverte du Hoggar & Le Combat de Tit – Mars– Avril–Mai 1902*, p. 246.

95. Bovill, E. W., *The Niger Explored*, p. 163.

Bibliography

Barbier, J. V., *A Travers le Sahara – Les Missions de Colonel Flatters d'Après des Documents Absoluements Inedits*, Paris, 1884

Benhazera, M., *Six Mois Chez les Touareg du Ahaggar*, Algiers, 1908

Bernard, A. & Lacroix, N., *La Pénétration Saharienne 1830–1906*, Algiers, 1906

Bernard, Captain F., *Quatre Mois Dans le Sahara – Journal d'un Voyage Chez Les Tuareg, Suivi d'un Aperçu sur la Deuxième Mission de Colonel Flatters*, Paris, 1884

Bissuel, Captain H., *Les Touaregs de l'Ouest*, Algiers, 1888

Boahen, A. Adu, *Britain, the Sahara and the Western Sudan 1788–1861*, London, 1964

Bodley, R. V. C., *The Soundless Sahara*, London, 1968

Bourget, M. J. M., *L'Algérie Jusqu'à la Pénétration Saharienne*, Algiers, 1930

Bovill, Edward W., *The Niger Explored*, London, 1968

Bovill, Edward W., *The Golden Trade of the Moors: West Africa in the Fourteenth Century*, London, 1968

Briggs, Lloyd Cabot, *Tribes of the Sahara*, Massachusetts, 1960

Brosselard, Henri, *Voyage de la Mission Flatters au Pays des Tourags*, 1883

Brunon, M. R., *La Découverte du Hoggar & Le Combat de Tit – Mars–Avril–Mai 1902*, 1959

Cassou, Marcel *Le Transsaharien – l'Échec Sanglant des Missions Flatters 1881*, Paris, 2004

Clancy-Smith, Julia A., *Rebel and Saint: Muslim Notables, Populist Protest, Colonial Encounters (Algeria–Tunisia 1800–1904)*, California, 1994

Cook, James R., *New French Imperialism – 1880–1901 The 3rd Republic & Colonial Expansion*, 1973

Daumas, General Eugène (trans. Ohlendorf, Sheila M.), *The Ways of the Desert*, Texas, 1971

De Arteche, Jose, *The Cardinal of Africa: Charles Lavigerie, the Founder of the White Fathers*, London 1964

Derrécagaix, Lieutenant-Colonel V., *Exploration du Sahara. Les Deux Missions du Lieutenant-Colonel Flatters*, Paris, 1882

Dubois, Felix (trans. Diana White), *Timbuctoo the Mysterious*, London, 1897

Duveyrier, Henri, *Exploration du Sahara: Les Touareg du Nord*, Paris, 1864

Duveyrier, Henri, *Journal de Route*, Paris, 1905

Gardner, Brian, *The Quest for Timbuctoo*, London, 1968

Gautier, E. F., *Sahara, The Great Desert*, London, 1935

Gladstone, Penelope, *Travels of Alexine: Alexine Tinne 1835–1869*, London, 1970

Grévoz, Daniel, *Les Méharistes Français à la Conquête du Sahara 1900–1930*, Paris, 1994

Grévoz, Daniel, *Sahara 1830–1881: Les Mirages Français et la Tragédie Flatters*, Paris, 2000

Huré, Général R., *L'Armée d'Afrique 1830–1962*, Paris, 1977

Keenan, Jeremy, *The Tuareg: People of Ahaggar*, London, 1977

Keenan, Jeremy, *Sahara Man: Travelling with the Tuareg*, London, 2001

Leclerc, René, *Sahara*, Paris, 1954

Lhote, Henri, *Le Hoggar, Espace et Temps*, Paris, 1984

Lhote, Henri, *Les Touaregs du Hoggar (Ahaggar)*, Paris, 1984

Lorcin, Patricia M. E., *Imperial Identities, Stereotyping Prejudice and Race in Colonial Algeria*, Massachusetts, 1995

Martel, André, *La Politique Saharienne Ottomane. Le Sahara: Rapport et Contacts Humains*, Paris, 1967

Mélia, Jean, *La Drame de la Mission Flatters*, Paris, 1941

Morsy, Magali, *North Africa 1800–1900: A Survey from the Nile to the Atlantic*, London, 1984

Naval Intelligence Division, *Algeria Geographical Handbook, Vol. 3*, 1944

Nicolaisen, Johannes, *The Ecology and Culture of the Pastoral Tuareg*, Copenhagen, 1963

Pandolfi, Paul, *Les Touaregs de L'Ahaggar: Parenté et Résidence chez les Dag-Ghâli*, Paris, 1998

Peyre, Joseph, *Proie des Ombres*, Montreal, 1942

Porch, Douglas, *The Conquest of the Sahara*, London, 1985

Pottier, René, *Flatters*, Paris, 1948

Rouvillois-Brigol, Madeleine, *Le Pays de Ouargla (Sahara Algérien)*, Paris, 1975

US Government, *Handbook for Algeria*, 1964

Wellard, James Howard, *Samarkand and Beyond: A History of Desert Caravans*, London, 1977

Index